# Self-Knowledge and Agency

# Self-Knowledge and Agency

Edited by
Manidipa Sen

Decent Books
New Delhi

**Cataloging in Publication Data — DK**
[Courtesy: D.K. Agencies (P) Ltd. <docinfo@dkagencies.com>]

**Self-knowledge and agency** / edited by Manidipa Sen.
p. cm.
Contributed articles.
Includes bibliographical references and index.
ISBN 13: 9788186921593

1. Self-knowledge, Theory of. 2. Agent (Philosophy) 3. Ethics. I. Sen, Manidipa.

DDC 126 23


*First published in India,* 2012
ISBN 13: 978-81-86921-59-3 ISBN 10: 81-86921-59-1



*Published and printed by:*
Decent Books
*'Suryodaya'*, D-36/A-1, Mohan Garden
Najafgarh Road
New Delhi – 110 059
Ph. (011) 2535-3435

*Distributed by:*
D.K. Printworld (P) Ltd.
*Regd. Office:* 'Vedaśrī', F-395, Sudarshan Park
(Metro Station: Ramesh Nagar)
New Delhi – 110 015
*Phones:* (011) 2545 3975; 2546 6019; *Fax*: (011) 2546 5926
*E-mail:* indology@dkprintworld.com
*Website*: www.dkprintworld.com

# Preface

This collection of essays represents a body of work that deals with questions concerning how we know our own minds and how this kind of knowledge has a bearing on our being agents. The epistemological enquiry concerning how, if at all, we can know ourselves is one of the most contentious issues in contemporary Philosophy of Mind. Debates centering on agency, freedom, and moral responsibility cannot be dissociated from this epistemological query. Hence, the need was felt to have an International Conference in the newly established Centre for Philosophy in the School of Social Sciences at Jawaharlal Nehru University, New Delhi, on the topic of Self-knowledge and Agency. Held in January 2007, with philosophers from India and abroad participating in it, the Conference was funded by Jawaharlal Nehru University. I am grateful to the then Vice-chancellor and the Rector of the University for this grant to facilitate organizing the conference. I also take this opportunity to sincerely thank all those who actively participated in the Conference by either presenting papers, commenting on papers that were presented, or chairing the academic sessions.

The essays that appear in this volume (except for the ones written by Joanrdon Ganeri and me) were presented at the Conference. I am extremely grateful to the contributors of this volume for being so patient with the delay in bringing out this publication, and for their very valuable contributions.

I also wish to express my deepest gratitude to my

colleagues at the Centre for Philosophy (JNU), Satya P. Gautam, R.P. Singh and Bhagat Oinam, for their encouragement, support and invaluable advice in organizing the conference, whose fruitful outcome is this collection of thoughtful essays.

Publication of the book in its present form was made possible thanks to a generous grant from Jawaharlal Nehru University, without which it would have been impossible to bring out this volume. Thanks are also due to Mr Rajendra Agarwal of Decent Books for his able assistance in editing the volume, and expediting the publishing process.

**Manidipa Sen**

# Contents

# Acknowledgement

The editor sincerely acknowledges the permission from the authors of the following articles for their republication in this volume:

1. Fiona Macpherson, "A Disjunctive Theory of Introspection: A Reflection on Zombies and Anton's Syndrome", appeared in *Philosophical Issues*, vol. 20, no. 1, 2010, pp. 226-65.
2. Bijoy Boruah and Bhaskarjit Neog, "Collective Agency and Social Action", appeared as "Collective Agency" in *Journal of Indian Council of Philosophical Research*, vol. XXXVIII, no. 3, 2011, pp. 1-32.
3. Jonardon Ganeri, "Self and Morality: Some Indian Perspectives on Sorabji", appeared as "Self and Morality: Some Indian Comments on Sorabji" in *Antiquorum Philosophia*, vol. 2, 2008, pp. 25-35.

# Introduction

*Manidipa Sen*

INQUIRY concerning the nature of self-knowledge and the role of human beings as subjects of experience and agents of actions are closely, if not, inseparably related to one another. Also closely related are issues concerning the normative dimensions of the mental and questions regarding identity and individuality. The aim of this collection of essays is to address these issues by focusing on firstly, the epistemological questions, and subsequently on questions regarding the relationship between these epistemic concerns and concerns pertaining to agency and morality. As it is well known, recent debates in Philosophy of Mind, Philosophy of Action, and Moral Philosophy have highlighted these interrelated problems. One may say that the famous inscription in the temple of Delphic oracle "Know thy self", the pronouncement that had been the guiding principle behind the different philosophies of antiquity, is significant in its own way even for philosophers of today. Philosophers in recent times have made important contributions to problems concerning first-person epistemology and related issues of agency and identity. The essays in this volume, therefore, aim at addressing one or several of these interrelated debates on self-knowledge and agency. We will, in the introduction, give a brief overview of the recent debates central to self-knowledge and agency before looking at the specific problems that each essay addresses.

***

Questions concerning the knowledge of one's own mental states and processes have always intrigued philosophers, not only because of the special epistemological questions that it raises, but also because of its relevance to problems of human agency, freedom and moral responsibility. Two interrelated questions are clearly relevant to self-knowledge: (1) Is it at all possible to have self-knowledge? and (2) If it is so possible, how do we acquire it? The first question is, in a very important way, related to the second. Unless we are able to give a satisfactory answer to the question regarding how we acquire self-knowledge, our positive answer to the first question becomes an empty claim. Furthermore, these two queries may be said to be related to deeper ontological questions concerning whether we have a self, and if we do have, what its nature could be. The whole issue of self-knowledge, and the related ethical questions, therefore, would require different articulations in terms of the ontological perspective one adopts regarding the nature of the self.

Broadly, two different kinds of answers are given to the second or the "how" question — one associated mainly with Descartes, and the other with anti-Cartesians like Gilbert Ryle — the former upholding an observational model of self-knowledge, while the latter upholding some form of an inferential model. Descartes takes mental states to be genuine conscious episodes and processes to which the subject has a privileged access, and which are immediately given to the subject as her own intimate mental states and processes. Privileged access to our own mental states and processes is due to the three characteristics that this form of knowledge is said to have: immediacy, authoritativeness, and salience.[1] This familiar picture about psychological facts further suggests that these are facts about individuals which hold independently of their relation to the external world, and hence they may be

1. For a detailed discussion see the Introduction of the book *Knowing Our Own Mind*, Crispin Wright, Cynthia Macdonald and Barry Smith (eds.), Oxford: Clarendon Press, 1998.

individuated independently of the individual's contact with her external environment.

The non-observational or the inferential model, on the contrary, bases this kind of knowledge on the behaviour of the subject from which they are supposed to be derived and on the basis of which they are justified. The anti-Cartesian picture of psychological states is further motivated by the views that since mind and world are not two independent categories, the world enters constitutively into the individuation of mental states. Hence, to have a full understanding of such states or to individuate them, it would not be sufficient to know what goes on inside the head.

This above account of the mind as being part of a larger world paves way for an externalist interpretation of the mental. In accordance with this interpretation, and as against the Cartesian model and an internalist model of the mental, many philosophers have tried to develop a picture of the mental which states:

- Mind is essentially intentional, and hence is directed towards objects.
- Mind is essentially embodied, and hence cannot be studied in isolation from the body.
- Mind is essentially interactive, and hence is constantly negotiating with other minds.

However, philosophers[2] have tried to argue that the problem with first-person epistemology is that it seems to hover between a Cartesian as well as a non-Cartesian paradigm. From the point of view of the fact that mind is not self-contained with regard to itself, and that some domains of the

2. See Crispin Wright, "Self-Knowledge: A Wittgensteinian Legacy", in *Knowing Our Own Minds*, Oxford: Clarendon Press, 1998; Paul Boghossian, "Content and Self-knowledge", in *Philosophical Topics*, 17, 1989.

mental may remain elusive for us, we need to reject the privileged access position of the observational model. Whereas, the fact that we are in some way immune to the error of misidentification when we use the pronoun "I" together with the obvious acceptance of the fact that at least some of our mental states are available to us in a somewhat groundless, authoritative and transparent manner lead philosophers to argue for a privileged access thesis regarding our own minds.

One of the root causes of this vacillation may be in our trying to integrate the subjective as well as the objective perspectives about ourselves. On the one hand, we have access to certain parts of our experience as it were "from the inside". On the other hand, we too have an outside. We are part of the world, with certain properties which are available to us just as much as they are available to others. So being objects of nature, we learn about ourselves as objectively as anyone else does. This, as such, doesn't create any problem unless we appreciate the fact that: (a) they provide very different answers to the same problem, and (b) that these different answers may conflict with each other. How are we going to integrate these two features of the mental — the subjective and the objective, the inner and the outer — is a philosophical problem, which has to be addressed by any theory regarding knowledge of our own mental states and processes.

In order to try and find a solution to this problem, one needs to ask the more basic question regarding whether these two so-called different ontological perspectives are really that different. One can try to address this problem by radicalizing our notion of subjective as well as the objective and conceive of them as not to be excluding one another.[3] What kind of

3. See for example, Greg McCulloch's *The Life of the Mind: An Essay in Phenomenological Externalism*, London: Routledge, 2003, where an attempt of this sort has been made; see also Donald Davidson's "The Myth of the Subjective", in his *Subjective, Intersubjective, Objective*, Oxford: Clarendon Press, 2001.

epistemological move needs to be made in order to assimilate within the epistemological framework a radicalized notion of the subjective? — An answer to this question may throw some light on the debate between the observational and non-observational models of self-knowledge.

In spite of the irresolvable differences between the observational and the inferential paradigms of knowledge of our own minds, they both are based on the same assumption that self-knowledge is an epistemic achievement. So, for these opposed accounts, knowledge of our own minds, as articulated in self-ascriptive sentences, are genuine assertions that are either true or false. A large number of philosophers (Donald Davidson, Crispin Wright, Tyler Burge, Akeel Bilgrami, Richard Moran, Dorit Bar-On, to name a few) have rejected this original assumption. Inspired by Kant and Wittgenstein, they have tried to explain self-knowledge as either being constitutive of the very notion of intentionality we work with or self-ascription as having an expressivist explanation. In addition, or in line with these concerns, a model of self-knowledge may be constructed on the basis of experiential and communicative dimensions which are peculiar to human existence. None of these alternatives fit into the traditional dichotomy of the observational and the non-observational paradigms regarding self-knowledge. Hence, a radically different kind of understanding of this sort of knowledge has been sought by many philosophers, which has led to what may be termed as an "anti-explanatory" account of knowing our own mental states and processes.

Our interest in understanding knowledge of our "I"-thoughts and their articulations, like, "I am in pain", are integrally related to an understanding of statements having as their subject the pronoun "I". Since "I" is guaranteed against lack of reference or mistaken reference, it seems to function in a different way from other referential expressions, in particular, proper names. An anti-explanatory model mentioned previously is a critique of the robust epistemology and referentiality that philosophers have tried to build up in order to account for our thought and talk about ourselves. The expressivist account, which is a classic anti-explanatory model of self-knowledge, as articulated in Wittgenstein's *Philosophical Investigations*, states that instead of taking knowledge of our minds as articulated in self-ascriptive sentences to be genuine assertions that are either true or false, they should be interpreted in a different light. Hence, for these philosophers, the reference of "I" in the sentence "I am in pain" is neither the body, nor the immaterial mind, nor the conglomeration of the two. "I", in fact, does not have any reference, or to put it more strongly, "I" is not a genuine referring expression. The problem is that we cannot make a mistake in our reference with the use of the word "I". But one cannot be said to be involved in the act of reference unless one is in a position to choose that reference from a host of others, and hence is prone to making a mistake. So, according to these philosophers, an expressivist reading of sentences involving the use of the pronoun "I" is required.

Another way of my thinking of myself as the reference of "I", consists in distinguishing myself from the reference of "you" or "her", and in this sense we can and do choose to refer to one person with the use of the pronoun "I" from among or different from others. This may be regarded as a way of bringing in the reflexive dimension of self-knowledge and self-reference, which really amounts to an identification and recognition of oneself as the subject of experience. Furthermore, this would ultimately result in a knowledge of who one is and what one is thinking — that is, knowledge of one's own identity. In addition, one may say that our "I"-thoughts and accompanying self-ascriptions make sense to us only in the context where we can position ourselves *vis-à-vis* the other (the reference of "you" or "she"). It is not only one's relation to the outside material world, but also one's relationship to other human beings which provide content to self-identity, and hence to self-knowledge.

After having problematized these different aspects of self-knowledge and self-reference, one may argue that a fundamental requirement for any theory regarding the nature of self-knowledge is to answer two kinds of questions.[4] The first concerns questions about the nature of the knowledge of one's particular mental states — particular pains and pleasures, whereas, the latter concerns questions about the nature of our knowledge of the kind of thing we are. Obviously, these two issues are inseparably related to each other. In fact, one may maintain that a theory concerning our knowledge of particular mental states and processes has no value unless it is a pointer to the more general theory about our knowledge of the kind of thing we are. Hence, one would like to explore whether and in what way from the specific questions regarding the knowledge of and reference to "I"-thoughts, one may extrapolate a theory concerning the kind of thing we are.

Issues concerning self-knowledge have important ramifications on the question of human agency and moral responsibility. An argument, according to Akeel Bilgrami[5] relating to these two issues, may be offered from the point of view of the constitutive thesis. Briefly put, the argument runs as follows: Since we cannot have agency without intentionality, and self-knowledge is constitutive of all intentional acts in general, it is also constitutive of the very idea of agency. Furthermore, since human agency is constitutive of moral responsibility, so would self-knowledge be.

4. See Quassim Cassam's Introduction to the edited volume *Self-Knowledge*, Oxford: Oxford University Press, 1994.

5. Due to Akeel Bilgrami, *Self-knowledge and Resentment*, Cambridge, Mass.: Harvard University Press, 2006.

This is in outline some of the major problems relating to the notion of self-knowledge and the role of human beings as agents. The essays in this volume touch upon these issues discussed above. A brief description of the essays, given below, will make it evident how this cluster of problems centring around self-knowledge and agency are dealt with by the contributors of the anthology.

* * *

All the essays in this volume are concerned with the problem of self-knowledge. Some of the essays, however, directly deal with the epistemological issues central to an understanding of self-knowledge, whereas others look into the relationship between self-knowledge, agency, intentionality, morality and what is it to be a rational human being. We will, in our exposition, start with those essays that deal with the problem of self-knowledge as primarily an epistemological problem and move on to essays that explore the relationship between self-knowledge and human agency. The essays in the volume are also ordered in this way.

As we have highlighted earlier the close relationship between self-knowledge and thoughts involving the pronoun "I", the first essay of this anthology looks into precisely this relation. Amita Chatterjee, in her article entitled "From Self-ascription to Self-knowledge", which is also the first essay of the volume, deals with the connection between how from our talk about our own mind an account of self-knowledge may be derived. The pronoun "I", and the vagueness surrounding its use leads philosophers to conclude that "I"-thoughts have a special status, and the knowledge of "I" is privileged in a significant sense. For example, the distinction made by Wittgenstein between the subject and the object use of "I" and also the fact that "I", in its subject use is immune to error of reference, leads to a whole array of debates as to how we are to understand sentences where the pronoun "I" is used.

Chatterjee wants to enquire whether "there is a special route from our self-ascription to self-knowledge". A connected question that she wants to address is, whether the mastery of the personal pronoun by the speaker is a necessary condition for self-ascription. After having distinguished between genuine I-thoughts from pseudo I-thought, the author goes on to ask "whether success of self-ascription depends on using "I" or its surrogate as a special name, or whether self-ascription goes through without using any name?" The answer to this question is given by distinguishing between cognitivist model of reference as opposed to non-cognitivist model of reference. And the author thinks that it is the non-cognitivist model which certainly fares better in our understanding of "I"-thoughts. The non-cognitivists try to argue that for us to use the personal pronoun "I" in a significant sense we need not have a robust sense of "I", that is, a propositional knowledge that the speaker is so and so or such and such. Hence the rather weak account of self-ascription precludes the possibility of knowledge of a substantive self of the Cartesian variety, though, according to Chatterjee, "it does not rule out our having knowledge of something responsible for our ego-sense". This sense may be understood in terms of an unity of experience, a sense of self which is not given but created.

An epistemic account of self-knowledge is very often influenced by an account of perception. Through perception we have a direct and immediate access to the world. Since our knowledge of our own mental states seems to be an immediate and direct encounter with those mental states, philosophers have thought of a perceptual model of accounting for self-knowledge. Hence, they have regarded introspection to be a form of direct access to our mental states on a par with perception. However, a direct perceptual account of the knowledge of external world, as we know, faces difficulties due to the phenomena of illusion and hallucination, and thus more sophisticated accounts of perception have been propounded by philosophers, like, the disjunctivist theory of perception. As Fiona McPherson points out, disjuctivist accounts of perception "have held that there are substantial dissimilarities (either metaphysical or epistemological or both) between veridical perceptual experiences occurring when one perceives and perceptual experiences involved in hallucination." McPherson, in her article, "A Disjunctivist Theory of Introspection: A Reflection on Zombie and Anton's Syndrome", proposes a disjuctivist view of introspection, drawing parallels between introspection and perception, which she thinks is best suited to account for cases like Anton's syndrome and zombies, where introspection seems to go wrong. She also argues that though she favours a disjunctivist view of introspection, she denies disjunctivism with regard to ordinary perception, and hence tries to show in what ways these two forms of disjunctivism are compatible with and distinct from each other.

The article entitled "The Epistemic Illusion of First-Person Authority" by Monima Chadha, is concerned directly with the epistemological question as to whether we have an authoritative knowledge of our own current mental states, like belief, such that the way we know our mind is a qualitatively different way from the way we come to know someone else's mental states. There are two ways of cashing out the idea of first-person authority: epistemic and non-epistemic. The epistemic account of first-person authority rests on the idea that we have a special perceptual or perceptual-like access to our own mental states, and hence the distinctive features of ascription of such states to ourselves are derived from the special way of knowing our own minds. This perceptual model of self-knowledge, as we mentioned earlier, has come under heavy attack in recent times by philosophers who hold that the term "knowledge" in the context of the use of the word "self-knowledge" is misguided as knowing about current beliefs and desires does not consist in acquiring some new information about ourselves — it is far from being a mere cognitive achievement. Hence, as Chadha rightly points out, philosophers have subscribed to various kinds of "non-epistemic strategies" to understand the presumption of first-person authority in the context of so-called self-knowledge. One such important strategy is found in Donald Davidson's work, where Davidson "traces the explanation of first-person authority to the requirement of interpretation". According to Davidson, understanding talk about our own current mental states requires interpretation on the part of the hearer, and this interpretation, in turn, is based on taking the speaker to be authoritative about her own current self-ascription. Without this presumption of authority, interpretation, which is the basis of understanding, can't even get off the ground. Chadha, in this article, criticizes Davidson and other interpretativists by showing that there is really no radical asymmetry between first- and third-person ascriptions of intentional states, and hence the experience of authority that we seem to have with reference to our ascriptions of current mental states is a mere illusion. She does this by taking clue from the works of developmental psychologists, like Alison Gopnik. This opens up a whole lot of discussion on the "theory-theory" account of mind as opposed to a "simulation-theory" account. The author still thinks that first-person authority may be presupposed in order to sustain the interpretative strategy, but this experience of first-person authority is still an illusion.

Does intentional character of mental content pose a challenge to authoritativeness of self-knowledge? According to our everyday common sense understanding of self-knowledge, it does not. We not only have a privileged access to our current phenomenal experiences, like a severe tooth-ache, but we are also in a better position to describe what our current intentional states are, at least to a very large extent better placed than anybody else. This view has been challenged by many, including Alison Gopnik, in her influential paper "How we know our minds: The Illusion of First-person Knowledge of Intentionality" (in *Behavioral and Brain Sciences* 16, 1993). The present essay by Manidipa Sen is an attempt to show that the arguments put forth in this article based on certain experimental evidence from the behaviour of three and four-year-old children are based on both a faulty picture of intentionality as well as a faulty picture of how we come to know our own intentional states. Hence, if we can give an alternative account of knowledge of our own intentional states, then the account of first-person authority cannot be regarded as a mere illusion. Therefore, this essay and the essay by Chadha can be read together in order to get an alternative perspective on self-knowledge and first-person authority.

Yet another important problem with regard to self-knowledge concerns the ambiguity between knowing our particular mental states and knowing the kind of entity a self is. Madhuchhanda Sen, in her paper "Self and Its Knowledge" tries to show that an account of self-knowledge necessarily depends upon an account of the self. As we have already noted, we can give an account of how we know our particular mental states or processes without necessarily committing ourselves to a metaphysical knowledge of the self, and most of the discussions on self-knowledge in contemporary analytic philosophy have revolved around an account of knowledge of particular mental states. Sen is of the opinion that the term "self-knowledge" is ambiguous, and can be understood in, in fact, three very different ways: "Self-knowledge in the sense of self-consciousness, theoretical knowledge regarding the true nature of the self, and self-knowledge in the sense of self-realization". However, Sen emphasizes that even if we can distinguish these three kinds of self-knowledge we cannot significantly talk about any one of them without talking about the other two. Taking clue from classical Indian philosophy, Sen shows the connection between metaphysical account of the self and the nature of self-consciousness. A question that has been raised over and over again by philosophers is whether the self can itself be an object of knowledge. If we take self-knowledge to be a cognitive achievement, then we have to take the self to be known to us with the help of certain accredited means of knowing. But then the question that has bothered philosophers is whether the subject itself can be the objcct of knowledge? In the first part of her paper, Sen takes up this issue, and tries to weave together different responses to this question found in different schools of classical Indian philosophy. Parallels can be drawn between the way classical Indian philosophers have tried to address this question with the ways in which constitutivists, in contemporary philosophy of mind, have tried to do the same.

The problem as to how we experience ourselves as selves, whether this experience can be captured in a purely epistemological framework, is a question that needs addressing when we are dealing with self-knowledge. One may say that though self-knowledge is not a form of knowledge as such, it does consist in a form of self-consciousness as experience of our current mental states. But this experiential dimension of self-consciousness has also been objectified as an instrumental capacity of human beings with some cognitive base and thus the claim made that the role of experience in consciousness is also objectively calculable. Paul Fletcher, in his article entitled "Self-knowledge and the Problem of Experience", articulates its aim as follows: "My desire is, . . . , to propose, however tentatively, that there are grounds for exploring a form of experience or a form of life that is not so strictly curtailed by epistemological limits". This is an essay which tries to go beyond the epistemological approach to self-knowledge. In an attempt to do so, Fletcher goes through the classic rendering of the role of experience in our knowledge found in Kant — a view, as we know, that goes beyond the rationalist and the empiricist paradigms of understanding of experience. In this rendering, Fletcher finds three essential features: (1) the relationship between the subject of experience and the subject of knowledge, and the subsequent notion of subject that arises from the way in which Kant construes this relationship; (2) The limits of possible experience, leading to a notion of subject which suggests that "the purpose of the subject is no longer to flee the sensible world"; and (3) Shifting the place of space and time from the natural world to the world of sensible intuition. But Fletcher questions Kant's notion of the relationship between the subject and the world by bringing in Wittgenstein's displacemnet of the inner-outer distinction. As he says, "Throughout his corpus he (Wittgenstein) shows how the inside is not separate from the outside by some impassable border but the threshold on a continuum". It is this idea of the threshold that can account for self-knowledge.

Where do we situate self-knowledge in the intentional act that assumes the existence of an agent? To put it in yet another way, how do we understand the role of agency in the act of intentionality, an act which establishes a relationship between the self and the world? According to Prasenjit Biswas, two accounts are in place in the philosophical literature regarding whether agency is embedded in the self. The two contrasting models, to describe in Biswas's terms are, "one the Self-model perspective that conceives of a necessary metaphysical dependence between the self and the body and the world . . . and the other, a linguistically and discursively constituted notion of agency that makes itself only as a nominal/pronominal index with an emptied out sense of agency." The first alternative leads to a robust sense of agency as opposed to that of the latter. Biswas wants to steer clear of these two opposed positions and wants to give an account of embedded agency through an account of "phenomenologically constitutive notion of agency", which avoids any robust metaphysical theory of the self, body and the world. It is an account of agency "which discloses the world in phenomenal properties of self-knowledge". As opposed to the naturalistic accounts of intentionality, as developed by Searle and Strawson, Biswas brings in the Husserlian notion of "affections", which, according to him, "is a nexus between streams of consciousness, lived experience and intentional correlates," to account for embedded agency. Husserl's idea of self as an enactive subjectivity, that is, a subjectivity-in-relation provides, according to Biswas, a better account of the place of an agent in the intentional act.

Not only are we agents, but we, as social beings, engage in collective actions. What kind of notion of agency do we have in such actions? Bijoy Boruah and Bhaskarjyoti Neog, in the article on "Collective Agency and Social Action" deal precisely with this question. They start by pointing out that agency can be understood as having two apparently contrary features: independence as well as interdependence. We cannot be an agent without being independent, since it is the agent who is ultimately responsible for his/her action, and this responsibility entails that he/she is not constrained in any way. These are actions performed by the individual herself, and hence the responsibility lies solely with the individual. Whereas, there are actions for which we have to be dependent on other individuals. These are the actions which, according to the author, "define our existence as a social being", and can be called "co-operative or collective actions". Now the interesting and important feature of these collective actions, as opposed to individual actions, is that an explanation of this kind of action cannot be derived from the intention of one individual agent, but from what may be termed "collective intention". Collective intention is not a mere addition of individual intentions of each one of the members involved in the collective action. How and to what extent is collective intention possible and what is the relationship between collective intention and social/collective action involving collective agency? — A number of philosophers have tried to address this question and have come to the conclusion, despite their differences in detail, that collective intention is certainly a necessary condition for the possibility of collective agency. Now the question that the authors raise in this paper is "whether collective intention is *sufficient* for collective agency?" They go on to show that the question of sufficiency is important because mere collective intentionality cannot be a driving force for collective agency, since "Collective Agency must be predicated upon the collectives' ability to form an internal evaluative perspective for the execution of its intention to accomplish the goal that it sets for itself". One can say that it is this evaluative perspective that makes a collective agency responsible for its actions, not just by having a collective intentionality, which can very well be understood instrumentally.

Rachana Kamtekar's essay "Updating Practical Wisdom" is a relook into the problem of practical rationality, a kind of rationality embedded in our actions, and which gives meaning to our agency. The issue of practical rationality is central to the problem of agency, since the very understanding of agency and corresponding understanding of action presupposes an understanding of rationality, and in particular, practical rationality. Practical wisdom, as enshrined in practical rationality, is distinguished from scientific knowledge and knowledge of first principles by Aristotle, because the latter are unable to guide us in living a good life. However, Kamtekar thinks that "Aristotle's own positive characterization of practical wisdom — a true and reasoned state of the capacity to act with regard to human goods, acquired by experience — is disappointingly thin". This thinness of the Aristotelian account is evident from the empirical studies conducted in social and cognitive psychology. Empirical findings in these two domains, according to Kamtekar, seem to show that we need to say more about practical wisdom than just "a sensitivity to all the ethically salient features of a situation". Kamtekar gives a detailed account of this empirical evidence, but does not think that they undermine practical rationality and therefore, practical wisdom altogether. Her conclusion is that "an Aristotelian ideal of virtuous character can be informed by empirical findings about the ways in which we can improve as reasoners."

One of the most important problems connected with an account of self-knowledge is the question of identity of self as a person. How do we understand this self-identity? Is it something given to be merely discovered by us? These questions of identity very often lead to discussions regarding how we can ontologically identify a person as the same person over a period of time. However, one may ask whether these ontological questions can be settled a priori without looking into the practical dimensions of identity. In her article "Negotiating Practical Identities", Meena Dhanda, addresses the problem of personal identity by considering how we negotiate with different and, sometimes, conflicting roles that we play in our lives that confer identities to us. In this context Dhanda starts by talking about moral identity. Though moral identity is acquired over a period of time, Dhanda is of the opion that "Moral identity is the identity of a person. It is not a matter of degree". There is, according to the author, a necessity of a person's having moral identity. Practical identity seems to be more fluid in the sense that it consists of roles that may be "radically questioned, redefined, or even opted out of". However, here also Dhanda thinks that these practical identities cannot be given up altogether since they are a result of or are embedded in inter-personal relationships of both institutional as well as personal kind. In developing this notion of practical identity Dhanda critically engages with the work of Christine Korsgaard, who regards practical identity as a description under which one values oneself. Dhanda, however does not think that all practical identities are "value-conferring". They may on the one hand be given, and on the other are not identities whose demands one must necessarily obey. She also thinks that negotiation of practical identities consists both in searching for one's identity, which is epistemic endeavour, and in making one's identity, which is more of an ethical enterprise.

Problem of self-knowledge, as it has been discussed earlier, is closely connected with the question of the true nature of the self. And the question concerning the truth of the self has been closely linked with question of how to lead a good life. These connections are evident in the philosophies of antiquity. Classical Indian philosophers, as well as their Greek counterparts, have always dealt with the epistemological, metaphysical and ethical issues concerning the self together, because of the obvious interconnection between these three ways of addressing the problem of self and self-knowledge. The last two essays in this volume are enaged with these interconnected concerns. Richard Sorabji, in his essay, "Self and Morality: Cross-Cultural Perspectives", compares the responses of classical Indian philosophers to some of the most important concerns related to self and morality in the Greek philosophy. Sorabji takes up five such topics where, he thinks, there are analogues in classical Indian philosophy: Reincarnation, Higher and Lower Selves, Bad Thoughts and Conscience, No Self, and Being True to your Individual Self. In discussing these five concerns related to a self who is an ethical being, Sorabji not only looks at Greek philosophers, but also takes into consideration Christian philosophers and Islamic philosophers. While discussing Indian philosophers and their views regarding these five concerns, he not only discusses views of different ancient schools of Indian philosophy, but also takes into consideration thinkers like Gandhi. A variety of ideas and positions are woven together in a rich tapestry of connected and parallel views of philosophers from varied religious and civilizational backgrounds.

Ganeri's paper is a response to Sorabji from the classical Indian philosophical perspectives. Sorabji mentions that Indian philosophers not only have specific positions with reference to the five topics that he discusses, but they also have very interesting and sometimes contrasting points of views about these topics. Ganeri's paper explores this remark and justifies it by going into a detailed discussion of the debates between different schools of Indian philosophers as a response to some of the concerns of their Greek counterparts. Not only does he look at various official schools of Indian philosophy, Ganeri takes into consideration views propounded in the *Mahābhārata*, *Manu-Smṛti,* etc. to strengthen his interpretation of the five topics that Sorabji himself deals with. So, these two essays complement each other in understanding the play of self and morality in the rich tradition of classical Indian and Greek philosophies.

A closer look into the debates that the authors in this volume deal with, hopefully brings out the importance of exploring the relationship between self-knowledge and agency. One cannot but emphasize that knowing our own mind or knowing ourselves is not merely an epistemological enterprise, neither can it be dealt with by overlooking the epistemological concerns that accompany it. We need to weave together these debates in order to have a better understanding of ourselves as authoritative self-ascribers and agents of actions.

# 1

# From Self-ascription to Self-knowledge*

*Amita Chatterjee*

> Self-knowledge is a notion that is not always fully examined when academics talk about "the self" because that academic self is often taken to be pretty abstract, and so far as it is specified the discussion can often be treated as being about other people's selves rather than one's own. But in everyday life self-knowledge is rather an important topic, one that crops up often in our personal affairs and has a strong moral bearing.
>
> — Mary Midgley[1]

WRITING a paper on self-knowledge is extremely difficult as both "self" and "knowledge" are perplexing polymorphous concepts. The varied understanding of the compound word is, therefore, a natural outcome of different understandings of the component words. *The Oxford English Dictionary* has listed six different senses of self-knowledge, viz. (1) interpersonal cognitive relations; (2) remembering on a first-hand basis one's past actions or experiences; (3) awareness of

* I wish to express my gratitude to Arthur Falk whose insightful e-mails a couple of years ago led me to write this paper. I am also indebted to the University Grants Commission for providing the funds for carrying out the background research under its scheme for "The University with Potential for Excellence".

1. Mary Midgley, "Being Scientific About Our Selves', in *Models of the Self*, ed. Shaun Gallagher and Jonathan Shear, UK and USA: Imprint Academic, 1999, p. 468.

any object; (4) immediate awareness of one's mental processes; (5) the totality of mental experiences that constitute our conscious being; and (6) the general mode of awareness that is distinct from the content that makes up the stream of consciousness. The first five definitions can be related to the content of experience of an embodied system while the last one tries to capture the ground of all conscious experiences, which is not directed towards any content.

In view of so many different concepts of self and correlative concepts of self-knowledge, I need to define the scope of my discussion in this paper. "Self" in the compound expression "self-knowledge" would neither refer to Pure Consciousness, nor to the insular Cartesian Self. I rather fancy that sense of self which lies at the root of an organism's creating its "other" as well as the distinction between its "internal systems" and its "external" environment, which puts all its experiences together and endows it with a feeling of continuity, which in dynamic interaction with many others makes the being what or who it is. However, in this paper, I shall confine myself to that understanding of self which is compatible with both, the official view of philosophers and the intuitive view of common man.

Ever since the publication of Galen Strawson's paper on "The Self",[2] people start their enquiries from the phenomenal sense of self. As a justification, it has been maintained that the phenomenal sense of self appears to be the same irrespective of cultural variance and ontological commitments.[3] However,

2. Originally published in *Journal of Consciousness Studies*, vol. 4, nos. 5/6, 1997, pp. 405-28; reprinted in *Models of the Self*, eds. Shaun Gallagher and Jonathan Shear, UK and USA: Imprint Academic, 1999, pp. 1-23.

3. Except Thomas Metzinger who thinks that it is to be explained away, all stalwarts in the field are of the opinion that the sense of self needs to be explained, whether they believe in the ontology of a core self or admit self merely as a narrative construction.

even the so-called phenomenal sense of self has been construed rather narrowly just to include the feeling/awareness of I, me and mine in total exclusion of you and what you think of me. This approach is in consonance with philosophical trend because philosophers have always tried to capture the salience of self in its subjectivity and reflexive awareness — "as a pure identity-pole".[4] In the human context, it is almost unanimously accepted that the criterion of having knowledge of self is the ability to entertain first-person thoughts. That is, I can have knowledge about myself only if I have belief about myself and I can have belief about myself only if I can entertain thoughts about myself and this latter ability is manifested through our use of indexical sentences. In all languages of the world there are special mechanisms of explaining I-thoughts. So I want to explore whether there is a sure route from our self-ascriptions to self-knowledge. In course of our exploration we need to understand the implications of different modes of self-ascription and if any form of self-ascription at all leads to self-knowledge, then what does it really amount to. However, our take-off point is problematic because there is a long-standing debate around the issue whether the mastery of first-person pronoun is necessary for self-ascription. Though it is essential to have some indexical belief to have self-knowledge and to act as an autonomous moral agent, yet it does not entail that to ascribe belief about oneself, one must have linguistic mastery of the first-person pronoun, "I".

It has been unanimously admitted that the human race is a race of self-ascribers. We do ascribe different "attitudes" to ourselves at different points of time. Those who believe that self cannot be experienced in terms of any empirical quality and those who believe that we can infer an ontologically existing self over and above our body depending on our

4. Shaun Gallagher and Dan Zahavi, *The Phenomenological Mind*, London and New York: Routledge, 2008, p. 200.

empirical experience are equally inclined to analyse self-ascriptions. It is possible to approach the topic of self-ascription from two different points of view — from those of philosophy of language and philosophy of mind. I shall approach the phenomenon of self-ascription from the perspective of philosophy of mind and not from the perspective of philosophy of language. The major difference between the philosophy of mind approach and the philosophy of language approach is this: the former (exemplified in the writings of Chisholm,[5] Lewis,[6] Falk[7] and Mellor[8]) emphasizes on understanding the exact nature of attribution involved in self-ascription, while the latter (adopted by Perry,[9] Kaplan,[10] et al.) enquires how important self-reference through the use of first-person pronoun is in the human communication process. The latter relies mostly on Gareth Evans's[11] propositional model of referential success, while the former offers a pre-propositional account of self-reference. The most important difference amongst two approaches with which I shall be concerned is: according to the former, I-thoughts or indexical beliefs are necessary, non-trivial conditions of one's agency and moral agency, while according to the latter, acceptance of a sentence containing the first-person pronoun "I" is necessary for explaining one's moral agency and change of behaviour.

---

5. *The First Person,* University of Minnesota Press, 1981.
6. "Attitudes De Dicto and De Se" (1979); reprinted in *Philosophical Papers,* vol. 1, Oxford, 1983.
7. *Desire and Belief,* Lanham: Hamilton Books, 2004.
8. "I and Now" (1989); reprinted in D.H. Mellor, *Matters of Metaphysics,* Cambridge University Press, 1991.
9. "Myself and I" (1998); reprinted in John Perry, *The Problem of Essential Indexical and Other Essays,* expanded edition, CSLI Publications, 2000.
10. "Opacity" in L. Hahn and P. Schilpp, eds., *The Philosophy of W.V. Quine,* Open Court 1998.
11. John McDowell, ed., *The Varieties of Reference,* Oxford: Clarendon Press, 1982.

Let us quickly enumerate the characteristic features of I-thoughts as accepted by the philosophers of mind.[12] The core instances of indexical self-reference are the beliefs in the indicative mood involving the first person and the present tense, e.g. "I am in pain now".

i. Unlike the word "this", the referent of an I-thought on any occasion of its use is not subject to variation by the speaker's intention to refer; it's user-proof. Even if I pretend to be someone else, I refer to myself.

ii. It's fail-safe because on any occasion of its use it succeeds in referring to oneself; no matter how uninformed or misinformed its believer happens to be about the referent. It refers without the believer needing to identify the referent. Antonio Damasio's patient RB lost all autobiographical memory and didn't know anything about him; yet he could successfully refer to himself.

iii. It's infallible, for it always hits the right referent, no matter how totally wrong its believer may be about the referent when using it. I may go crazy and believe that I am Laxmibai, the Queen of Jhansi, yet the person I refer to is still me.

iv. One who entertains an I-thought must have a capacity to distinguish the object of his I-thought from all other things.

v. Only ascription of an I-thought gives the believer a unique perspective.

By virtue of these features, a genuine I-thought can be distinguished from pseudo-I-thoughts. Pseudo-I-thoughts also involve self-reference but only a genuine I-thought is a non-

12. See Anscombe, "The First Person" (1975); reprinted in G.E.M. Anscombe, *Metaphysics and the Philosophy of Mind,* University of Minnesota Press, 1981. See also Falk (2004).

trivial necessary condition of a believer's action or attitudinal change. We have come across at least three types of pseudo-I-thoughts in the literature.

(a) One such case is where Pratiti has a belief that just happens to apply to her. Suppose Pratiti believes that the girl Rahul is in love with is beautiful. But Pratiti does not know that Rahul is in love with no one else but Pratiti. So Pratiti's belief about Rahul's fiancée applies to Pratiti herself. But without the belief of the form "I am the one whom Rahul loves" Pratiti cannot act appropriately. In the parlance of philosophy of language, Pratiti's belief about Rahul's fiancée is *de dicto* and not *de re*. Arthur Falk has given another example to drive this point home. A story in the Old Testament runs as follows. Prophet Nathan told King David about a man who forcefully took away one of his sheep and misbehaved with him. David accused the man in Nathan's story of injustice and ordered punishment for him. Only then Nathan disclosed that this man was none other than King David. "Until the moment David realized 'I am the man' he had no idea that he believed of himself that he was unjust; his belief simply had been *de dicto*. Nathan had arranged to create first the wrath that the behaviour itself warranted, and then the self-recognition in the story, so that the wrath has turned toward David, *de re* and David replied with repentance, "I have sinned against the Lord".[13] The moral of the story: once there is a genuine I-thought, there follows the appropriate change in attitude.

(b) Suppose Pratiti believes that Pratiti is dehydrated but because of a lesion in her brain she has forgotten that she is Pratiti and therefore does not make any effort

13. Falk (2004), p. 236.

to get a glass of drink. Though Pratiti's belief about herself is a *de re* belief, yet it is not of the right type and that is why it does not evoke the right sort of response in Pratiti. Pratiti could have acted appropriately, had she also possessed the auxiliary belief that "I am Pratiti". Absence of such auxiliary belief is commonly found in half-stunned states.

(c) Suppose Pratiti is recuperating from a serious illness. She was in a nursing home for quite some time and hasn't looked into a mirror since her admission. Suddenly, one day the nurse holds a mirror before her and Pratiti exclaims "This girl is surely very tired; all her energy appears to be drained out". But Pratiti hasn't realized that this girl is no other than herself. This is an instance which shows that even a *de re* belief with a demonstrative pronoun fails to constitute a genuine self-reference. Had she identified that tired girl with herself her sympathy would have changed to concern for herself. All of us heard about the story of Ernst Mach. Mach wrote, "Not long ago, after a tiring railway journey by night and much fatigued, I got into an omnibus, just as another gentleman appeared at the other end. 'What shabby pedagogue is that, that has just entered?' thought I. It was myself: opposite me hung a large mirror. The physiognomy of my class, accordingly, was better known to me than my own."[14]

The main insight that we have from such stories is that one's genuine I-thoughts or beliefs that can be expressed to others by using the personal pronoun "I" directly affect one's behaviour and dispositions, whereas beliefs directed toward the same content but not expressible through "I" don't by

14. See Ernest Mach, *Analysis of Sensations*, Open Court, 1897.

themselves affect behaviour. So it has been concluded that one's indexical beliefs are indispensable to one's action. Here I must draw your attention to one important point. When we call a belief indexical, we don't mean that the indexical belief's content contains indexical words, but only that the content can be expressed by using indexical sentences when the believer wishes to communicate it to others.

Philosophers of language, e.g. John Perry, on the other hand, insists that what all the deviant cases mentioned above lack is the mastery of the indexical pronoun "I" and use of a sentence containing the first-person pronoun "I". According to Perry, Pratiti, David, Mach and others — all believed singular complete propositions, yet they failed to act appropriately. It is the mastery of the pronoun "I" that leads one to act appropriately in a context in accordance with the available information to reach one's goal. While a philosopher of mind says that if there is a change in action or attitude of a person, there must have been change in the indexical belief, Perry instead upheld that change has taken place in the sentence-content and not necessarily in the belief-content. Why did Perry and other like-minded philosophers uphold such a counter-intuitive view? The reason is: indexical beliefs are intensional entities and there are lots of problem regarding the individuation and regimentation of intensional entities. So if cases can be explained without reference to intensional entities, why should we unnecessarily accommodate these entities? The response here is somewhat Quinean. However, these philosophers wanted to distance themselves from Quine's idea of ego-centric propositional attitudes which Quine wanted to explain by stimulus-meaning and he was even ready to ascribe them to non-human animals like cats and dogs.

It is possible to contest Perry's view both on empirical and philosophical grounds. Empirically speaking, there are cases of entertaining indexical beliefs without any mastery of the first-person pronoun. Two-year-old Thomas, for example, regally declares, "Thomas wants to have a bath", "Thomas wants to have a cookie", and thus expresses his own desires without ever using "I". Some psychologically disturbed patient, on the other hand, appropriately and fluently uses the pronoun "I" without having any idea whom this "I" refers to. This brings us to the philosophical arguments against Perry's position. Underlying this position there is a deep-rooted faith in what Gareth Evans calls Russell's Principle. According to this principle, it is not possible for a person to have a thought about something unless he knows which particular individual in the world he is thinking about. So to have I-thoughts "I" must have genuine reference and the most important way of discharging this requirement is to think of the object as the unique satisfier of some description. Hence without mastering the use of "I", it is not possible to attain reference-success. This position is vulnerable on two grounds; first, "I" is to be used as a special name to have genuine self-reference. This Special Name Theory, we shall see, does not enjoy immunity to error through misidentification. Secondly, it has been pointed out by Bermudez that if the capacity to think "I" thoughts depends on the linguistic mastery of the first-person pronoun, then a non-circular analysis of self-knowledge is impossible. Bermudez christens this problem "the paradox of self-consciousness".[15]

Let me first enquire whether success of self-ascription depends on using "I" or its surrogate as a special name or whether self-ascription goes through without using any name. Let me explain the difference between these two positions with the example of Pratiti again. The Special Name theorists hold that Pratiti does not only express her belief with a first-person pronoun, but also is in possession of a private and

15. Jose Luis Bermudez, *The Paradox of Self-Consciousness*, Cambridge, MA: MIT Press, 2000.

incommunicable vivid name of herself, the reference of which she cannot ever fail to grasp. This is due to a special sort of knowledge that accompanies the mastery of first-person pronoun. Without positing a special vivid name one cannot explain how any reference to the self is ever established. The alternative to this view was suggested by Anscombe, David Lewis and Chisholm and has been developed in details recently by D.H. Mellor and Arthur Falk. As opposed to the Special Name Theory, Falk calls it the No Name Theory. Briefly stated, the No Name Theory says that Pratiti's *de re* belief about herself does not depend on any name of the *res* occurring in Pratiti's mind. She does not use any inner name equivalent to the "I" she uses to present her beliefs to others. She simply makes attributions to herself directly. This theory has an advantage over the Special Name Theory. We have seen in cases of pseudo-ascription that even when the believer uses her name to ascribe a belief, she may not know the identity between the name-bearer and herself, and thus, misidentify to whom the belief applies. But on the No Name hypothesis Pratiti does not have the opportunity of being mistaken at all. She does not have the opportunity to go wrong in the use of a name, because she does not use a name. Now the question remains how Pratiti does ascribe belief to herself or what is the nature of direct self-ascription? An answer has been proposed by Falk, Mellor and Shoemaker[16] independently of each other. They proposed a non-cognitive/non-propositional model of reference instead of the generally admitted cognitive model of reference. On a cognitive model of reference, to refer to something is to know enough about it so that what one knows can serve to distinguish it from other things. Such a theory of reference, however, leads to a vicious circle, since to know something one must first refer to it. One may save

16. "Introspection and the Self", in S. Shoemaker, *Midwest Studies in Philosophy: Studies in the Philosophy of Mind*, 10, 1986.

the situation by positing different kinds of knowledge, e.g. knowledge by acquaintance and knowledge by description. Or one may offer a non-propositional/non-cognitive model of self-ascription. Depending on the connection established previously between self-ascription of belief and one's purposeful action, a belief in the first person and present tense is identified as being about that which is moved by the belief. In the context of our example, if Pratiti believes that she herself is dehydrated then she will do something to quench her thirst. Hence the referent of Pratiti's belief can be identified as that which drinks because of the belief. Falk calls this the kinetic theory of core instances of indexical reference. The theory depends on a very simple thesis: If indexical reference is indispensable for purposeful action then purposeful action is sufficient for indexical reference. Here I shall quote two very important passages from Falk to make this theory of direct self-ascription clear.

> When a person is aware that her beliefs and desires interface directly with her muscles and glands — her machinery for action — that direct awareness of something about the state of her own agency leads her to choose to publish those attitudes in language using the first-person pronoun, present tense and indicative mood. The main point is to resist the idea that to use the pronoun "I" or "now" we need to introspect something I-ish or Now-ish. Once a person has many standing and recurrent beliefs in the first person, there is some point to introducing a self-concept to label the dossier, so to speak, for mental house-keeping purposes. Only extensive self-reportage creates the need for such a self-concept; it's not that the self-concept comes first and makes self-reportage possible.[17]

> Each of us is like a great ship plying the ocean. Its parts must communicate with each other, and so must ours. It must also communicate with other ships. The prerequisites

17. Falk, 2004, p. 268.

> of two types of communication should not be confused. On the deck is the communication officer, using full resources of our language with other ships. When commands go down to the boiler room, however, the niceties of speech don't count. When the boiler room gets words from above, "Full steam ahead" no one down there acts perplexed and wonders "When?" or "Which one?" This is direct attribution. Only the one subject can be intended and only the one time. Worries about the boiler room crew not knowing how to identify the intended subject and the intended time are unwarranted.[18]

Like Falk many neuro-scientists also maintain that our beliefs about ourselves enjoy immunity to error through misidentification, if those are derived from our direct proprioceptive experience. Even schizophrenics who have deluded notion of agency and think that someone else has inserted thoughts and beliefs in their minds cannot denounce their proprioceptive experience. For they never deny owning such thoughts though they are sure that they were not responsible for having such thoughts.

The analogy of dossier or information file has also been used by Gareth Evans, John Perry and Francois Recanati[19] to explain the origin of our self-concept. Though they approached the problem of self-knowledge from the perspective of philosophy of language, some part of their story can be easily appropriated for our purpose. It is evident from the previous account that all our ego-centric thoughts are based on special type of perception. Recanati concurs by saying,

> The concept Ego is associated with special way of gaining information about a person which we have by virtue of being

18. Falk, 2004, p. 268.
19. *Direct Reference: From Language to Thought*, Oxford: Blackwell Publishers, 1993.

> that person and so forth. It follows that the information which is relevant to my first-person thoughts is the type of information which I gain "from the inside", as when I feel that the wind blows my hair about or that I have a toothache.[20]

Such perceptual information are however temporary and unstable. Besides such information some stable but descriptive information also forms part of our ego-concept, e.g. I was born in Calcutta in 1950 of Indian parents; my grandparents came from the erstwhile East Pakistan, now called Bangladesh. Such autobiographical information are an essential constituent of my self-concept, but have not been known by direct perception. These are called encyclopedia entries in my self-file. So a self-file contains information which are gained through direct acquaintance as well as those which have been derived from others. When all such information are integrated in one single folder our ego-centric thoughts are unified and produce a sense of continuity and intimacy which are considered the characteristic features of self-knowledge.

This account of self-knowledge is not incompatible with the story told by the developmental psychologists. They have been trying for a long time to draw our attention to the fact that the sense of the proto-self or the sense of self-other boundary is rooted in the organism's background body sensation. "As soon as the infant becomes able to focus on its body parts and their internally causally coherent behaviour, it is equipped to develop a sense of self."[21] Let me elucidate this point a little. The developing child may first acquire a

20. *Direct Reference: From Language to Thought*, Oxford: Blackwell Publishers, 1993, p. 123.

21. Marcel Kinsbourne, "Awareness of One's Own Body: An Attentional Theory of its Nature, Development and Brain Basis", in *The Body And The Self*, eds. Bermudez, Marcel and Eilan, Cambridge, MA: MIT Press, 1998.

sense of self when it becomes selectively able to attend, in however ill-differentiated a fashion, to its individual body parts in the somatosensory modality. Its visual channel soon reveals which body parts are always present and hence one's own and which external objects are present only sometimes. The focus of attention, a body-part, is experienced as emerging from a ground. This ground is the familiar feeling that one's body exists as a backdrop to whatever one is experiencing or doing and this ever present somatosensory background may be the basis for constructing the continuity of the experiencing self. A decontextualized construct of a self as mental and distinct from the body is a later emerging abstraction, according to the cognitive developmental psychologists like Vygotsky and Gibson. Underlying the person's feeling of the ownership of the body would be the ownership of the rest of the body by each body part, specifically whichever body part happens to be the focus of attention at the time. The body part at the focus of attention owns its background of body sensation. The construct of the self is abstracted from this origin in sensation. Thus the self has no specific location but rather is co-extensive with the field of bodily sensations. This background awareness of one's body puts the stamp of personal experience and makes all his experience part of his autobiography.

Thus we can round up how one directly attributes certain simple beliefs to oneself. Our self-ascription, however, goes beyond my current indexical states. We do ascribe about ourselves a large number of dispositional states regarding our competences, interests and skills. Such ascriptions depend not only how I perceive myself but also on how others perceive me. Though a complete account of self-knowledge should include these aspects, philosophers have always set them aside. It is not only through the body sense alone that an infant becomes aware of one's self. Its self-experience is enriched by what it sees in the adult expressions which most of the time mirrors its own. Contrary to the accepted view that infants imitate the adults, there are ample evidences to show that it is the adult who very often imitates the infant's expressions. Besides, the discovery of mirror neurons in the brain has enabled us to conjecture how an infant learns other minds through empathy. Mirror neurons fire when the agent imitates somebody or perceives others to do something. Mirror neuron firings enable one to understand how another being feels while performing a certain act. Gradually, by cashing on such beliefs a baby learns to decipher what others think of her and that shapes in a very significant way how the baby looks upon herself. These external influences blend so well with the infant's internal experiences that it appears that one's self-knowledge always springs from within. That is why I think that a complete understanding of self must contain within it not only the concepts of I and me but also that of you and what you think of me.

This thesis will appear more plausible if I describe the minimal conditions of our psychological self-awareness. Proprioceptive self-awareness provides us with a "contrast space" where an organism can numerically distinguish itself from its other. It may also give some non-conceptual awareness of bodily self and its physical environment but its perception of itself as a psychological subject is constitutively linked to its awareness of others' mind. Following Bermudez[22] I would like to formulate this thesis rather weakly and contrast it with the analogy-based understanding of other minds and a strong symmetry thesis offered by Gareth Evans and P.F. Strawson. The weak reading of the so-called symmetry thesis claims only this: not all of a subject's psychological representation can be applicable only to the first person. This thesis is not compatible with the analogical theory which

22. "Ecological Perception and the Notion of a Non-conceptual Point of View" in Bermudez, Marcel and Eilan (1998).

upholds that psychological self-awareness is independent of awareness of other minds. The argument from analogy does not advocate for a constitutive connection between first-person and third-person ascription of psychological properties because according to this theory, "our capacity to ascribe psychological properties to others is an extension from our logically independent capacity to ascribe psychological properties to ourselves". The strong symmetry thesis, which Evans and Strawson advocate, depends in a significant way on their theory of concept mastery, and whenever they talk about psychological self-ascription, they mean concept-involved self-ascription. Let me cite from Strawson:[23]

> A necessary condition of one's ascribing predicates of a certain class to one individual, i.e. oneself, is that one should be prepared, or ready, on appropriate occasions, to ascribe them to other individuals, and hence that one should have a conception of what those appropriate occasions for ascribing them would be.

But, we have ample evidence from developmental psychology that a nine-month-old human baby can distinguish between her own mental state and that of other, albeit non-conceptually, but cannot do so between six and nine months when her capacity to ascribe the same psychological representation and others is yet to develop. The core of psychological self-awareness consists of awareness of a set of categories. So a suitably self-aware subject should be able to distinguish himself as a perceiver within a contrast space of perceivers, as an agent within a contrast space of agents, and as a bearer of reactive attitudes within the contrast space of other bearers of reactive attitudes. Developmental psychologists have shown that these three abilities are developed well before the development of concepts and language and that is evident

23. *Individuals*, London: Methuen, 1959.

from their experiments on joint vision, interactive play and social referencing.[24]

Daniel Stern[25] has shown how at the age of nine-months an infant can take initiative in generating states of joint visual attention. To quote,

> Infants begin to point at about nine months of age, though they do so less frequently than mothers do. When they do, their gaze alternates between the target and the mother's face, as when she is pointing to see if she has joined in to share the attentional focus. . . . These observations lead one to infer that by nine months infants have some sense that they can have the same attentional focus, that their mother can also have a particular attentional focus, that these two mental states can be similar or not, and if they are not they can be brought into alignment and shared.

This illustrates how an infant acquires self-awareness relative to the category of perceivers. This experiment warrants the ascription of recognition to the infant that the mother perceives the world from a perspective that is different from the infant's own, but that the infant can learn about by adjusting the focus of her attention. Built into this recognition on the part of the infant is an awareness of herself as a perceiver, in particular, as a perceiver who is trying to perceive what her mother perceives.

That approximately at the same time an infant comes to know herself as an agent is evident from the study of interactive play. Trevarthen and Hubley[26] conclude from their

---

24. See "An Ecological Perspective on the Origins of Self" in Bermudez, Marcel and Eilan, 1998.
25. *The Interpersonal World of the Infant*, New York: Basic Books, 1985.
26. "Secondary Intersubjectivity: Confidence, Confiding, and Acts of Meaning in the First Year", in Lock ed., *Action, Gesture, Symbol: The Emergence of Language*, London: Academic Press, 1978.

experiments that around forty-five weeks an infant gives a play object happily to the mother when asked to do so. They play the game of passing the ball and when the infant gets back the possession of the ball, she again happily holds out the ball to the mother and urges her to play. What is distinctive of this type of interactive play is that it offers a case of psychological self-awareness relative to the category of agents. The pleasure that the infant takes in the various games is not just pleasure at her own agency but pleasure at successfully carrying out an intention such pleasure shared with the other participants in the game reflects an awareness that they too are agents.

Now we come to the third feature of core psychological self-awareness which also gets manifested in the last quarter of the first year. The phenomenon on which experiments have been performed is known as social referencing. In all experiments on social referencing infants look towards their mothers for guidance when they encounter a surprising or alarming event and the mother's facial expression is highly effective in determining the infant's subsequent behaviour. The best explanation of this phenomenon requires attributing to the infant a comprehension that her mother reacts to things and events in the same way as she does, that she also finds events surprising or alarming. Social referencing implies the presence of psychological self-awareness relative to the category of bearers of reactive attitudes. These phenomena can be understood in the analogy of some linguistic acts. Joint visual attention can be considered a primitive analogue of the linguistic act of reference and social referencing is a primitive analogue of the linguistic act of predication. Distinctive psychological self-awareness thus develops in pre-linguistic children. These findings of developmental psychologists also support the weak symmetry thesis which admits a constitutive link between psychological self-awareness and other-awareness. Prior to nine months, an infant cannot enter into a triadic relation. Her attention is directed either to an object or to the onlooker caregiver. It is only when she is nine-months old she is aware of another perceiver who can perceive the same thing thus demonstrating that self-awareness is constitutively related to her awareness of other minds.

The weak symmetry thesis is not incompatible with the claim that our ways of finding out about our own psychological states can differ fundamentally from our ways of finding about the psychological states of other people. Nor does it rule out the possibility that one's awareness of one's own psychological representations is richer and more vivid than her awareness of the psychological states of others, in spite of the impossibility of a psychologically self-aware subject being completely unaware of the existence of other minds. The weak reading of the symmetry thesis, therefore, has the additional advantage of applying to the low functioning autistic child whose understanding of others is really impoverished compared to normally interacting babies.

The account of self-ascription that we have developed is sufficient for explaining our phenomenological sense of self as well as our belief about self. It cannot warrant our positing a Cartesian self, though it does not rule out our having knowledge of something responsible for our ego-sense and the sense of the unity of experience. However, this account is completely neutral about the ontic status of this "something" and is supportive of any version of a created self — real, conceptual, narrative, phenomenological or neural.

# 2

# A Disjunctive Theory of Introspection*

## A Reflection on Zombies and Anton's Syndrome

*Fiona Macpherson*

REFLECTION on sceptical scenarios in the philosophy of perception, made vivid in the arguments from illusion and hallucination, have led to the formulation of theories of the metaphysical and epistemological nature of perceptual experience. In recent times, the locus of the debate concerning the nature of perceptual experience has been the dispute between disjunctivists and common-kind theorists. Disjunctivists have held that there are substantial dissimilarities (either metaphysical or epistemological or both) between veridical perceptual experiences occurring when one perceives and perceptual experiences involved in hallucination. Common-kind theorists have denied this.

In this paper, I examine the nature of introspection — a faculty that has often been compared with and contrasted to perception. I reflect on cases where introspection goes wrong in ways analogous to that in which our perceptual faculties can go wrong and formulate, what I take to be, an attractive theory of introspection. The cases that I focus on, in which things go wrong, are the case of zombies and the case of subjects with Anton's syndrome. (Anton's syndrome is a condition in which people who are blind claim that they can

* Appeared in *Philosophical Issues*, vol. 20 no. 1, pp. 226-65.

see.) I suggest that, just as it is possible to be a disjunctivist about perception, it is possible to be a disjunctivist about introspection. I argue that this is a good view of one type of introspection, namely introspection of states that have phenomenal character, such as perceptual experiences. It has a good account to give of the cases in which such introspection seems to go wrong and it yields a plausible metaphysical and epistemological view of the nature of introspection.

However, while I favour a disjunctive view of introspection, I do not favour a disjunctive view of perception. And, I suspect, that many disjunctivists about perception would not wish to condone my disjunctivist theory of introspection. I therefore go on to examine to what an extent disjunctivism about perception and disjunctivism about introspection are compatible, and thus to establish whether one must choose between the theories or not. I also identify why I favour a disjunctive theory of introspection but not of perception.

The structure of the paper is as follows. First, I discuss a reconstruction of an argument of Sydney Shoemaker's. The argument is valid and starts from premises, some of which concern introspection of states that have phenomenal character. The conclusion of the argument is that zombies are not possible. I believe that we have two reasons to reject the conclusion. One reason stems from consideration of the conceivability of zombies. The second reason stems from consideration of the nature of Anton's syndrome. Discussion of these two reasons, comprises section two of the paper. If the conclusion of Shoemaker's argument is false then we have to reject one of its premises. It is not a straightforward matter deciding which to reject. In the third section of the paper, I propose a disjunctivist view of introspection about our states that have phenomenal character. In the fourth section, I elaborate and defend the theory and show that adopting this disjunctive view allows one to endorse the view of Anton's syndrome that I advocate. In the fifth section, I show how this view provides us with a response to Shoemaker's argument. In this section I also argue that one should distinguish between different types of zombie. It turns out that Shoemaker's argument is right with respect to some zombies and wrong with respect to others. In the sixth section of the paper, I compare and contrast my disjunctive theory of introspection to disjunctivist theories of perception, explain to what extent they are compatible, and why I hold a disjunctive theory of introspection but not of perception.

**Shoemaker's Argument**

Three pieces of terminology common in the philosophy of mind are "phenomenal character", "zombie" and "ersatz states". The first refers to that aspect of mental states, paradigmatically had by perceptual experiences, sensations, moods and emotions, which is to be identified with "what it is like" to be in such states, to use Nagel's (1974) well-worn phrase. I will take it in this paper, as is fairly standard, that "phenomenal character" is a neutral term to refer to that aspect of mental states. Using the term does not commit one to a particular theory of phenomenal character; in particular, it does not commit one to a dualist or non-physicalist or non-representationalist theory of phenomenal character (nor, of course, does it commit one to a physicalist or functionalist theory). Much has been written on the topic of the nature of phenomenal character, but entering this debate is not required for the purposes of this paper.

"Zombies", as defined in philosophy, are creatures that are functionally identical to particular normal human beings; humans that we presume have states with phenomenal character.[1] However, zombies lack all states with phenomenal character.

1. Sometimes zombies are defined as being functionally identical to humans, sometimes physically identical and sometimes both. It is functional identity that matters here.

An "ersatz state" is a state which has the same functional role as some mental state that has phenomenal character, but which itself lacks phenomenal character. For example, an ersatz pain is a state that has the very same functional role as a pain state, but which lacks phenomenal character — there is nothing that it is like to be in that state. Zombies are replete with ersatz states.

Shoemaker (1975) has argued that there could not be ersatz mental states. He illustrates the point using an example involving a genuine pain state that has phenomenal character and a putative ersatz pain state. Suppose, simplifying for the sake of argument, that the functional role of genuine pain states is as follows: they are caused by bodily damage and they cause observable behaviour such as crying and running away, and cause the formation of a judgement that the subject of the state is in pain, where this involves the subject judging, in effect (that is, even if they would not express their judgement using just these words), that they are in a state with a nasty phenomenal character and that this judgement, in turn, causes the subject to produce the words, "I'm in pain". Now suppose that there could be an ersatz pain state. This would be a state that had the very same causal role. It would be caused by bodily damage and then it, in turn, would cause behaviour such as crying and running away, and cause the formation of a judgement that the subject of the state is in pain, where this involves the subject judging, in effect, that they are in a state with a nasty phenomenal character, and then it, in turn, would cause the subject to produce the words "I'm in pain". Shoemaker argues that if there could be such ersatz states then this would introduce an intolerable scepticism concerning the knowledge we — subjects who have states that have phenomenal character — typically take ourselves to have about our own phenomenal states. He says:

> with what right does each of us reject the suggestion that perhaps his own case is such a case, and that he himself is

> devoid of states having qualitative character? Indeed, with what right do we reject the suggestion that perhaps no one ever has any feelings (or other states having qualitative character) at all? . . . To hold that it is logically possible (or, worse, nomologically possible) that a state lacking qualitative character should be functionally identical to a state having qualitative character is to make qualitative character irrelevant . . . to what we can take ourselves to know in knowing about our own mental states . . . [If] we take qualitative character to be something that can be known in the ways we take human feelings to be knowable (at minimum, if it can be known introspectively), then it is not possible, not even logically possible, for a state that lacks qualitative character to be functionally identical to a state that has it.[2]
>
> — 1975: 295-7

Thus, Shoemaker urges, we should reject the idea that ersatz states are nomologically or logically possible and thus preserve the idea that we can, and often do, have knowledge that we are in a state with phenomenal character.[3]

Now, picking up on the idea mooted in the first sentence of the above quotation, we can imagine a subject that completely lacks states with phenomenal character — a zombie — and formulate a version of Shoemaker's argument that shows that zombies are not possible. Although Shoemaker (1975) does not explicitly present such an argument, I will, nonetheless, call the following argument "Shoemaker's zombie argument".

**Premise 1** If zombies are possible then ersatz states are possible.

2. Shoemaker's term "qualitative character" can be taken to be interchangeable with "phenomenal character".
3. Of course the man on the Clapham omnibus would not typically express his knowledge using this terminology, but that is beside the point.

**Premise 2** If ersatz states are possible we do not know whether we have states with phenomenal character.

**Premise 3** It is not the case that we do not know whether we have states with phenomenal character.

**Conclusion 1** It is not the case that ersatz states are possible (by modus tollens using premises 2 and 3).

**Conclusion 2** It is not the case that zombies are possible (by *modus tollens* using conclusion 1 — hence premises 2 and 3 — and premise 1).

I find this argument, *prima facie*, problematic. As the argument is valid, we either have to accept the conclusion or reject one or more of the premises. Yet, the premises all seem like ones we should accept. Premise one, one might think, looks to be simply definitional of a zombie. Premise two expresses the sceptical worry that Shoemaker claims ersatz states would engender. Premise three looks to be a plausible claim about self-knowledge that we really do not want to give up. However, I think that we have two good reasons to reject the conclusion. This is why the argument is *prima facie* troubling. I do not want to accept the conclusion, yet it is not obvious that any premise should be denied. This paper addresses the question of what one should do in the face of this apparent dilemma.

In the next section, I will give the two reasons that I believe support the rejection of the conclusion. But, in the rest of this section, I would like to make a few other comments on the argument.

As I said at the start of the paper, I will be outlining a theory of introspection that is constructed by thinking about cases in which introspection apparently goes wrong. This is a methodology similar to that commonly used in philosophy of perception. One can think of Shoemaker's zombie argument as akin to the argument from hallucination, which is frequently considered in philosophy of perception. The argument from hallucination starts from the claim that it is a possibility that any, or even all, of our perceptual experiences could have been had when hallucinating and thus when not seeing the world. This alleged possibility is then used to raise the sceptical challenge of whether we really know about the objects and properties that appear to be before us when we have visual experiences or, if we do, how we can have such knowledge, given that the argument claims that the experiences we have are compatible with us not seeing and merely hallucinating. In a similar fashion, the zombie argument suggests the possibility that any, or all, of our introspective judgements to the effect that we are in a state with phenomenal character might be had when there is no state with phenomenal character being introspected. It can be used to raise the sceptical challenge of whether we really know that we are in states with phenomenal character or, if we do, how we can have such knowledge given that the argument claims that the introspective judgements we make are compatible with us not introspecting states with phenomenal character. It is this sceptical challenge that is articulated in the second premise of Shoemaker's zombie argument.

One response to the sceptical challenge, as it is raised by the argument from hallucination, is dismissive. One might think that the argument raises the mere possibility of error, and one might think that such a mere possibility does not undermine our claims to know things by perception. And one might adopt a similar response to the sceptical worries raised by Shoemaker's zombie argument. Thus, one might think that the mere possibility of introspective error does not undermine our claims to have knowledge of our own states with phenomenal character, and thus that premise two is false.

I have two responses. First, *ultimately*, I agree that the

mere possibility of error does not show that we cannot have knowledge. The purpose of this paper is to spell out exactly why, and in what circumstances, one can think that that is the case. However, I think that the possibility of error does raise a challenge — and one that ought to be addressed, not simply dismissed. The task of explaining how we can have knowledge, given the possibility of error, has to be undertaken, and I believe that it is a substantial task.

Second, note that in the perceptual case, those who endorse the idea that the mere possibility of error does not undermine our knowledge need to, and often do, differentiate between those possibilities that undermine our claims to knowledge and those that do not. For example, a "safety principle" might be invoked that claims a subject only knows that *p* if, in all close possible worlds, if the subject believes that *p*, then *p* is true.[4] The point of such a principle is to claim that only if the possibility of hallucinating without realizing that one is, rather than perceiving, is in a nearby possible world — as opposed to a distant one — would our claim to know something by perception be undermined by the possibility of error. Alternatively, a form of reliabilism might be endorsed to the effect that if perception is a reliable process then it can yield knowledge, even if there are unreliable methods of forming beliefs too, such as hallucinating.[5] Thus possibilities of error whilst using a reliable process do not undermine our knowledge, but possibilities in other circumstances may. There are other responses that play a similar role of differentiating the possibilities that it is claimed raise a skeptical challenge and those that do not.

I do not find such responses particularly attractive responses to scepticism. They do not address the question of whether our beliefs are ever justified. These theories do not

4. See, for example, Sosa (1999) and Pritchard (2005).

5. See, for example, Goldman 1979.

tell us whether we do know things — they can only tell us the conditions that would be required for knowledge.[6] Thus, the theories provide what I will call conditional responses to scepticism. They say, *if* certain external conditions are met, then we know. Now perhaps this is the best we can do in response to external world scepticism, but it seems to me that this answer is *particularly* unsatisfactory when it comes to knowledge of my own mind. The knowledge that I have that I am not in the sceptical situation — my knowledge that I do have states with phenomenal character — is not conditional. I know that I have states with phenomenal character unconditionally. I know it, even though I don't know whether the externalist conditions apply.

To make the same point another way, it has been frequently pointed out that if the conditions that such externalists require for knowledge are in place, and on account of that we can be rightly said to have justified beliefs and knowledge, we would still not be able to make rational claims that we know things because whether or not we are justified or whether or not we know, is a matter beyond our ken. For example, Crispin Wright says:

> Cartesian doubt is already a second order doubt — a doubt about the extent of the knowledge we can rationally lay claim to. — 2008: 401

Now while this doubt may seem near insurmountable with respect to our knowledge of the external world, is it with respect to our internal world? Surely we *are* in a position, with respect to knowledge of our own minds, to make the rational claim that we know that we are in states with phenomenal character. If so, the externalist approach cannot do justice to the epistemic situation that we find ourselves in with respect to introspective knowledge.

---

6. See Klein, P. (2009: section 1).

In fact, something even stronger seems to be the case here. I could know that I have states with phenomenal character even if the externalist conditions did not hold. For example, if the safety principle didn't apply to my situation — that is, if in the actual world I were in a state with phenomenal character, but in close possible worlds I were not in a state with phenomenal character but nevertheless falsely believed I was in a state with phenomenal character — then I still think that I could know that I am in a state with phenomenal character now in this world. Similarly, suppose introspection is not a reliable process because both zombies and non-zombies use introspection to ascertain whether or not they are in states with phenomenal character and I am the only non-zombie on Earth, so most cases of introspecting lead to false beliefs about being in states with phenomenal character. Still, in such circumstances, I think that if I were in a state with phenomenal character, I could know that I were. In short, it seems to me that the introspective knowledge, that I have of my own consciousness, does not depend for its existence on conditions external to me. This intuition may be thought by some to be controversial, and I have not argued for it here, but it is a standard internalist one and if, like me, you share it then you will have all the more reason to adopt my account of introspection.

I take it to be a substantial advantage of my theory of introspection that it shows how we can know that we are in states with phenomenal character unconditionally — even if we don't know what external conditions hold, and in spite of the external conditions that hold. At the very least, non-externalist approaches to the problem of scepticism, particularly in the introspective case, are worth exploring. One should take this paper as such an exploration.

Earlier in this section, I said that I believe that Shoemaker's zombie argument raises sceptical possibilities in the same way that the argument from hallucination does (even if I think that there are dissimilarities in the plausible responses to that form of scepticism). However, one might challenge this analogy. One might think it distinctive of the argument from hallucination that the evidence that one has when perceiving and hallucinating that one uses to form one's perceptual beliefs is the same — the same type of perceptual experience — and this commonality of evidence is crucial in raising this kind of sceptical worry.[7] One might think that the situation is not the same in the introspective case. When one has states with phenomenal character and is not a zombie, typically the evidence that one has and that one uses to form the belief that you are in a state with phenomenal character is a state with phenomenal character. But zombies, by definition, don't have this evidence; they lack states with phenomenal character. Thus, there is no commonality of evidence in the two cases.

In response, I think that Shoemaker's argument raises the worry that the difference of evidence that we normally think obtains in the case of internal knowledge is screened-off from us. The thought is this: you might be convinced that you don't just have beliefs that you have phenomenal character — you also have the requisite phenomenal character which constitutes your evidence for your beliefs about it. But the zombie will be likewise convinced. The zombie really believes that they are in a state with phenomenal character and not just in a state of believing that they are. No matter how convinced you are that you have further evidence than the zombie, so too the zombie is convinced. So the worry becomes, do you really have access to some different evidence from the zombie? Isn't all you have access to your own beliefs about phenomenal character and doesn't the zombie share those too?

7. Of course, not all philosophers will accept this point. Particularly, perceptual disjunctivists will try to resist this. But I am here exploring only one line of thought that might be brought to bear against the sceptical challenge under discussion.

Ultimately, of course, I want to reject this picture. I don't think that our phenomenal character is screened-off from us by our beliefs about phenomenal character. But I think that we need to respond to the potential worry that it might be. We need to make sure that we have a theory of introspection that shows how I can have knowledge of my phenomenal character, despite the possibility of zombies. My disjunctivist theory of introspection will do precisely that.

## Rejecting Shoemaker's Conclusion: Possibility and Anton's Syndrome

Recall the final conclusion of Shoemaker's argument: it is not the case that zombies are possible. Why should one reject the conclusion? There are two reasons. The first reason is that zombies either are conceivable or, at least, appear to be so. Although the relation between conceivability and possibility is hotly disputed in the literature, I am inclined to think that the conceivability or apparent conceivability of zombies provides us with a reason, even if a defeasible one, to think that they are possible.

I believe the onus is on someone who denies that zombies are possible to show us why, despite their apparent conceivability, they are either not possible or not conceivable.[8] For example, when Kripke (1970) argued that water was necessarily $H_2O$, he was faced with an objection that it seemed to some that they could conceive of water that turned out not to be $H_2O$. Such people would have no doubt said that they

8. Of course, one might claim that Shoemaker's zombie argument is a way to show why. I agree, and think that in face of both the argument and the point about conceivability we have a dialectical stalemate. However, that itself is reason to doubt the conclusion of the argument, if there are no further considerations to adduce. It is in that sense only that the onus is on someone to tell us why zombies are either not conceivable or not possible despite their being conceivable.

could imagine going to another planet, finding water on it, and carrying out scientific analysis of the water that revealed it to be XYZ and not $H_2O$.[9] But Kripke had a fitting reply. He said that such people were not conceiving of *water* not being $H_2O$. Rather, they were conceiving of some clear colourless liquid, perhaps a liquid that filled the same functional role as water on Earth (for example, filled the rivers and fell as precipitation), turning out to be XYZ. Of course, as is well known, Kripke held that this type of strategy was unavailable to explain away cases where one imagined some element of the mind that had phenomenal character was present while some physical feature of the world was not present. While there can be a difference between water and something that appears to be water, he claimed that there was no difference between something that was a phenomenal state, like a pain or a feeling of heat, and something that merely appeared to be, or felt like, that phenomenal state. He would presumably have extended this reasoning to cases like that of the zombie, where one imagines some element of the mind that has phenomenal character being absent while some functional role is present, arguing that there is no easy way to explain away the apparent conceivability of such cases for there is no difference between the absence and the apparent absence of a phenomenal state. Thus, I believe the *prima facie* conceivability of zombies gives us some reason to reject the conclusion of Shoemaker's zombie argument.

The conceivability of zombies gives us a reason to believe in the logical and metaphysical possibility of zombies and of ersatz states. But recall that Shoemaker was even more concerned by the nomological possibility of ersatz states. The second reason to doubt Shoemaker's argument is a reason to think that such states, or at least states with the problematic feature of ersatz states, are nomologically possible, and perhaps

9. This scenario was presented by Putnam (1973).

indeed actual. The remainder of this section of the paper deals with this reason, which arises on consideration of Anton's syndrome.

Anton's syndrome is as classified as a delusion. The DSM-IV definition of a delusion is:

> A false belief . . . that is firmly sustained despite . . . incontrovertible and obvious proof or evidence to the contrary. — 1994: 765

Other delusions include the Capgras delusion, whose sufferers believe that someone close to them (commonly a spouse) has been replaced by an identical impostor, and the Cotard delusion, whose sufferers believe that they are dead.

Anton's syndrome is a delusion in which subjects who are blind report that they can see. Moreover, they report that they can see particular things on particular occasions. They often try to explain away their failure to identify things in front of them by maintaining that they can see but that there is a problem on that specific occasion, such as the lights are dim, or they are not wearing the correct glasses, or they were not paying attention when asked.[10]

Here are three excerpts of a dialogue between a doctor (G.G.) and a subject (H.S.) who has Anton's syndrome, that helps to illuminate the condition and which brings out a variety of features of the delusion:

G.G.: What can you see of me?

H.S.: The head and . . . you are wearing a white coat.

10. See, for example, Goldenberg et al. (1995), Hirstein (2005), McDaniel and McDaniel (1991), Raney and Nielsen (1942), Redlich and Dorsey (1945), Stuss and Benson (1986), and Swartz and Brust (1984). It has often been determined that suffers have some form of brain damage. There are no reports of Anton's syndrome in congenitally blind subjects but Anton's syndrome can come and go over a continued period of blindness.

G.G.: (covers his face with a black fan — the part of the conversation in italics takes place while the face is hidden behind the fan): *Do you see my eyes?*

H.S.: *Yes.*

G.G.: *Do I wear glasses?*

H.S.: *I think not.*

G.G.: *Do you see whether I wear glasses?*

H.S.: *I think that you do not wear glasses but I am not sure whether this is right.*

G.G.: *Do you see whether I have a beard?*

H.S.: *I do not think so.*

G.G.: *Is there anything particular about my face?*

H.S.: *No.*

G.G.: *Do you see my face?*

H.S.: *Yes.*

G.G.: *Is my face light or dark?*

H.S.: *You've got some brown tan, not very light.*

G.G.: *Are my hair long or short?*

H.S.: *A normal haircut.* (Goldenberg et al. 1995: 1377-78)

The doctor was, in fact, wearing a white coat. The subject, H.S., did not know this, however, and was drawing on her general knowledge of the situation (that doctors typically wear white coats) when giving an account of what she could see, as Anton's syndrome sufferers often do.

G.G.: (Opens and shuts scissors): Do you have an idea what that might be?

H.S.: Are those scissors?

G.G.: Do you see them?

H.S.: Only vaguely. I guessed a little.

G.G. (Silently hides scissors beneath the table [the part of the conversation in italics takes place while they are hidden]) What can you see of these scissors?

H.S.: *Upside are the handles where you take them, and below them is the part for cutting.*

G.G.: *Are you seeing this?*

H.S.: *Yes.* (Goldenberg et al. 1995: 1378)

In this case, it looks as if H.S. is using information gleaned from other sensory modalities, here audition, when making claims about what she can see. [H.S. has claimed to see an exercise book.]

G.G.: Is there anything on its cover?

H.S.: I think there is something written on it.

G.G.: What could that be?

H.S.: I do not know.

G.G.: Do you see what type of writing that is?

H.S.: I do not know how to call that type of writing. There are small letters.

G.G.: Capital letters?

H.S.: No, no capital letters

G.G.: Latin Script?

H.S.: Yes. (Goldenberg et al. 1995: 1379)

In this final dialogue, we can see that what the subject says about what they can see appears to be influenced by the series of leading questions from the doctor.

The standard interpretation of delusions is the two-factor theory. The theory posits that the in delusions the subject has:

(1) an anomalous experience that explains why they form the delusional belief.

(2) an abnormality in their reasoning process that explains

> why the subject does not reject that belief in the face of what should be conclusive counter-evidence.[11]

For example, in the Capgras delusion, it might be claimed that subjects have an anomalous experience of the feeling of unfamiliarity when looking at their spouse. They form the hypothesis or belief that they are not looking at their spouse, but at an impostor. Some abnormality in their reasoning process then explains why this belief is not overturned in the face of conclusive counterevidence.

---

11. See Davis et al. (2001) and (2005). It is important to note that I will be suggesting an alternative to two-factor theories *that posit an anomalous conscious experience as the first factor*. This is how twofactor theories were originally explicated in the literature. It is possible to hold a theory that does posit two factors to explain delusions but in which the first factor does not involve a conscious experience. It may seem obvious that two factors are required to explain delusions: one factor to explain the formation of the delusional judgement, another to explain why this judgement is maintained in the face of conclusive counter-evidence. (The possibility of someone who forms the delusional judgement but who then jettisons it when faced with counter-evidence, attests to the need for two factors of this kind.) Anton's syndrome is slightly more complicated than standard delusions in that it seems that two judgements are involved: the judgement that a visual experience is being had and the judgement that the subject is seeing. As we will see, there are people who make the former judgement but not the latter: Charles Bonnet subjects. And it would seem possible to have people who make the former judgement and who then formed the second judgement but who then relinquish it in the face of counter-evidence. This suggests that perhaps at least three factors are required to explain Anton's subjects. (Perhaps even four factors are required if Anton's syndrome subjects are not having visual experiences but judge that they do, and if it is possible to have subjects who form this judgement but then give it up in the face of counter-evidence.) Thus, the thrust of my argument will not be that it is not the case that two or more factors are required to explain Anton's syndrome. Rather, it will be that one of the factors required to explain it is not a conscious visual experience.

The explanation that is most commonly offered of Anton's syndrome, in line with the two-factor theory, is that subjects are undergoing a visual experience — or one rather like it, such as an experience had when visually imagining — as of the object, say a jotter, which they claim to see. This then leads them to form the hypothesis or belief that they are seeing a jotter, which is not overturned in the face of conclusive counter-evidence. Such evidence may include the fact that the doctor has told them that they are blind and that what they claim to see is frequently not there, and the evidence from their own non-visual senses, such an touch, which frequently conflicts with the subjects' claims about what they are seeing.

However, it is not obvious that the two-factor theory is the best theory of Anton's syndrome. There is a competing explanation. The alternative is that the subjects are not undergoing a visual experience at all. They merely judge that they can see and can see particular objects and properties on certain occasions. I will not make a full and thorough case for this here, but I will give three reasons that cast doubt on the claim that the subjects are undergoing a visual experience.

The first reason to doubt the two-factor theory is that, according to it, the existence of the visual experiences is supposed to explain rationally why the subject forms the belief that they are seeing. It is supposed to make the formation of such a belief reasonable: the subject who forms such a belief forms it on account of a reason accessible to them — the visual experience that they have. But, it is not obvious that having such an experience completely explains in rational terms the formation of the belief. This is because having visual experiences is not sufficient for a blind person to form the belief that they are seeing.

Consider a different condition, known to psychologists as Charles Bonnet syndrome. In this syndrome, blind subjects, who are otherwise normal, report complex, vivid, visual hallucinations. But many report that they are not tempted for a moment to believe that they are seeing. The following quote about such subjects is telling:

> The patients described the content of their hallucinations as people, animals, plants, a large variety of inanimate objects, and sometimes complete scenes. . . . The hallucinations occurred both in black and white or colour. They could be clearer, equally clear, or less clear in comparison to reality. . . . 49 patients (82 per cent) stated they were always immediately aware of the unreal nature of their hallucinations. — Teunisee et al. 1996: 795

One might think that the experiences in Anton's syndrome are more like perceptual experiences than those in Charles Bonnet syndrome, and that this explains why the Anton's subjects believe that they can see, whilst the Charles Bonnet subjects do not. However, this is not true. Vivid and complex experiences that are like perceptual experiences involved in seeing are often reported in Charles Bonnet syndrome, whilst the experiences of Anton's subjects are frequently described as vague, blurry and reflective of poor vision (Raney and Nielsen 1942 and Goldenberg et al. 1995). Thus, it is not the case that the Anton's experiences are more vivid compared to the experiences in the Charles Bonnet cases, which might have explained why only the Anton's subjects form the belief that they are seeing.

Moreover, one might have thought that the experiences in Anton's syndrome and those in Charles Bonnet syndrome differ as to whether they are under the conscious control of the subjects of the syndrome. If those in Anton's syndrome are not consciously willed, but those in Charles Bonnet syndrome are, then this might explain why only the Anton's subjects believe they can see. However, in both syndromes the experiences are not under the conscious control of the subjects of the syndrome.

Therefore, the difference in the beliefs formed by Anton's and Charles Bonnet subjects cannot be attributed to such a factor.

Another reason to question whether the Anton's subjects are having visual experiences comes from detailed study of their reports. Consider the dialogues between G.G. and H.S. above. Sometimes H.S. reports that she sees some objects (such as the eyes of the doctor), but then she cannot report on the presence or absence of obvious features of those objects (such as whether there are glasses on top of the eyes). Moreover, what H.S. reports as being what she sees is clearly influenced by information gleaned from her other senses (as when she hears the snipping noise of the scissors), what people say is in front of her, and leading questions (as in the case of the writing on the exercise book). Moreover, subjects often change their reports of what they see in response to similar factors. These facts are not conclusive, but they suggest that perhaps such subjects are not having visual experiences at all.

It might be objected at this point that the above facts about the reports of H.S. would be fully explained if what is happening in Anton's subjects is that their visual experiences are changing in response to information gained from their other senses or from information given by others or from leading questions. Thus, perhaps what other people say and what noises the subject hears interact with the subject's experiences and changes their content and character.

Now while this could happen, note how unusual that would make the subjects' experiences. Imagine that you are sitting in front of a doctor. You visually experience the doctor and his white coat. Then the doctor mentions that he is bald and you suddenly now visually experience his baldness. An accomplice now tells you that the doctor is lying and that in fact he has long hair. Now you have a visual experience as of the long hair of the doctor. Suddenly the doctor mentions that he is thinking of dying his hair and only now do you experience the colour of his hair.[12] Further, all of a sudden you hear a snipping sound and suddenly you visually experience a pair of scissors in the hand of the doctor. You are asked to comment on the writing on a book. You cannot make it out, but as the doctor asks you more and more questions so your visual experience alters, allowing you to at least comment on the font of the letters, if not what words the letters spell out. Such a pattern of experiences would be highly unusual. A normal person would certainly be disturbed by such a pattern and would report this. But Anton's subjects do not. Again, this fact is not conclusive, but highly suggestive that perhaps Anton's subjects do not undergo visual experiences at all.

My preferred alternative explanation is that Anton's subjects lack visual experience and, in the face of this, they confabulate. In describing what is happening as confabulation, I am not suggesting that the patient deliberately lies or makes something up. On the contrary, I assume the confabulation in such cases is not premeditated nor under the control of the subject.

Psychologists report that subjects are prone to this type of confabulation in response to a lack of information or in response to an absence of relevant experience. The confabulation in Anton's syndrome appears to be an instance of this kind of confabulation and would thus not be unusual.[13]

---

12. Note that this is precisely what Goldenberg et al. suppose is happening, although they don't comment on quite how bizarre this situation is: "Visual sensations could also be *induced* by telling the patient that in front of her was a visible object" (1995: 1379, emphasis added).

13. See for example, Gazzaniga and LeDoux (1978) and Gazzaniga (1998). They note that split brain subjects often confabulate about their behaviour when they, or the relevant hemisphere of their brain that is posited to contain language, lacks access to visual experience accessible only to the other hemisphere. As Joseph puts →

In the case of Anton's subjects, what is confabulated is nonetheless responsive to the subject's doxastic background. The beliefs that they do form reflect, and are coherent and consistent with, what the subject believes to be true of the world. They draw upon the, often minimal, information or misinformation that they already possess about the world in forming their beliefs about what they see.

So, on my account, the Anton's subjects lack visual experience and, faced with such an absence, confabulate and report that they are seeing. No doubt, the organic brain damage that such subjects have suffered is responsible for this happening. However, what the subjects report that they see is intelligible. It is intelligible in light of their doxastic background. Their beliefs — be they based on general knowledge, or on what their other senses tell them, including what they hear other people saying — influence what they report seeing. This theory renders the Anton's subjects as reasonable or rational as the competing two-factor theory. (Though not, of course, *completely* reasonable or rational for the subjects report seeing and experiencing when they are not, according to this theory.) It explains why the reports of the subjects do not look like typical reports of visual experiences: the subjects are not reporting what they do because they have certain visual experiences. Rather, as the subjects' background beliefs change, so too does what is confabulated. Finally, this theory is more parsimonious than the two-factor theory, making it at least a very plausible alternative to it.

Anton's subjects seem to make two types of judgements.[14] First, they report, and thus seem to judge, that they are seeing

→ it, "confabulation is . . . likely when the language axis is functionally isolated from a particular source of information about which the patient is questioned" (1986: 516).

14. The reason I qualify this statement with "seem" will become apparent at the end of section three below.

things. But, second, they also report, and thus seem to judge, that they are having visual experiences. To use technical vocabulary, which the subjects themselves would probably not use, they seem to judge that they are in states with visual phenomenal character. They report that they have visual "perceptions" or "sensations" and comment that they are "blurry" or "vague" or "weak".[15] Goldenberg et al. say of H.S. that:

> The patient insisted on the visual nature of her sensation. She recognised that her visual sensations were not like normal visual perceptions, but at the same time would not accept the possibility that they were only mental images.
>
> — 1995: 1378

Suppose that Anton's subjects do make such judgements. The two-factor theory would say that the first type of judgement is false, whilst the second type is true. My confabulation theory would say that both types of judgement are false.

With an overview of Anton's syndrome in place, let us now return to considering their place in the overall dialectic. Clearly, if there are *actual* cases (as my theory says there are) in which subjects judge that they are in a state with phenomenal character when they are not, then they are relevant to an assessment of Shoemaker's argument. They would be cases that whilst not ersatz cases — cases in which a state that lacks phenomenal character has *exactly* the functional role of a state

15. Whether blurriness is a property of experience or can be explained merely in terms of how the world is represented to be by some experiences (as representationalists would believe) is disputed in the literature. The same debate could, no doubt, be had about weakness and vagueness. I do not wish to take a stance on this issue here. One might agree with the representationalist yet nonetheless think that attributions of such qualities to their "perceptions" or "sensations" by naïve subjects reflect their thoughts about their experience, which is the only point I wish to make here.

that has phenomenal character — none the less share the features of ersatz states that raises the sceptical worry concerning introspective knowledge. They would be cases in which someone falsely judges that they are in a state with phenomenal character (in this case a visual phenomenal state) when they are not.[16] It is the possibility of judging that one is in a phenomenal state, such as a pain or a visual experience, when one is not, that raises the sceptical worry that perhaps any or all of our judgements are false and that we are not in a phenomenal state when we judge that we are. If my theory of Anton's syndrome is correct then this shows that such cases are actual. Even if my theory turns out to be false, by looking at this case in detail we seem to have opened up the nomological possibility, and, at the very least, the metaphysical possibility, of there being such cases. And it is, of course, the mere possibility of such cases that is required for Shoemaker's argument to get off the ground.

To reiterate the above in another way, define the simplest "good case" as being a case where a subject has a state with phenomenal character and then introspects and judges that they are in a state with phenomenal character. Define the

16. Not only am I not claiming here that Anton's subjects have ersatz states, I hope that it is obvious that I am not claiming that Anton's subjects are zombies. For example, when Anton's subjects report that they are in a state with no visual phenomenal character, they are probably in some states with phenomenal character, such as auditory or haptic states. Thus, when I say that Anton's subjects seem to falsely judge that they are in a state with phenomenal character I mean, of course, that they seem to judge that they are in a state with phenomenal character over and above the states that they are in that actually do have phenomenal character. One can easily imagine a "pure" Anton's case in which the subject has no phenomenal states (for example, suppose we temporarily deaden all their other senses) and then they go on and form the erroneous judgement that they are having a state with phenomenal character.

simplest "bad case" as being a case in which a subject is not in a state with phenomenal character but nonetheless judges that they are.[17] It is the existence of bad cases that raises sceptical worries. The conceivability of zombie cases and my account of Anton's subjects provide reasons to believe in the metaphysical and nomological possibility of such cases.

Thus, we have some reason to reject the conclusions of Shoemaker's zombie argument, namely that zombies and that ersatz states are not possible. We have some reason to believe that states with the problematic feature of ersatz states are possible and, thus, we should be concerned to address the sceptical worry that such cases raise.

## A Disjunctive Theory of Introspection

The key to responding to the sceptical worry, I believe, is to deny that it is possible for someone to be in a state with no phenomenal character and yet to judge that they are, or for someone to be in certain phenomenal states (such as non-visual states) and to judge that they are in an additional phenomenal state (such as a visual state). I will deny these possibilities, yet at the same time, I will maintain that Anton's subjects are not having visual experiences. How is it possible to do both of these things at once? The way forward is to follow the example of disjunctivism in the philosophy of perception, but to apply it, not to perceptual experiences, but to introspective states.

17. Zombies are cases that fit the simplest bad case description. Anton's subjects that conform to my confabulation theory typically will not, as no doubt they will often be in *some* phenomenal states when they judge that they are having a phenomenal visual experience, for example they may be having auditory and tactile experiences. Anton's subjects typically conform to a non-simple bad case template: they judge that they are having an additional phenomenal state over and above those that they are actually having. These non-simple bad cases also raise Shoemaker's skeptical worry.

For purposes of comparison and elucidation, I will very briefly outline one form of disjunctivism about perceptual experiences. A common disjunctive theory of perceptual experiences would be that, even though when someone perceives and when they merely hallucinate they have perceptual experiences that seem the same to them, these experiences are actually very different kinds of mental state. In the "good case", when perceiving, the person is undergoing a visual experience that has what is seen as a constituent of the experience. In doing so, they are directly aware of what they see. In the "bad case" where the person is hallucinating, they are not having that type of visual experience. The thing that is seen in the good case is not a constituent of the experience in the bad case. The person is in a state that is indiscriminable from the visual experience in the good case but, metaphysically, the states are very different. This metaphysical disjunctivism could be supplemented by an epistemological disjunctivism. This view would say that the experience in the good case and that in the bad have different epistemological significance. The experience in the good case can justify the belief of, and yield knowledge in the subject of the experience concerning what is seen. The experience in the bad case cannot justify belief and does not yield knowledge.[18]

I do not advocate disjunctivism for perceptual experiences, but I want to advocate a particular form of disjunctivism for introspective states of the kind that amount to putative introspections of states with phenomenal character.

The theory is this. We distinguish a good case and a bad case. In the good case, one is in a state with phenomenal character, say a visual experience (of course, it does not matter whether the experience is one had whilst perceiving or when

18. More detail of the nature of disjunctivism and its various forms can be found in Haddock and Macpherson (2008).

hallucinating). One then introspects this state and comes to be in a certain introspective state which has a content, namely something to the effect, "I am in a state with phenomenal character". I will call this introspective state a judgement. In fact, we will see below that the introspective state has both features like judgements and features traditionally associated with an inner-perceptual state.

In the simplest bad case, one is not in a state with phenomenal character, such as a visual experience. Nonetheless, one then goes into a state of a certain kind. This is a state that is, for the subject, indiscriminable from the state of judging that one is in a state with phenomenal character. The key thought is that the state one goes into is not an inner judgement. For want of a better term, we might call it a pseudo-judgement.

What indiscriminability means here has to be carefully spelled out. To do so, I will elaborate on the good case and the bad case once again, in turn. In the good case, when one forms a judgement that one is in a state with phenomenal character, I claim that that judgement is partly constituted by the phenomenal character of the state that it is about. This is why I think it is correct to say that in making the judgement one comes to be directly aware of the phenomenal character of one's visual experience — because that phenomenal character is literally a part of the judgement. This is to say that one's judgement does not involve a representation of the phenomenal character, if that idea is cashed out as follows: that, were the same type of judgement made on another occasion, that judgement might be capable of misrepresenting that a state with phenomenal character was present in one. If there is representation of phenomenal character by the judgement state, it is such that it is guaranteed to be accurate, for the existence of the judgement necessarily involves the existence of the phenomenal state, which is a part of it. If one thought that the nature of representation is such that it can occur only if there is the possibility of misrepresentation, as some but not all people do, then the most accurate description of the case at hand would not be that the judgement represented the state with phenomenal character but, rather, *presented* it to the subject of the judgement. Whether one chooses to say that the judgement represents or not seems to me to be a terminological matter of how one should define "representation".

Thus, the inner judgemental states are like judgements in that they involve an affirmation of a content such as: "I am in a state with phenomenal character". But they are like perceptual states in that having them essentially involves being in a state with a certain phenomenal character — the phenomenal character of the state of which they are an introspection. Moreover, the state provides one with an awareness of the phenomenal character of the state being introspected in a way that is direct and unmediated, because the state is literally composed of that phenomenal character. Thus the similarity between the nature of my introspective states and the nature of perceptual experiences, as they are conceived of by the perceptual disjunctivists, as providing direct and unmediated access to the world and being partly constituted by the world, is clear. Thus, my view of introspection shares some similarities with a view of introspection that that treats it as unmediated direct observation.[19]

19. See Gertler (2008) for an excellent taxonomy of views of introspection and a detailed description of standard unmediated observation views of introspection. Other recent accounts of introspection in the literature, different to my own, that nonetheless involve the claim that introspective states are partly constituted by the states that they are introspections of include Papineau (2002) and Chalmers (2003).

One might ask: is introspection going on in the bad case? The answer is, in part, a terminological matter. But before explaining why this is the case, let me first articulate one confusion that might be motivating this question. One might think the following: what is being given is a disjunctive theory of introspection, so there must be two kinds of introspection — a good and a bad case. So surely a proponent of my theory must think that introspection is going on in the bad case. But there doesn't look to be introspection in the bad case — for there is no mental state to introspect.

In response, I would urge comparison with the disjunctive theory of perception. That does not say that there are two types of perception, but rather that there are good cases in which perception takes place, and bad cases in which perception does not take place, merely hallucination. The theory is disjunctivist because it says that the bad hallucinatory cases are cases in which what is going on is to be analysed in terms of some form of indiscriminability from perception. Similarly, a disjunctivist about introspection needn't be forced into saying that introspection is taking place in the bad case, merely something is going on that should be analysed in terms of some form of indiscriminability from introspection. With that in mind, I think that whether one says introspection is going on in the bad case, will depend on whether one takes introspection to be a success term or a term for some sort of process. On one hand, if one takes "introspection" to be a success term then one takes it that it can only go on if the process delivers some accurate verdict on what is going in inside one's mind. If that is how one understands introspection then it will be right to say that there is no introspection going on in the bad case. On the other hand, if one takes introspection to be some kind of process then one might think that in the bad case a process goes on which bears enough resemblance to the introspective process in the good case, to count as a process of introspection.

If this is one's view of introspection then it would be correct to say that introspection is taking place in the bad case. As I said above, which option one chooses is a mere terminological matter.

Now, to further elucidate my theory: in the good case, if one introspects one's introspective judgement that one is in a state with phenomenal character, it yields a higher-order judgement to the effect that one is judging that one is judging that one is in a state with phenomenal character.[20] I claim that that higher-order introspective judgement, and any further higher-order introspective judgements (judgements that one is judging that one is judging that one is in a state with phenomenal character, and so on), are also partly constituted by the phenomenal character of the original phenomenal state that one first introspects. Thus, to speak slightly metaphorically, one can think of the phenomenal character of the original state passing on up the line of increasingly higher-order introspective judgements, partly constituting each in turn, in just the way that it constituted the original introspective judgement. Thus, the phenomenal character that is present in the original experience and that is present in the original introspective judgement is also present in all the higher-order judgements.

Compare this with what happens in the bad case. One is in a state that lacks phenomenal character. One then goes into a state that is indiscriminable to one from making a judgement that one is in a state with phenomenal character. The state is indiscriminable from a judgement in this sense: when one is in it one cannot tell that one is in such a state, rather than the relevant judgement state, by reflection alone. Crucially, this does not mean that were one to introspect this pseudo-judgement that one would go into the same judgement state

20. In this sentence, I am stipulating what happens in the perfectly good case. I am not claiming that this is the only thing that can happen if one has accurately introspected and judged that one is in a state with phenomenal character.

that one would go into were one to introspect the counterpart to the pseudo-judgement that exists in the good case. Rather, one would go into a state that was indiscriminable from a higher-order judgement. Thus, one would not judge that one was judging that one was in a state with phenomenal character. One would go into a state that was indiscriminable to one from such a judgement, in the sense outlined above. Thus, again to speak slightly metaphorically, one can think of the absence of phenomenal character being passed on up the line, thus affecting every higher-order introspective pseudo-judgement in the bad case, thus yielding states that are indiscriminable from the counterparts to these states that exist in the good case — not yielding genuine judgements.[21]

Consequently, note that I do not spell out what it is for two states to be indiscriminable by saying that they are so if and only if they have all the same effects in a subject, as Fish (2008) does when elucidating his version of (perceptual) disjunctivism. Indeed, Fish becomes more specific, following Sturgeon (2000), claiming that:

> On this account, to say that two mental states are indistinguishable would be to say that they register equivalently in introspection, where this is understood as requiring the two states to generate equivalent introspective beliefs. — 2008: 151

21. To clarify my terminology here, the state with phenomenal character that gets introspected in the good case has as its *counterpart* the state that lacks phenomenal character in the bad case. The *counterpart* of the judgement that one is in a state with phenomenal character that exists in the good case is the pseudo-judgement in the bad case that is indiscriminable from this judgement. Similarly the higher-order judgement that one is judging that one is judging that one is in a state with phenomenal character, which exists in the good case, has a *counterpart*, namely, the pseudo-judgement that is indiscriminable from it — and so on for all further higher-order judgements and pseudo-judgements.

Indeed, no other theory could be at further remove from mine for, according to my (introspective) disjunctivist theory, the states in the good case and in the bad case never yield the same higher-order introspective states.

A further point to note is that although the bad case is indiscriminable from the good case, *what it is like* to be in any of the states in the bad case is not *what it is like* to be in any of the counterpart states in the good case. On the contrary, in the good case, the phenomenal character of the state that is introspected is part of the phenomenal character of the introspecting state and each subsequent higher-order introspecting state. In the bad case that phenomenal character does not exist, for the counterpart to the state that is introspected in the good case lacks phenomenal character. Of course, this does not mean that there must be no phenomenal character at all to making a pseudo-judgement in the bad case (unless one is considering a zombie that by definition has no states with phenomenal character). In non-zombie creatures, there may be something it is like to make pseudo-judgements. You might think this if you think that there is something that it is like to make ordinary conscious judgements and to have conscious occurrent beliefs — it is just that such pseudo-judgements will not have exactly the same phenomenal character as their counterpart judgements which exist in the good case. It might even be the case that a pseudo-judgement and its counterpart in the good case have some phenomenal character in common. However, there will always be an element of phenomenal character that is present in the good case that is absent in the bad, namely, the phenomenal character of the experience that the judgement in the good case is about.

I have said that the bad case is indiscriminable from the good case in the following sense: when you are in it you cannot tell that you are in the bad case rather than the good case, by reflection alone. That is to say, you cannot *know* that you are in the bad case and not in the good case by reflection alone.[22]

22. This formulation clearly draws on Siegel (2004) and (2008), and Martin (2004), which in turn draw on Williamson (1990). Williamson claims, "*a* is indiscriminable from *b* for a subject at a time if and only if at that time the subject is not able to discriminate between *a* and *b*, that is, if and only if at that time the subject is not able to activate (acquire or employ) the relevant kind of knowledge that *a* and *b* are distinct" (1990: 8) Siegel modifies this notion in order to yield an account of indiscriminability that accounts for cases in which what we are interested in is the indiscriminability of mental states that are had at different times: "*X* is indiscriminable from *Y* by a subject *S* at time *t* iff *S* cannot know at time *t* by introspection alone that *X* is not *Y*" (2008: 209). Note that one problem that Siegel (2008) raises for perceptual disjunctivists who employ this type of notion of phenomenal character, namely, that they cannot account for the hallucinations of cognitively unsophisticated creatures, such as dogs, who can hallucinate yet are not able to form the relevant judgements does not apply to my account. This is because I use the notion of indiscriminability not to define hallucinations, but pseudo-judgements, which are not obviously such that cognitively unsophisticated creatures can have them. In fact, if there is a problem in this vicinity for my account it will be to say what, in addition to the lack of indiscriminability from the good case, makes a pseudo-judgement a pseudo-judgement and not some other state. While I don't provide an answer to this in this paper, I can do two things. First, I can claim that the indiscriminability condition is merely a necessary condition on being a pseudo-judgement. Therefore, note that in no way am I restricted to saying that indiscriminability from the good case is all that there is to being in the pseudo-judgement in the bad case. (Some disjunctivists in the case of perception take themselves to be resitricted in a parallel way. They claim that all there is to having a perceptual experience is to be in a states indiscriminable from the good case.) Thus, there is no bar to my providing additional necessary or sufficient conditions for being a pseudo-judgement. Second, I can gesture, even if only exceptionally roughly, towards the kind of condition that might be given. One might think that a necessary condition for having a pseudo-judgement is that one must have a disposition at that time to utter the words, "I am having an experience", or words with a similar meaning.

However, I hold that the good case is not indiscriminable from the bad case in this sense: when you are in it you can tell that you are in the good case and not in the bad case, by reflection alone. Thus, you can *know* that you are in the good case by reflection alone. Indiscriminability, in this sense, is not a symmetric relation. *X* can be indiscriminable from *Y*, but *Y* need not be indiscriminable from *X*.

Some might wonder whether indiscriminability really can be a relation that is not symmetric. For example, if one focuses on cases where one is comparing two things, *X* and *Y*, simultaneously, say things that are observable in front of one, and one thinks of indiscriminability as being a matter of not being able to tell things apart, then one is apt to think that indiscriminability must be symmetric. After all, if one can tell that one of the things on the bench is distinct from the other (is *X* and not *Y*), then this gives one a way of identifying the other object — it is not the first object *X* (and therefore must be *Y*).[23]

However, not all cases are like this. Specifically, many cases in which one is presented with only one of the items at a time are different. This is because, in some cases, one's ability to tell which item is before one will be altered by the nature of the item that one is presented with. This will often happen when these items are states of one's self.

There are several examples of this kind. At one end of the spectrum is the case of sobriety and drunkenness. It seems plausible that on many occasions when I am sober I can know that I am sober. I can tell that I am not drunk. However, there are some (admittedly not all) states of drunkenness that are such that when I am in them I am unable to know whether or not I am sober or drunk.[24] My ability to tell whether I am

23. See Williamson (1990: 10-11) who makes this case for the notion of indiscriminability that I attribute to him in the previous footnote.

24. The relevant states in which I cannot tell are, I think, those in which I am barely drunk and those in which I am completely plastered.

sober or drunk is affected by the very state of sobriety or drunkenness that I am in.

Further along the spectrum is a case discussed by Bernard Williams (1978: Appendix III). Set aside cases of dreaming used to motivate scepticism: cases of dreaming that are supposed to be subjectively exactly like being awake in all respects. Restrict your attention to the kind of dreams that we typically have, which are not like this. Williams claims that there are some instances of being awake such that when one is awake one can know that one is awake and not dreaming (dreaming scepticism aside). But there are some cases of dreaming such that one cannot tell whether one is awake or dreaming. This is because one's ability to tell whether one is dreaming or not is affected by whether one is doing so. Often, of course, when one wakes, one regains one's ability to tell dreams apart from wakefulness, and one can use this ability, plus one's memory of one's dream, and come to know, after the fact, that one was dreaming. I take it that this is a fairly common occurrence.

At the far end of the spectrum are the following cases: being conscious and being unconscious, and being alive and being dead. It is often possible to tell and to know that one is conscious or alive and impossible to tell or to know that one is unconscious or dead (unless of course there is an afterlife).

In the case of introspection, the fact that you can know by reflection alone that you are in a state with phenomenal character, despite the fact that there is a corresponding bad case which is such that when you are in it you cannot know by reflection that you are not in the good case and are in the bad case, is the key to understanding how the view will overcome the sceptical challenge raised by Shoemaker's zombie argument. I will explicate exactly how this should be done in section five.

That is the disjunctive theory of introspection that I endorse. In the next section, I will do four things. First, I will explain how one who holds this theory, and who holds that Anton's subjects do not have visual experiences, should construe what is happening in the minds of Anton's subjects. Second, I will defend the view that pseudo-judgements are not judgements from a variety of criticisms and say more about precisely which mental states it is possible for people in the bad case to have. Third, I will compare and contrast my disjunctive theory of introspection with another form of disjunctive theory about introspection that one might adopt. Fourth, I will discuss an extension of my account that would cover other types of introspective judgements about experience.

## Elaborating and Defending the Theory

So, what should one say of Anton's subjects if you accept that they are not having visual experiences and you accept my disjunctive theory of introspection? Anton's subjects appear to make judgements, which they seemingly express by saying that they are having a visual experience. But they are not really making such judgements. For, on the disjunctive view of introspection, you need to have the requisite experience in order to make the judgement — and I have argued that the Anton's subjects are not having such experiences. Anton's subjects do not make judgements that they are in states with phenomenal character; they merely go into states that for them are indiscriminable, by reflection, from making such judgements. Thus, the way I spoke of the Anton's subjects in section two was deliberately imprecise. On my view, the subjects lack visual experiences and they make pseudo-judgements that they are having visual experiences.

One might object here that there are lots of reasons to think that the Anton's subjects are making false judgements in the bad case and not pseudo-judgements, for example, the behaviour of the subjects and what they say. Can I really maintain that they are not? My answer comes in four parts. First, there are other theories of belief or thought which hold that in some cases there is not a belief or thought present when many, including the man on the Clapham Omnibus, would think otherwise. One example is the singular thought theory. Proponents of this view would say that an apparent demonstrative thought like "that is a banana" is not a thought at all if there is nothing answering to the "that". One tries to essay a thought, and perhaps even thinks that one has, but yet one fails — the phenomenology of the situation notwithstanding.

The second part of my answer is that I have a reason to explain why the subject can't make the relevant judgement. On my theory, the judgement partly consists in a certain phenomenal character and, in the cases we are concerned with — the bad cases — that phenomenal character is not present. This mirrors the answer that a singular thought theorist will give about why an apparent demonstrative thought has failed: because a certain object — one that the "that" should refer to — is not present. Thus, on my view of introspection, a certain sort of error becomes impossible: judging that one is in a state with phenomenal character when one is not. However, one is not thereby rendered infallible in all one's judgements about whether one is in a state with phenomenal character, nor are one's phenomenal states self-intimating. For all I have said, there is nothing to guarantee that if one is in a state with a certain phenomenal character one will either judge that one is, or not judge that one is not.

The third part of my answer to the question about whether I can maintain pseudo-judgements are not really judgements comes from considering exactly what mental states I think it is possible for subjects in the bad case to have. According to my theory of introspection, subjects in the bad case cannot judge that they are in a state with phenomenal character, although they go into a state that is for them indiscriminable from making such a judgement. One might ask whether such subjects can go into related mental states. For example, can such subjects entertain the thought that they are in a state with phenomenal character?

To answer this question, one should distinguish between different types of concepts. There is a fine-grained view of concepts of phenomenal character that holds that there are, in fact, two concepts of phenomenal character. One concept of phenomenal character, $PC_1$, is such that you cannot have it unless you have been in states with phenomenal character.[25] Another concept of phenomenal character, $PC_2$, is such that you can have it without actually having been in a state with phenomenal character. Thus, a zombie that has never had states with phenomenal character can have the latter, but not the former, concept. Corresponding to each of these overarching concepts of phenomenal character, are more specific phenomenal concepts. For example, there is a phenomenal concept of colour, $\text{PC-COLOUR}_1$, that you cannot have unless you have had an experience of colour. It is a concept of what it is like to experience colour that draws on one's knowledge of what it is like. There is another phenomenal concept of colour, $\text{PC-COLOUR}_2$, that you can have if you have never experienced colour. It is a concept of what it is like to experience colour that does not draw on the knowledge of what it is like to experience colour. People who are congenitally blind can have the latter but not the former concept of colour. Thus they can entertain the thought that they are in a state with $\text{PC-COLOUR}_2$ but they cannot entertain the thought that they are in a state with PC-

25. Among those who hold this view are Chalmers (2003) and Tye (2003).

$COLOUR_1$. Likewise, there could be two such different concepts for each particular shade of colour.[26]

Now to return to the question: can subjects who are in the bad case entertain the thought that they are in a state with phenomenal character? The answer to this question depends on the nature of the subjects in question. If the subject is a zombie then they could not entertain the thought, "I am in a state with $PC_1$", on the ground that they lack the concept $PC_1$. But they could entertain the thought, "I am in a state with $PC_2$". However, not all subjects who can be in the bad case are zombies. A subject with Anton's syndrome could entertain the thought, "I am in a state with $PC_1$", because they can have this concept if they have, or have had, some states with phenomenal character (which, of course, typically, they will).[27] One can have a thought — even a thought that involves some $PC_1$ concept — without actually being in the state that has that phenomenal character, simply by drawing on, through memory, one's knowledge of what it is like to be in that state. For example, one can entertain the thought that one might be in terrible pain right now had the hammer hit one's thumb — a thought that employs a PC-$PAIN_1$ concept — without being in terrible pain. Indeed, most thoughts are such that one can think them in the absence of the presence of that which is thought about — as fantasy attests.

26. In fact, there may be particular shades of colour, such as Hume's missing shade of blue, which are such that if one has seen the shades of colour on either side of the spectrum of the missing shade of blue then one could come to have the first type of phenomenal concept of that shade without actually having experienced that shade. Such cases do not detract from the general point though.

27. There are no cases reported in the literature of congenitally blind subjects with Anton's syndrome. But even if there were, such subjects would have had non-visual states with phenomenal character.

Therefore, on my disjunctive view of introspection, there could be subjects that can entertain the thought that they are in a state with phenomenal character but, at the same time, are unable to judge (judge falsely) that they are in a state with phenomenal character, and the concept of phenomenal character in question can be either of the $PC_1$ or the $PC_2$ kind. One consequence of my view then is that the conditions in which one can entertain some proposition are not the same as the conditions in which one can judge that proposition to be true.

But now the questions arises, is it plausible to think that one can entertain a thought — and thus, as one might say, have access to the relevant content — without being able to make a judgement with the very same content? One might wonder why, if one can entertain the thought, one can't make the corresponding judgement in the bad case. Indeed, one might be tempted to think that if a view has the consequence that one can entertain a proposition but not judge it to be true, then the view is advocating something so implausible that it should be rejected.

I think not, however. One reason comes from noting that this consequence of my theory is not particularly odd. There are many cases where people think that we can take one propositional attitude to a content but not another. Here are four:

1. Those who think conceivability implies possibility think one can entertain some impossible scenario, but not conceive of it.
2. Many people think that one can entertain or suppose an explicit contradiction but one cannot consciously believe it (or judge it to be true).
3. Some people think that one can entertain the thought, "I do not exist", but one cannot believe it (or judge it to be true).
4. Some people think that one can entertain or suppose that, "I do not exist", but one cannot have a true belief

that (or judge truly), "I do not exist, or have a false belief (or judge falsely), "I do exist".

If you are inclined to think that any of these cases are plausible then I suggest you should not be dismissive of a view that has similar consequences.

The second reason comes from making clear that my theory explains why one cannot make the introspective judgement at a certain time, despite one being able to entertain the content. The reason is that the introspective judgement has the phenomenal character of the state being introspected as a constituent. And in the bad case, there is no relevant phenomenal character present to form part of the state. Thus the introspective judgement can't come into existence. On my view the process by which one forms the introspective judgement is very different from that by which one comes to have the introspective thought. The introspective judgement involves direct access to the phenomenal character that one is judging to be present. That the introspective process cannot take place should not affect the existence of a very different process that leads to the entertaining of a thought.

The fourth and final part of my answer to the question about whether I can maintain that pseudo-judgements are not judgements, urges someone who thinks I cannot to consider a slightly less radical-sounding variant of my view which would say that pseudo-judgements are judgements, only that they are radically different from non-pseudo introspective judgements in all the ways that I have claimed above. (Call these latter judgements, introspective "full-blown-judgements".) This would still be a disjunctive view that advocates the existence of two different kinds of introspective judgement.

I suspect that I could make all the essential points of this paper whilst giving up the claim that pseudo-judgements are not judgements. According to the less radical-sounding variant, full-blown-judgements and pseudo-judgements differ in phenomenal character. Zombies can't have introspective full-blown-judgements but we (non-zombies) do, and because we can know that we do scepticism does not arise.

I suspect that this variant of the theory is little different from the more radical-sounding alternative. On both versions, pseudo-judgements are like ordinary non-introspective judgements in many respects, none the less, their nature is quite unlike that of introspective full-blown-judgements. Whether one thinks the epithet "judgement" should apply to pseudo-judgements, I suspect, might lie in one's willingness to flag up what seem to me to be the crucial and vitally important differences that exist between them and the full-blown-judgements, perhaps at the expense of advocating a radical-sounding view.

I will now compare and contrast my disjunctive theory of introspection with another form of disjunctive theory about introspection that one might adopt. One feature of my view, that in the bad case a subject cannot judge that they are in a state with phenomenal character although they go into a state that is for them indiscriminable from making such a judgement, is similar to a feature of the singular thought theory outlined above. According to the singular thought view, one cannot form a demonstrative thought, belief or judgement to the effect that "that is a banana" if there is no appropriate object around — in this case something answering to the "that". One can imagine a disjunctive theory of introspection somewhat different to my own that explained the differing natures of judgement and pseudo-judgement by saying that in the good case, the judgement, "I am in a state with phenomenal character" contains a hidden demonstrative. It is really a judgement to the effect, "*That* is a state with phenomenal character". In the good case, one can have this thought as there is a phenomenal state answering to the "that". In the bad case there is nothing answering to the "that" and thus whilst one is trying to essay the judgement "That is a state with phenomenal character", one fails to do so.

A version of this singular thought introspective disjunctivism might employ the notion of a quotational concept of phenomenal character. A quotational concept is one that has its referent as a constituent of the concept. A quotational concept of phenomenal character is one that has the phenomenal character as a constituent. It represents its referent as "That state": where the blank is completed by the phenomenal character of the relevant state.[28] Quotational concepts are clearly different from $PC_1$ or $PC_2$ concepts of phenomenal character. The latter two do not have phenomenal characters as constituents and one can be in them without having to be in a state that has a particular phenomenal character. On the singular thought view, in the good case, one would judge, "I am in a state with phenomenal character", employing a quotational concept of phenomenal character. In the bad case, one couldn't make that judgement, although one could make a similar judgement employing a different concept of phenomenal character, such as $PC_1$ or $PC_2$.

According to such a singular thought view, in the good case, the introspective judgement is a demonstrative judgement that can't be made in the bad case, and the content of the judgement can't be *entertained* in the bad case either. The lack of the relevant state with phenomenal character precludes the employment of the relevant demonstrative concept required to judge *or to entertain* the content in the bad case. This is one crucial respect in which my view is different from this view. Recall that on my view, in the bad case, the subject can't make a judgement with a certain content but they *can* entertain the content. The content can be entertained as it is not a singular content. It can't

28. The existence of such concepts is advocated by Chalmers (2003) and Papineau (2002).

be judged because the introspective judgement doesn't consist solely in what one might call a "brute affirmation" of a content. Rather, the introspective judgement consists of an affirmation of a content that involves a direct awareness of the phenomenal character of the state that one is introspecting.

I think that my disjunctivist theory of introspection view is preferable to a singular thought disjunctivst theory of introspection. For the reasons already given, I don't see it as a negative that on my view in the bad case one can entertain the content even if one can't make an introspective judgement with that content. In fact, it seems a positive for, in the absence of a visual experience, it certainly seems to me that I can entertain the thought that I am having a visual experience. And it seems that this thought has the same content as the content of the judgement that I make when I do have a visual experience and introspect.

On the singular thought view, in the absence of visual experience, when I seem to be entertaining the thought that I am having a visual experience, two things might be taking place. On the one hand, I could be having no thought at all and be merely trying, but failing, to entertain a thought with a hidden demonstrative — thus being seriously deluded about whether I am even thinking. On the other hand, if I am entertaining a thought that I am having a visual experience, then it must be a thought that involves a $PC_1$ or $PC_2$ concept of phenomenal character — not one with a hidden demonstrative. This means that I am not entertaining the thought with a content that is the same as the content of the judgement I make when introspecting and which the singular thought theorist thinks involves a hidden demonstrative. But it certainly *seems* to me as if I do entertain the very same content, when lacking a visual experience, that I judge, when having a visual experience — and the singular thought theorist should agree with this as their theory claims that the demonstrative is "hidden". If this is the case, then I am wrong as to which thought and/or judgement I am having.

On either hand, I am wrong about my thoughts or judgements. Positing such massive error in normal subjects is an unattractive feature of this view. (The error that my view posits only occurs when subjects seem to falsely judge that they are in states with phenomenal character when they do not judge at all. But every view has to think that such subjects are in error — if you don't posit the sort of error that I do then you have to claim that the subjects falsely judge that they are in a state with phenomenal character when they are not. But the subjects that the singular thought theorist claims are in error needn't be in error at all on my view. Thus, the singular thought theorist has to posit more error on the part of subjects.)

Moreover, the singular thought theory allows that one might judge falsely that one is in a state with phenomenal character if that judgement involves a $PC_1$ or $PC_2$ concept. But then it seems Shoemaker's sceptical worries can arise again concerning these types of judgements. Combine this thought with the thought that subjects often may not know whether they are making the sort of judgement that involves a demonstrative concept or not (because the demonstratives in question are "hidden") and one can see that the singular thought theory allows sceptical worries to re-emerge involving introspective judgements.

Finally in this section, I will discuss an extension of my disjunctive account of introspection that is not only disjunctive about introspecting and judging whether a state has phenomenal character, but also disjunctivist about introspecting and judging whether a state has a *particular* phenomenal character, such as that had when I perceive red things. (Call that phenomenal character red.) The extended account would be that one can only judge that one is in a state with a particular phenomenal character, say red', if one is in a state with red′ phenomenal character. If one is not in a state with red′ phenomenal character then one might go into a state which is indiscriminable from judging that one is in a state with red′ phenomenal character — a pseudo-judgement to the effect that one is in a state with red′ — but one would not really be making the judgement. Much more could be said to elaborate on such an extended account. I merely record the existence in logical space for such an extended account here. I neither commit myself to it nor reject it.

### Responding to Shoemaker's Zombie Argument

In the previous two sections, I outlined my disjunctive theory of introspection. In this section, I will explain how one can use this theory to respond to Shoemaker's zombie argument.

The theory I've outlined supposes that there cannot be states lacking phenomenal character that give rise to judgements that one is in a state with phenomenal character. This gives no reason to reject the third premise of Shoemaker's argument:

**P3** It is not the case that we do not know whether we have states with phenomenal character.

We should instead either accept Shoemaker's conclusion that zombies are not possible or reject one or both of premises one or two:

**P1** If zombies are possible then ersatz states are possible,

**P2** If ersatz states are possible we do not know whether we have states with phenomenal character.

When considering these options we should remember that there are more or less fine-grained, and more or less abstract, specifications of a functional system that we can give. For example, simplifying for the sake of argument as we did in section one, suppose that it is true that the functional role of genuine pain states is as follows: they are caused by bodily damage and they cause observable behaviour such as crying and running away, and they cause the formation of a judgement by the subject of the state that they are in pain, which in turn causes the subject to produce the words "I'm in pain". It might be possible to give a more fine-grained, and yet compatible and true, functional specification of genuine pain. For example, pains might be states caused by c-fibre firing that is caused by bodily damage and states which cause activation of motor neurons which cause crying and running away, and states that cause the subject of the state to judge that they are in pain, which in turn, causes the subject to utter the words, "I'm in pain". Likewise, a more abstract, yet compatible and true, specification of the functional role may be possible: pain is caused by bodily damage and itself causes crying and running away and causes the subject of the pain to go into some intermediate mental state, which causes the subject to produce the words, "I'm in pain".

With this point in mind, I suggest that zombies are possible, so long as the functional roles that their mental states instantiate, and share with the mental states of normal humans that have phenomenal character, do not specify that the effects of those states involve introspective judgements about phenomenal character.[29] For example, one effect of the genuine pain states of normal humans that the pain-like states of zombies can share is that they cause the subject to go into some intermediate mental state (a judgement in the case of normal humans; a pseudo-judgement in the case of zombies), which in turn causes the subject to utter the words, "I'm in pain". But if we give a more detailed specification of the effect of genuine pain states, stating that their effect is that they cause the subject to judge that they are in pain, then we mention an effect that the states of zombie pain-like states cannot have.

29. In a later article, Shoemaker (1981) makes a version of this response, distinguishing functional roles that include introspective beliefs and those that don't.

Thus, when someone claims that they can conceive of zombies, I would argue that they are conceiving of creatures that have a functional specification identical to that of a normal human, but a functional specification that does not involve introspective judgements about phenomenal character. The functional specification is less specific and more abstract, merely involving some mental state that is (a) either a judgement or is indiscriminable from a judgement by reflection by the subject of the state and (b) has some of the effects of a judgement.

This "limited" type of zombie is possible and their existence does not raise the sceptical worry concerning knowledge of our own mental states. This is because, as I argued in section three, the existence of states indiscriminable from judgements to the effect that the subject is in a state with phenomenal character (by reflection by the subject of those states) does not mean that someone who is really judging that they are in a state with phenomenal character cannot know that they are in the state with phenomenal character and know that they are really judging that they are. Thus, Shoemaker's conclusion that zombies are not possible should be rejected in the case of these limited zombies. When considering this type of zombie then we should either reject either premise one or two:

**P1** If zombies are possible then ersatz states are possible,

**P2** If ersatz states are possible we do not know whether we have states with phenomenal character.

Which we should reject will turn on how exactly we define ersatz states. For now we can see that there are actually two different ways of making more precise the definition of ersatz states:

(i) Ersatz states are states that lack phenomenal character but that have the functional role of mental states that have phenomenal character, where it is specified that such roles involve the subject of the state introspectively judging that they are in a state with phenomenal character.

(ii) Ersatz states are states that lack phenomenal character but that have the functional role of mental states that have phenomenal character, where it is not specified that such roles must involve the subject of the state introspectively judging that they are in a state with phenomenal character.

If we adopt (i) then we should reject premise one for there can be limited zombies that do not have ersatz states in this sense. And we should accept premise two, for the ersatz states specified in (i) raise the sceptical challenge to our knowledge. However, if we adopt (ii) then we should reject premise two. It does not follow that the existence of ersatz states as specified in (ii) raise the sceptical challenge. And if we adopt (ii), we should accept premise one: the existence of limited zombies does entail the existence of ersatz states as specified in (ii). The difference between these positions is merely terminological.

I have claimed that "limited" zombies are possible, but I also claim that not all types of zombie are possible. There cannot be zombies of the sort that instantiate the functional role identical to that of phenomenal states, where the role is specified to involve an introspective judgement by the subject of the state to the effect that they are in a state with phenomenal character. We should accept Shoemaker's conclusion concerning such "unlimited" zombies: they are not possible. Thus a restricted version of Shoemaker's conclusion can stand.

Accepting this restricted form of the conclusion means that we do not face the skeptical worry that we, ordinary subjects of conscious experience, lack knowledge about our experiences and their phenomenal character. For we, and only we, will introspectively judge that we are in states with phenomenal character and, when we do so, we can know that we are in states with phenomenal character and know that we so judge. Moreover, the existence of the unlimited type of zombie is not supported by my interpretation of what is going on in the minds of Anton's subjects. Further, there is a story to be told to explain away the claims of those who might hold that they can conceive of unlimited zombies: they are merely conceiving of limited zombies. Therefore, the reasons that I adduced to resist Shoemaker's conclusion that zombies are not possible does not exist in the case of unlimited zombies.

My disjunctive theory of introspection makes a sharp distinction between judgements and pseudo-judgements. In turn, this allows us to distinguish between two types of zombie: limited and unlimited. The possibility of the existence of limited zombies is supported by what we can conceive and by my account of Anton's syndrome. My disjunctive theory of introspection shows that the possibility of limited zombies and of people with Anton's syndrome who conformed to my theory of it would not raise an intolerable scepticism concerning knowledge of states with phenomenal character. People who have conscious states with phenomenal character can know that they do.

It is the possibility of unlimited zombies that raises the more worrying sceptical challenge. I have shown how one might resist concluding that such zombies are possible. If some people hold, contrary to what I have claimed, that such zombies are possible, then the sceptical challenge remains to be addressed by them and will have to be tackled by them in an alternative way.

## Disjunctive Theories of Introspection and of Perception

I have advocated a disjunctivist theory of introspection but, as I have already mentioned, I do not advocate a disjunctive theory of perception. I wish to say a few words about why one might endorse the former but not the latter. First, I will say a little about the compatibility of my introspective disjunctivism and perceptual disjunctivism in its metaphysical form. Then I will discuss the metaphysical and epistemic benefits of introspective and perceptual disjunctivism.

Perceptual disjunctivism comes in many forms.[30] As outlined in section three, there are metaphysical and epistemological versions of perceptual disjunctivism (often held together). The core thesis of metaphysical disjunctivism is that the experience in the good case (when veridically perceiving) and the bad case (a hallucination that seems the same to the subject as the experience had when veridically perceiving) are not of the same fundamental mental kind. In the good case, the relevant part of the world partly constitutes the experience; the bad case does not have this constituent. This claim seems compatible with the introspective disjunctivism I have outlined above. However, a stronger form of metaphysical disjunctivism is often held, in which in addition to the above claim, it is held that it is a sufficient condition for a state to be a perceptual experience (either one involved in perceiving or one involved in hallucination) that it is indiscriminable from a veridical perceptual experience.[31] This claim is often articulated further by saying that what it is for a state to have perceptual phenomenal character is just for it to be indiscriminable from an experience had in the good case.

*Prima facie*, my disjunctive theory of introspection is incompatible with this strong form of perceptual disjunctivism. This is because my theory suggests that there can be a subject that is in a state that is indiscriminable from having a veridical perceptual experience but who is not having a perceptual experience. This is because a subject might be in a state that lacked phenomenal character altogether, but they would be in a state

30. See Haddock and Macpherson (2008).

31. See Martin (2004) and (2006), Fish (2008) and Sturgeon (2008).

that was indiscriminable from an experience had in the good case. So on my account, a subject can lack a perceptual experience with phenomenal character yet he can satisfy the strong perceptual disjunctivist analysis sufficient for being in such a state. (Recall that I suggested that this was what was happening in the case of Anton's syndrome and of zombies.) Other quite different examples of this type — where intuitively a subject is not in a state with perceptual phenomenal character yet satisfies the indiscriminability condition — have been concocted by A.D. Smith (2008) as problem cases for this strong disjunctivism.

However, some people might resist the thought that these positions are incompatible. Fish (2008), for example, is happy to endorse the idea that hallucinations lack phenomenal character, although he claims they will seem to have it.[32] Thus, he could say that the Anton's subjects, as I conceive of them, are having hallucinations and are having perceptual experiences, it is just that such states lack phenomenal character, therefore that it is unproblematic if those states satisfy the indiscriminability condition. However, this view only gains compatibility between the views by stretching the notion of

32. M.G.F. Martin (2006) also claims that hallucinations can lack phenomenal character. However, he claims that one can distinguish between states that are hallucinations that have phenomenal character and states that lack it, when both are indiscriminable by reflection by the subject of those states from veridical perceptual experiences, by introducing a notion of impersonal discriminability. This notion is such that we consider not just what the subject of the state can discriminate but what an ideal subject could discriminate and thus what is discriminable *simpliciter*. The idea is that only states that have perceptual phenomenal character will be impersonally indiscriminable from veridical perceptual experiences. States that lack such phenomenal character could be impersonally discriminated, even if the subject of the state can't actually discriminate it. However, Martin's notion of impersonal indiscriminability has been strongly criticized by Siegel (2004) and (2008) and Smith (2008).

hallucination and perceptual experience to include states that lack phenomenal character. This is certainly stretching the term beyond its usual usage, and in a way that I would resist. I believe that we should take it as a given that perceptual experiences are states with phenomenal character. So the moral is that if one thinks that one can have hallucinations and perceptual experiences without being in a state with phenomenal character then one can think that my disjunctive view of introspection and strong metaphysical disjunctivism about experiences are compatible, but if one wishes to uphold the more traditional philosophical terminology where hallucinations and perceptual experiences must be states with phenomenal character then the views are incompatible.

Turning now to metaphysical considerations for favouring introspective disjunctivism over perceptual disjunctivism, one feature of perceptual disjunctivism, of the sort I outlined above, that some people do not like is its commitment to the idea that what one sees, say a table or a dog, is literally a part of one's mental state. Some people worry about whether physical objects at a remove from one's body can be part of one's mental states. Such people may be conservative in their mereological principles or perhaps they think that mental states are not physical states and so are concerned about how such states can have physical components. I won't argue that these worries are legitimate or justified. But if one held them then this would give one a reason to reject perceptual disjunctivism. However, one wouldn't have reason to reject my disjunctive view of introspection. This is because my view only holds that mental states, or the phenomenal characters of mental states, can be parts of other mental states.

Finally, are there any epistemological reasons to endorse introspective disjunctivism but reject perceptual disjunctivism? I think that introspective disjunctivism overcomes scepticism concerning knowledge of our own minds but it is not so clear that epistemological disjunctivism about perception is as successful at dealing with external world scepticism. Epistemological perceptual disjunctivism says that the veridical experience had whilst perceiving in the good case has a different epistemic status from the visual experience in the bad, hallucinatory case. The former can yield knowledge of the external world, the latter cannot.

Recall that I claimed that when introspecting one's state with phenomenal character one can know that one is in a state with phenomenal character and one can further introspect and, all being well, one can come to know that one knows. One reason in favour of the thought that one can really know, and know that one knows, in the introspective case is that how things are in the good case and the counterpart bad case are radically different phenomenally for one in the two cases. The phenomenal character that exists in the good case, not only the phenomenal character of the experience but also the phenomenal character of the judgements, does not exist in the counterpart states in the bad case.

Now consider what McDowell says when considering perception and hallucination and what he claims is their distinctive epistemic status when he is promoting his epistemic perceptual disjunctivism:

> The root idea is that one's epistemic standing on some question cannot intelligibly be constituted, even in part, by matters blankly external to how it is with one subjectively. For how could such matters be other than beyond one's ken? And how could matters beyond one's ken make any difference to one's epistemic standing? — 1982: 215

McDowell is *not* here promoting the attractive idea of the last paragraph that the phenomenal character of one's experience in the bad case and the good case must be different if they are to have a different epistemic status, as he might seem, at first blush, to be doing. For McDowell also claims that how things appear to one will be the same in both hallucination and perception, despite their distinctive epistemic status. Rather McDowell claims that, in the good case, one sees that *p* and he holds that this factive state is a state of one's subjectivity and that, when one sees, that is the fact being made manifest to one's subjectivity. One might think of McDowell's epistemological disjunctivism as trying to do justice at the same time to the fact that the states in the good and bad cases seem the same to one and the fact that one's mind must, in some sense, be different in the two cases if the states are to differ epistemically.

Does McDowell do enough to persuade us that the mind of a subject is sufficiently different in hallucination and perception to warrant attribution of different epistemic status? One might think not. One might hold that a difference in phenomenal character is precisely what *is* required in order to warrant attribution of a different epistemic status to the states. (At least if one has internalist symapathies one will.) If one thinks that then one will think that my theory of introspective disjunctivism does what McDowell's theory of perceptual disjunctivism does not: it guarantees that the minds of subjects are sufficiently different when they introspect and gain knowledge of their mind compared to when they merely seem to do this. According to my theory there is no doubt that the minds of the subjects *are* sufficiently different when introspecting accurately and when pseudo-judging. The ground for making an introspective judgement about experience is the very experience and its phenomenal character that one is judging. And one has the ground literally in one's mind when one accurately judges that one has an experience. Of course, one does not have this ground when one lacks an experience but pseudo-judges that one is experiencing. The having or lacking of this ground clearly makes a phenomenal difference to one's mind.

Most people hold that, in the case of perception, the

ground for making a judgement about the external world is an experience of the world not the external world itself. If one is not a disjunctivist about perception, one will think that this experience can exist in both the good and the bad case and thus that one has the same grounds in both cases. McDowell and other disjunctivists resist this thought, holding that the experience in the good case is partly constituted by the external world, therefore claiming that one's grounds in the two cases are not the same. But, as we have just seen, McDowell does not think that when the fact partly constitutes one's experience in the good case it manifests itself by presenting a different phenomenal character to one's mind compared with the bad case. Thus, one might think that the fact is not really "made manifest" to the subject in the crucial way to guarantee a distinctive epistemic status.

Of course, some disjunctivists might insist that in the good perceptual case one's phenomenal character is literally constituted by the external world and its properties and, as this is not so in the bad case, the phenomenal character in the two cases is different after all. However, it would not be unreasonable, in my opinion, to think that this is gross *terminological hoodwinking*. The experience in the good case and the bad case are such that *in principle* one could not tell them apart just by reflection on those experiences — nor could any expert tell them apart in principle just by reflection. *What it is like* for the subject in each case is *in principle* the same. Therefore, if one labels any differences between the good case and bad case experiences as being differences of phenomenal character one is certainly not using that term with its standard usage.

In opposition to the picture presented by perceptual disjunctivists, the mental states of the subjects in the good and bad introspective states are truly very different in phenomenal character according to my theory. The good case is discriminable from the bad case. There is a phenomenal difference between the good and bad introspective cases and it is this difference in phenomenal character that underpins the claim that one has knowledge in the good introspective case. As stated in the previous paragraph, however, I believe that there is not a difference in phenomenal character between the good and the bad perceptual cases and this shows that attribution of knowledge in the good perceptual case cannot be done for the same reason as it is in the good introspective case. Whether it can be done for any good reason in the perceptual case remains an unanswered question.

## Conclusion

I have claimed that in response to Shoemaker's argument we either need to explain away the seeming possibility of zombies or show that one of the premises concerning introspective knowledge about our experiences is false. Prima facie, the conceivability of zombies and the confabulation theory of Anton's syndrome seem to imply that Shoemaker is wrong about introspective knowledge. I have proposed a view of introspective knowledge about phenomenal character of a disjunctive sort in which if a subject has no state with phenomenal character then they can't form a judgement that they are in a state with phenomenal character. This view is interesting as it uses a disjunctivist style of consideration usually favoured by non-Cartesians about the mind to argue for what is in many respects a fairly traditional, Cartesian view of the mind. This view allows one to accept the confabulation theory of Anton's syndrome, it partially vindicates the conclusion of Shoemaker's argument, and makes clear which kind of zombies are possible and which are not.[33]

33. I would like to thank Michael Brady, David Chalmers, Max Colheart, Stuart Crutchfield, Duncan Pritchard and Nicholas Silins for helpful discussion. I would particularly like to thank William Fish who helped me work out the case for my theory of Anton's syndrome in detail.

## References

Brueckner, A. and M.O. Fiocco (2002), "Williamson's Anti-Luminosity Argument", *Philosophical Studies*, 110: 285-93.

Chalmers, D. (2003), "The Content and Epistemology of Phenomenal Belief", in Q. Smith and A. Jokic (eds.), *Consciousness: New Philosophical Perspectives*, Oxford: Oxford University Press.

Davies, M., M. Coltheart, R. Langdon, and N. Breen (2001), "Monothematic Delusions: Towards a Two-Factor Account", *Philosophy, Psychiatry and Psychology*, 8: 133-58.

Davies, M., A.A. Davies and M. Coltheart (2005), "Anosognosia and the Two-Factor Theory of Delusions", *Mind and Language*, 20: 209-36.

DSM-IV (1994), *Diagnostic and Statistical Manual of Mental Disorders, Fourth Edition*, Washington DC: American Psychiatric Association).

Evans, G. (1982), *The Varieties of Reference*, Oxford: Clarendon Press.

Fish, W (2008), "Disjunctivism, Indistinguishability and the Nature of Hallucination", in A. Haddock and F. Macpherson (eds.), *Disjunctivism: Perception, Action, Knowledge*, Oxford: Oxford University Press.

Gazzaniga, M.S. and J.E. LeDoux, (1978), *The Integrated Mind*, New York: Plenum Press.

Gazzaniga, M.S. (1998), *The Mind's Past*, Berkeley: University of California Press.

Gertler, B. (2008), "Self-Knowledge", in E.N. Zalta (ed.), The Stanford Encyclopedia of Philosophy (Winter 2008 Edition), http://plato.stanford.edu/archives/win2008/entries/selfknowledge.

Goldenberg, G., W. Müllbacher, and A. Nowak, (1995), "Imagery Without Perception – A Case Study of Anosognosia for Cortical Blindness", *Neuropsychologia*, 33: 1373-82.

Goldman, A. (1979), "What is Justified True Belief", in G. Pappas (ed.) *Justification and Knowledge: New Studies in Epistemology*, Dordrecth: D. Riedel.

Haddock, A. and F. Macpherson, (2008), "Varieties of Disjunctivism", in their *Disjunctivism: Perception, Action, Knowledge*, Oxford: Oxford University Press.

Hirstein, W. (2005), *Brain Fiction: Self-Deception and the Riddle of Confabulation*, Cambridge MA: The MIT Press.

Joseph, R. (1986), "Confabulation and Delusional Denial: Frontal Lobe and Lateralized Influences", *Journal of Clinical Psychology*, 42: 507-20.

Klein, P. (2009), "Skepticism", *The Stanford Encyclopedia of Philosophy,* (Spring 2009 Edition), E.N. Zalta (ed.), http://plato.stanford.edu/archives/spr2009/entries/skepticism/.

Kripke, S. (1970), *Naming and Necessity,* Cambridge MA: Harvard University Press.

Martin, M.G.F. (2004), "The Limits of Self-Awareness", *Philosophical Studies,* 120: 37-89.

——— (2006), "On Being Alienated", in T.S. Gendler and J. Hawthorne (eds.), *Perceptual Experience,* Oxford: Oxford University Press.

McDaniel, K.D. and L.D. McDaniel (1991), "Anton's Syndrome in a Patient with Posttraumatic Optic Neuropathy and Bifrontal Contusions", *Archives of Neurology,* 48: 101-5.

McDowell, J. (1982), "Criteria, Defeasibility, and Knowledge", *Proceedings of the British Academy,* 68: 455-79. [Reprinted in J. Dancy (ed.) *Perceptual Knowledge,* Oxford: Oxford University Press, 1988, page numbers refer to this reprint.]

Nagel, T. (1974), "What Is It Like to Be a Bat?", *The Philosophical Review,* 83 (4): 435-50.

Neta, R. and G. Rohrbaugh (2004), "Luminosity and the Safety of Knowledge", *Pacific Philosophical Quarterly,* 85: 396-406.

Noe, A. (2002), "Is the Visual World a Grand Illusion?", *Journal of Consciousness Studies,* 9(5-6): 1-12.

Papineau, D. (2002), *Thinking About Consciousness,* Oxford: Oxford University Press.

Pritchard, D. (2005), *Epistemic Luck,* Oxford: Oxford University Press.

Putnam, H. (1973), "Meaning and Reference", *Journal of Philosophy,* 70: 699-711.

Raney, A.A. and J.M. Nielsen (1942), "Denial of Blindness (Anton's Symptom): Two Clinical Cases", *Bulletin of the Los Angeles Neurological Society,* 7: 150-1.

Redlich, F.C. and J.F. Dorsey (1945), "Denial of Blindness by Patients with Cerebral Disease", *Archives of Neurology and Psychiatry,* 53: 407-17.

Schaffer, J. (unpublished manuscript), "The Debasing Demon".

Schwitzgebel, E. (2002), "How Well Do We Know Our Own Conscious Experience? The Case of Visual Imagery", *Journal of Consciousness Studies,* (2002) 9(5-6): 35-53.

——— (forthcoming), "The Unreliability of Naïve Introspection", *Philosophical* Review.

Shoemaker, S. (1975), "Functionalism and Qualia", *Philosophical Studies*, 27: 291-315.

——— (1981), "Absent Qualia are Impossible", *Philosophical Review*, 90: 581-599.

Siegel, S. (2004), "Indiscriminability and the Phenomenal", *Philosophical Studies*, 120: 91-112.

——— (2008), "The Epistemic Conception of Hallucination", in A. Haddock and F. Macpherson (eds.) *Disjunctivism: Perception, Action, Knowledge*, Oxford: Oxford University Press.

Smith, A.D. (2008), "Disjunctivism and Discriminability", in A. Haddock and F. Macpherson (eds.), *Disjunctivism: Perception, Action, Knowledge*, Oxford: Oxford University Press.

Sosa, E. (1999), "How to Defeat Opposition to Moore", *Philosophical Perspectives*, 13: 141-53.

Sturgeon, S. (2000), *Matters of Mind: Consciousness, Reason and Nature*, London: Routledge.

——— (2008), "Disjunctivism about Visual Experience", in A. Haddock and F. Macpherson (eds.), *Disjunctivism: Perception, Action, Knowledge*, Oxford: Oxford University Press.

Stuss, D.T. and D.F. Benson (1986), *The Frontal Lobes*, New York: Raven.

Swartz, B.E. and J.C.M. Brust (1984), "Anton's Syndrome Accompanying Withdrawal Hallucinosis in a Blind Alcoholic", *Neurology*, 34: 969-73.

Teunisse, R. J., J.R. Cruysberg, W.H. Hoefnagels, A. L. Verbeek, and F.G. Zitman (1996), "Visual Hallucinations in Psychologically Normal People: Charles Bonnet's Syndrome", *The Lancet*, 347: 794-97.

Tye, M. (2003), "A Theory of Phenomenal Concepts", in A. O'Hear (ed.), *Minds and Persons*, Cambridge: Cambridge University Press.

Williams, B. (1978), *Descartes: The Project of Pure Inquiry*, Harmondsworth: Penguin Press.

Williamson, T. (1990), *Identity and Discrimination*, Oxford: Basil Blackwell.

——— (2000), *Knowledge and Its Limits*, New York: Oxford University Press.

Wright, C. (2008), "Comment on John McDowell's 'The Disjunctive Conception of Experience as Material for a Transcendental Argument'", in A. Haddock and F. Macpherson (eds.) *Disjunctivism; Perception, Action, Knowledge*, Oxford: Oxford University Press.

# 3

# The Epistemic Illusion of First-person Authority[1]

*Monima Chadha*

## Introduction

ON the Cartesian picture we have direct and incorrigible access to objects before the mind and this immediacy accords self-knowledge its privilege and infallibilty. This thesis has been under threat from several quarters. The advent of externalism has posed a serious threat to the thesis that the content of our thoughts is internal to the mind. In the last two decades there has been much discussion about whether self-knowledge is compatible with externalism. Externalism denies that mental contents are intrinsic to the thinker, the content of what we think and mean depends on our natural, social and linguistic environment. Psychological research also suggests that a large part of what goes on in our minds is inaccessible to introspection, and also that our reports of our mental states are often wrong (Nisbett and Wilson 1977). Most contemporary philosophers deny "privileged and infallible" access, in the Cartesian sense. However, they usually hold the thesis that we normally have a "peculiar" epistemic access, that is, a person has a special way of finding out about his or her own mental

1. I use the term "epistemic illusion" in the sense used by Edmund Wright (1983). Examples include sticks dipped in water which appear to be bent, mirages, etc.

states that is quite different from the way one finds out about other's mental states (Byrne 2005). Contemporary philosophers do not hold that peculiar access guarantees infallible knowledge of our own mental states, but they grant the intuitive thesis that it is easier to obtain knowledge of one's own mental states than knowledge of most other subject matters. Byrne (2005) refers to this latter thesis as "privileged" access. Byrne rightly notes that privileged access does not entail peculiar access, nor vice versa. Ryle, for one, held that we have privileged access without peculiar access. However, the orthodox view in the philosophical community is that people have privileged and peculiar access to their own mental states. The philosophical problem of self-knowledge then is to offer an explanation of how we have privileged and peculiar access to our own mental states. Contemporary philosophers, engaged in this enterprise, want to explain the special status of self-ascriptions or avowals of mental states.

The philosophical literature produced in the last two decades explores both epistemic and non-epistemic strategies to explain the special features of self-knowledge.[2] Those who favour the epistemic strategy hold that the special status of first-person ascriptions must be due to some special perceptual or quasi-perceptual mechanism on which they are epistemically grounded or some epistemic method that has been used to produce them.[3] I will not go into the details of what's wrong

2. There have always been the sceptics who do not think that there is a problem about the special status self-knowledge. For a recent account of the sceptical position, see Medina (2006).

3. The epistemic strategy has been pursued by many philosophers, most famously, Armstrong (1968), Burge (1985, 1988, 1996), Heil (1988, 1992), Shoemaker (1988), Peacocke (1996, 1998) and more recently Byrne (2005), MacDonald (1998). While, I think, it is fair to group together all these accounts under the epistemic umbrella, I admit there are important differences in the accounts offered by these theorists. For example, Armstrong, Burge, Heil and →

with particular accounts offered by those who favour the epistemic route. This dismissal is not just to keep things manageable, but also because I share the sentiment expressed by Bilgrami (1998) and Byrne (2005) more recently, that although epistemic accounts succeed in offering a neat explanation of peculiar access, in so far as they depend on a broadly perceptual-causal mechanism, the justification they offer for why we are usually right in our self-ascriptions are at the best reliabilist and inductivist. The epistemic accounts are, therefore, poignantly insufficient to offer a satisfactory solution to the philosophical problem of self-knowledge.

Those who subscribe to the non-epistemic strategy give up on the whole idea of "objects of thought before the mind" and aim to provide a non-epistemic rationale for the presumption of FPA. Such accounts draw inspiration from Wittgenstein and Davidson. The idea is that normally, sincere, intentional, self-ascriptions or avowals are not mediated by inference, perception, or any other cognitive process. For Davidson first person authority is a necessary presupposition for our interpretative practices. This is what is generally termed as the "constitutive thesis" which provides the framework for non-epistemic accounts of self-knowledge. For these theories self-ascriptions enjoy a presumption of truth without which we cannot explain our ordinary, everyday linguistic, moral and legal practices. Davidson himself shies away endorsing the non-epistemic conception. He finds it is a "strange idea" that claims made without epistemic support should carry "more authority than" claims made with such support (Davidson 1984: 103). Even if they succeed the non-epistemic accounts can only give a normative explanation of

---

→ MacDonald defend an inner sense account, whereas others like Shoemaker favour what has come to be known as the broad perceptual model.

privileged access, but in so far as they have nothing to say about peculiar access, they do not even come close to addressing the challenge posed by philosophical problem of self-knowledge.

Davidson's characterization of FPA conforms to the philosophical problem of self-knowledge. First-person authority is the thesis that subjects have a privileged non-evidence-based form of epistemic warrant for self-ascriptions of psychological concepts that does not attach to third-person evidence-based ascriptions of the same concepts. The explanation of FPA purports to offer an account for the peculiar and privileged access we have to our own mental states. Though Davidson rejects the perceptual analogy and the thought that beliefs are representations immediately present to the mind, he remains within the field force of epistemic accounts. I think, Davisdon's account is best described as an exercise in "descriptive epistemology", in the spirit of Strawson's infamous "descriptive metaphysics", rather than normative epistemology. My focus in this paper will be on Davidson's account as a project in descriptive epistemology. In section 2, I begin by setting out Davidson's explanation for FPA. The problem Davidson sets out for himself "is to explain the asymmetry in the way a person knows about his contemporary mental states and the way in which others know about them" (Davidson 1986: 51). Philosophers who favour this Davidsonian interpretative stance persist with efforts to account for asymmetries in first- and third-person ascriptions in an attempt to account for FPA. I argue that Davidson and other interpretativists should shy away from explaining the asymmetries in question, for they put pressure on the defining principles of interpretation theory.

I suggest we reject the need for a further explanation of FPA, since there is no epistemic asymmetry between first- and third-person ascriptions of intentional states. Counterintuitive though it may be, the denial of epistemic asymmetry in first- and third-person ascriptions is supported by empirical findings. In section 3, I depend on experimental evidence from social and developmental psychology to argue against the intuitive belief that our knowledge of our own intentional states is substantially different from our knowledge of the intentional states of others. (Gopnik 1993a, b). This is reflected in the developmental evidence which supports the systematicity and symmetry in the errors in first- and third-person ascriptions. We may entertain FPA as a necessary presupposition needed to sustain our interpretative practices, while recognizing it, in deference to empirical evidence, as an epistemic illusion.

**The Interpretativists' Strategy**

Davidson's explanation of what it is for a thinker to grasp and ascribe a thought is based on taking the interpretative stance. An interpreter depends on linguistic and non-linguistic behavioural clues, collateral information, training and imaginative surmise to understand and ascribe thoughts to another.[4] Our interpretative practices are based on the presumption that the speaker knows what he or she believes when he or she speaks, without such a presumption interpretation cannot get off the ground. Davidson says:

> The explanation comes with the realization that what a person's words mean depends in the most basic cases on the kinds of objects and events that have caused the person to hold the words to be applicable; similarly for what the person's thoughts are about. . . . The agent herself, however, is not in a position to wonder whether she is using her own words to apply to the right objects and events, since whatever she regularly does apply them to gives her words the

4. I will not spell out the details of Davidson's account here interested readers may look at the essays in his collected papers, *Inquiries into Truth and Interpretation*, Oxford University Press, 1984.

> meaning they have and her thoughts the contents they have. . . . First-person authority, the social character of language, and the external determinants of thought and meaning go naturally together. — Davidson 1986: 456

It is important to note that here Davidson is simply claiming that the interpretative stance requires FPA as a presupposition that grounds and explains the success of our interpretative practices. Davidson establishes FPA as a transcendental presupposition, in the Kantian sense, for it required as a necessary condition for the possibility of interpretation. Hacker offers a nice reconstruction of Davidson's transcendental deduction of FPA:

> We know that we communicate with one another. It is a requirement of communication that there be a presumption that the speaker knows what he means by his utterances. But if he knows that he holds true the sentence he utters and knows what he means, then he knows what he believes. So, there is a presumption, essential for the possibility of interpretation, and hence of communication, that a speaker knows what he believes when he avers that he believes something. — Hacker 1997: 290

Davidson's argument reveals important connection between FPA and the very possibility of interpretative practices. But what does it say about the problem Davidson sets himself "to explain the asymmetry between the way a person knows about his contemporary mental states and the way in which others know about them"? For his explanation, we must turn to the interpretation theory. A method of interpretation provides truth-conditions (T-sentences) for all sentences of the language concerned. The truth conditions of the sentence give its meaning independently of its use and the purposes that prompted it. The attitude of holding true, as directed towards sentences, forms the basis of interpretation. A sentence is held true by a speaker because of two factors: what the speaker takes the sentence to mean and what he believes. Interpretation proceeds with developing a theory that holds one factor steady and studies the other. The sentences held true provide the evidential basis for an interpretation theory, facts like the following "I am writing" is held true by *me* at time *t* and *I* was indeed writing at that time. For my hearer to know that I believe that I am writing he must know both that I hold this sentence true on this occasion of utterance and what I mean by it. We can assume that we both know that on this occasion I do hold the sentence I uttered to be true. And we can also assume that I know, though my hearer may not, what my sentence as uttered on this occasion, meant. There is no guarantee that the hearer is correctly interpreting the speaker's words. "The hearer's knowledge of what the speakers' words mean has to be based on evidence and inference; in effect, it is a hypothesis" (Davidson, 1991: 212). For the hearer cannot assume that a homophonic T-sentence is the best way of saying what the speakers words mean, that is, giving the truth-conditions of the speaker's utterance. It is a common fact that with sentences containing indexicals, as in the example above, this strategy will fail. By contrast, I know and can say what I mean by offering a homophonic T-sentence which gives the truth condition of my sentences. There is no special or mysterious way in which I know what my words mean. There is a presumption, Davidson says: ". . . that I am not generally mistaken about what I mean, is essential to my having a language — to my being interpretable at all" (ibid.). There are constraints on what a person can mean by his words, if he wants to be understood, he must intend his words to be interpreted in a certain way, and must provide his audience with the clues they need to arrive at the intended interpretation. So unless we presume that the speaker knows what he means, i.e. gets his own language right, interpretation cannot get off the ground, for there is nothing for the interpreter to interpret (Davidson 1987: 456).

Davidson's argument shows that there is an asymmetry between the knowledge one has of one's own words and the interpreter's knowledge of the meaning of one's words. Kirk Ludwig (1994) questions whether this asymmetry can serve as a source of FPA. Ludwig asks us to imagine the best possible case of another person knowing the meanings of one's words to see to what degree this reduces the asymmetry between the first- and the other-person ascriptions of mental states. Suppose, for example, you have an identical twin. Both of you were raised together, went to the same schools, have the same interests, and spend most of your time together. It seems reasonable to suppose that your knowledge of the meanings of each other's words will be almost perfect. Although there is still some sense in which you know better what you mean by your words than your twin does, your twin is in an excellent position to interpret your words. If, as Davidson is right, the asymmetry between self-ascriptions and other-ascriptions depends solely on the asymmetry between one's knowledge of the meanings of one's own words and other's knowledge of their meanings, in this case we should expect the asymmetry between self-ascriptions and ascriptions to one's twin will be almost completely eliminated. However, contrary to this expectation, the asymmetry is neither eliminated nor even reduced, because, as Ludwig rightly points out, most of what you think may never be indicated in any way in your behaviour. You can know about your dispositional states without consulting your behaviour, but without behavioural evidence of any kind your twin cannot have any knowledge of your behavioural states. One might think that when we turn attention to thoughts that are verbally expressed, an interpreter's almost complete knowledge of the meanings of the speaker's words may almost eliminate or reduce the asymmetry between the interpreter's knowledge of the speaker's thoughts and the speaker's knowledge of their own thoughts. But even this case does not give us reason to believe that Davidson's explanation of first-person authority will work. For the interpreter will still need to make an inference based on past experience, present circumstances, and behavioural evidence to believe that the speaker's assertion is sincere while the speaker needs no such evidence. Perhaps, one may want to be even more restrictive and suggest that Davidson's explanation seems adequate only if we restricted our attention to knowledge of thoughts which are verbally expressed, and which are assumed to be sincerely expressed. Even in this case Davidson's explanation has shortcomings. To account for asymmetry between the way we know what we self-ascribe and the way we know what we ascribe to others, we not only require an asymmetry in the knowledge of the meanings of our words but also require an asymmetry between one's own knowledge of which sentences one holds true and that of one's interpreter. Even if the speaker is in a better position to know what her words mean, she cannot be in a better position to know what she is thinking, for it is possible that the interpreter is in a better position to know what sentences the speaker holds true. As we said above, for Davidson, knowledge of one's beliefs is a function of knowledge of the sentences one holds true and the meanings of those sentences. If I am always in a better position to know and say what I believe than anyone else, then I must be in a better position to know what sentences I hold true and know the meanings of those sentences than anyone else. However, a central insight of Davidson's account, and the starting point of interpretation is that the interpreter is at least in as good a position as the speaker to know which sentences the speaker holds true. The attitude of holding true, as directed towards sentences, forms the basis of interpretation. Davidson cannot now claim that there is a presumption that the speaker knows what sentences she holds true, while there is no such presumption on the part of the interpreter. And, he should not claim this. Interpretation depends on the fact that the interpreter has access to the sentences held true by the speaker. Without this presumption, interpretation cannot proceed. It seems that Davidson is in a bind: on the one hand, we need the FPA as a presupposition to ground our interpretative practices; on the other hand, his attempt to account for FPA blocks the initial data for interpretation to get off the ground. Is there a way interpretativists can avoid this conundrum?

On behalf of the interpretativists, Richard Moran (1994) argues that we can save the asymmetries in first- and third-person ascriptions. He argues that differences in the manner in which we become aware of our own beliefs and those of others are mirrored in the different attitudes we adopt towards our own beliefs and those of others. In what follows, I argue that in his attempt to offer a normative justification for the asymmetries across first- and third-person ascriptions Moran exaggerates the differences in the attitudes we adopt towards our own beliefs and those of others. If we insist on these differences, as Moran, we are led to abandon the basic normative principles that guide interpretation. The normative principles constrain and enable our interpretative practices. Interpretation cannot proceed without the aid of these normative principles, so the interpretativists are back at square one.

Richard Moran focuses on two *prima facie* plausible asymmetries in the practice of first- and third-person attribution that cry out for an explanation. First, there is a strong requirement that a person must take his current beliefs to be true.

> I can take beliefs I ascribe to another person to be false, and I can see some of my own past beliefs as false, but I cannot take any belief I currently hold to be false. This requirement is different from any version of the principle of charity for the principle applies indifferently to a person's past and

> present configuration of beliefs. . . . By contrast, the requirement that a person views his own beliefs as true does not apply indifferently to his past and present beliefs . . . hence nothing like the principle of charity accounts for it.
>
> — Moran 1994: 165

And, secondly, the exercise of self-rationalizing involves securing a "special" kind of coherence between one's first-order states and second-order beliefs about them, which is different from the kind of coherence sought by the interpreter. To maximize coherence in the case of ascribing beliefs to others an outside interpreter may choose to revise the original ascription. In the case of other-ascription, an outside interpreter has three options: (a) to make the agent's beliefs cohere with each other and with the facts as the outside interpreter believes them to be; (b) ascribe some beliefs to another thinker that the outside interpreter knows to be false; (c) the outside interpreter changes his own view of the facts in light of the beliefs ascribed to another thinker. However, in the case of self-ascription the thinker is not seeking merely to maximize coherence, if he notices a conflict in beliefs it must be resolved. In such a case option (b) is not available to the agent herself. Furthermore, option (a) collapses into (c); for a thinker cannot alter his ascription of false or inconsistent beliefs without changing his view of the facts.

The second asymmetry can be explained by pointing to the dual role played by our concept of belief: as explanatory of behaviour and as bearer of truth-values. Furthermore, outside interpreters and agents are partial towards different aspects of the dual concept of belief. From the perspective of the believer the question of the truth of beliefs is prior to the question of how they dispose one to act. In contrast, the interest in the truth-value of the attributed beliefs is lacking, or at least bracketed by the interpreter. Thus, Moran claims that the interpreter is *only* interested in ascribing beliefs that explain an agent's behaviour; on several occasions false beliefs will serve better to explain an agent's behaviour than true ones. Moran is over-emphasizing the difference in interests of the interpreters at the cost of ignoring the normative principles that are fundamental to the interpretive strategy. Surely, there is something wrong here. The second asymmetry in the kind of coherence sought in the first- and third-person ascriptions can be dispelled by paying attention to the normative principles of charity and humanity. The principle of charity imposes the requirement of truth not just reasonableness in the beliefs of others. And, the principle of humanity requires that ". . . the imputed pattern of relations among beliefs, desires, and the world be as similar to our own as possible" (Grandy 1973: 443). The interpreter ensures that beliefs attributed by him *accord with each other* and with the *facts*. Accordance with facts extends the interpreters' charity in seeking to ascribe true beliefs to others. And, ensuring that the attributed beliefs accord with each other extends the interpreters' humanity in seeking to ascribe a maximally coherent set of first- and higher-order beliefs. As in the case of self-rationalizing where one makes an effort to resolve conflicts in one's own belief set, in the case of other interpretation one attempts to resolve conflicts in order to minimize disagreements and enable better understanding. Furthermore, the thinker/interpreter strives to ascribe a maximally true and coherent set of beliefs in the practice of attributing beliefs to oneself and another. As Davidson would say, interpretation cannot get off the ground unless there is widespread agreement between the speaker and the interpreter. Too many errors are destructive of understanding.

To reveal the first asymmetry Moran considers the following example. The interpreters' simultaneous beliefs that Desdemona does not love Cassio (first-order belief) and Othello believes that she does (second-order belief) are not logically contradictory. Similarly, Othello's simultaneous beliefs that Desdemona does not love Cassio and his second-order belief that he (Othello) believes that Desdemona does love Cassio are not logically contradictory. However, the maintenance of both beliefs simultaneously is an option available to the interpreter, not to Othello. Moran insists that the two beliefs conflict systematically and Othello must give up one or the other. Moran is right in insisting that this asymmetry cannot be accounted for by the humble principle of charity. However, one may question whether it is rational and possible for a thinker to have an ideally coherent set of beliefs, even when we restrict attention to the thinkers' current beliefs. Consider this variant of the preface paradox.[5] Mary is an obsessively scrupulous and meticulous author who doesn't write anything in her book unless she has triple-checked it and is virtually certain that it's true. Hence she justifiably currently believes that every sentence in her book is true. But Mary is also a student of human fallibility and knows all too well of the slips even the most careful writers can make. Hence, she is justified in believing that something in her long and complicated book is false. But putting these two things together, it appears that she is justified in believing both that every sentence in the book is true and that at least one of them is not true. The preface paradox gives us reason to suppose that it can sometimes be rational to hold conflicting beliefs.

The preface paradox brings to attention the obvious fact of the fallibility of our belief-forming mechanisms, and therefore, it is rational for one to believe concurrently that some (or at least one) of one's current beliefs are (is) false. This does not mean that the defect is located in a particular belief, or that the contents of my current beliefs are in any way logically inconsistent with each other. The second-order

5. The preface paradox was originally formulated by D.C. Makinson (1965), *The Stanford Encyclopedia of Philosophy* presents the following version of the preface paradox.

belief that it is likely that at least one of my current beliefs is false conflicts with taking each of one's current beliefs to be true. None the less, there is no rational ground for giving up any particular belief from one's current set of beliefs, including the second-order belief which secures epistemic humility on part of the thinker. In saying this I do not mean to be claiming that it will be perfectly rational for Othello to utter some version of Moore's paradox, namely "Desdemona does not love Cassio, but I believe she does". Rather the point is that it is rational for a speaker to simultaneously believe that all my current first-order beliefs are true and that it is highly likely that some (or at least one) of my current beliefs are (is) false, but I can't put my finger on those ones! So, like an interpreter, the rational thing to do for a thinker is to self-ascribe a maximally true and coherent set of beliefs. The interpretativists better not ignore the dictates of rationality. The interpretativists will be better off if they ignore the strong requirement since it conflicts with the obviously true and thus rational belief that our belief forming mechanisms, though reliable, are fallible.

The resistance to epistemic continuity across first- and third-person ascriptions is fuelled by an urge to offer an account of the pre-theoretic FPA. The intuitive plausibility of this thesis drives us to reject the epistemic continuity, however the epistemic asymmetry between first- and third-person attributions may be questioned if we pay attention to some empirical findings in psychology. This epistemic continuity between first- and third-person ascriptions is a welcome consequence of interpretation theory, for it fits nicely with the empirical evidence which we discuss in the next section.

### First-Person Authority and Asymmetry

Some studies in psychology suggest that errors we make in describing our own mental states are more widespread than the allowance made by philosophers. The systematicity and symmetry of first- and third-person errors suggest that our judgements about our own mental states are influenced by background theories about how these are caused and how they in turn cause behaviour. Some psychologists, famously, Nisbett and Wilson (1977) take the symmetry in the errors as a reflection of the mistaken *implicit theories* of how the mind works. Nisbett and Wilson propose that though it seems *as if* people engage in something that feels like introspection; in fact, when people are asked to report how a particular stimulus influences a particular response, they do so not by consulting a memory of the mediating process, but by applying or generating causal theories about the effects of that type of stimulus on that type of response. This denial of epistemic asymmetry between first- and third-person ascriptions is confirmed by evidence from developmental psychology.

Gopnik (1993) argues against the assumption that the process of discovering our own psychological states is fundamentally different from the process of discovering someone else's psychological states. It is commonly taken for granted that we simply observe our own psychological states. We do not infer them, and indeed do not use any theoretical account of mind at all. Suppose the common-sense account of "direct" access to one's own intentional states was true. Then we should predict that there is an asymmetry in children's correct or erroneous understanding of their own psychological states and their views of the psychological states of others. Developmental evidence shows that there is no such asymmetry. The philosophical problem of self-knowledge which asks for an explanation of privileged and peculiar access is based on this common-sense view. The task in this section is to show that the common-sense view is mistaken and therefore the philosophical quest for asymmetry in first- and third-person ascriptions is misguided.

Studies on children aged between 3-3½ years support a striking parallel between developing an understanding of ascribing intentional states to others and ourselves (Gopnik 1993b). In one experiment, children are presented with a variety of deceptive objects, such as a candy box full of pencils. The children are asked what they think is in the box. They report that they think that there is candy in the box. The box is then opened in their presence and they are allowed to see its contents, which turn out to be pencils, not candy. Children are then asked the false-belief question about their own immediately past belief, "When you first saw the box before we opened it, what did you think was inside it?" and about others' beliefs, "What will Nicky think is inside the box?" and the appearance-reality question, "Does it look as if there are candies in the box?" The pattern of results is similar in all the three cases: one-half to two-thirds of the children said they had originally thought there were pencils in the box. The children between age 3-3½ fail the false-belief task, whereas four-year-olds accept that they originally thought there was candy in the box. Wellman suggests that at age three children have a "copy theory of representation" according to which children think of beliefs, and other mental states as we adults sometimes construe perception, as a matter of direct relation between mind and objects in the world (Wellman 1990). Three-year-olds do not understand misrepresentation, such as false-beliefs, nor do they understand that beliefs may come from different sources and different degrees of belief. However, they have some preliminary notion of what Wellman calls "serious states", which include beliefs and perceptions without any distinction between them.

Moreover, children's ability to answer the false-belief question about their own belief is significantly related to their ability to answer the question about other people's belief as well as the appearance-reality question. Gopnik and Astington (1988) found a correlation between failing the false-belief test for oneself and failing it for another. These results have been replicated in other experiments performed by others (Meltzoff & Moore 1989, Wimmer and Hartl 1991). The experiments confirm that errors are not merely linguistic: the children do understand questions about the past. Nor can they be explained by simple memory problems. The very same group of children aged between 3 and 3½ did quite well on pretense and image tasks, which confirms that they are not merely reality-seduced. Nor is it just a matter of embarrassed deception or self-deception on part of the children. Changing one's mind does not always mean admission of a mistake or embarrassment. There is nothing wrong with admitting one is not hungry after being fed. When these children were subjected to similar desire tasks they behaved predictably: hungry children after being fed denied ever having the desire to eat. The results suggest the hypothesis that children believe and report the same things about others and themselves, credit others and themselves with specific mental states at the same time, and when they are mistaken, they are equally mistaken about others and themselves. So it seems that the children's understanding of intentional states evolves by parallel engagement with first- and third-person cases. The evidence suggests that crucial aspects of common-sense psychology, particularly the idea of intentionality, are constructed between age three and four. Investigators agree that there is a general shift in the child's concept of mind at about 3-3½ years, though there is debate about the precise characterization of the shift.

The developmental evidence suggests a close parallel between our knowledge of our own mental states and those of others, though it is obvious that the causal routes through which we acquire information about our own and other minds is different. How do we square this up? Gopnik suggests that there is a fundamental cross-modal representation system that connects the self and the other (Gopnik 1993a). The evidence for the existence of a fundamental cross-modal representation system comes from developmental studies (Meltzoff & Gopnik 1994; Meltzoff & Moore 1983). The imitation of facial gestures in very young infants, 12-21 days, suggests an innate mapping from internal kinaesthetic sensations to bodily movements in others.[6] Very young infants can and do recognize an equivalence between their own bodily movements and those of others. The infant's own facial gestures are monitored by proprioception; they are perceived, even though they are invisible to the infant. In imitation the infant maps an internal set of sensations, particularly kinaesthetic sensations, onto the behaviour of another person. For example, the infant maps the felt sensations of his own tongue onto the visually perceived tongue protrusion of another person. This initial understanding of the fact that the infant's felt body is like the seen body of another person might serve as a framework for the latter assumption that the infant's mind and the mind of another person are also similar. From a developmental viewpoint, knowing that we inhabit similar bodies to others, and assuming that they share our internal bodily states, is an important precursor to assuming that they share more abstract mental states as well. The bodily scheme constitutes the bridge between the self and the other and underpins the hypothesis that mental states are things had by others and us. Thus,

---

6. Learning theorists may object that the infants could have been trained to imitate during the first weeks of life. To resolve this point, Moore and Meltzoff (1983) tested 40 newborn infants in a hospital setting. The average age of the sample was 32 hours, the youngest was only 42 minutes' old. The results showed that the newborns imitated both the gestures shown to them, mouth-opening and tongue protrusion. Thus, they conclude that a primitive capacity to imitate is part of a child's innate endowment.

Meltzoff and Gopnik (1993) propose that the initial body scheme provides a "scaffold" on which the more sophisticated "theory of mind" can later be hung.

Extending this model to self-ascription of intentional states, Gopnik suggests "... we genuinely experience our own internal states and map it onto the expressions of others, and that these initial genuine perceptions are then shaped by psychological expertise" (Gopnik 1993a, 277). The experiences of internal states are mapped onto behavioural expressions of others internal states and only then we, so to say, *indirectly* see ourselves being in a certain intentional state. Similarly, our theoretical interpretations of the behaviour of others, attributing beliefs and desires to others, is achieved by mapping the attributions onto both the bodily expressions of others and our own internal bodily states. An analogy offered by Gopnik may help to get our mind around this seemingly counterintuitive suggestion. Our understanding of the physical world is based on an innate ability to combine information from many different sources into "a single type of subjective experience" with a distinctive character. So, for example, we combine both motion parallax and visual angle information to specify size and distance. Similarly, our understanding of the psychological world is based on information about our own internal states and about the movements of others is combined into "a single type of subjective experience" with a distinctive character. Gopnik concludes:

> The perceptually given mapping of feelings and behaviours that underlies early imitation, on this view, forms the genuine perceptual basis for our highly elaborated later theory of minds. This is not only true developmentally but also reflected in the phenomenology of our psychological experience. When we see beliefs, desires, or emotions of others on their faces or when we feel our own in our own guts we are really seeing and feeling the same things. The information from the two

> sources specifies the same underlying distal psychological objects.
> — Gopnik 1993a: 277

However, this engagement with the third-person cases is not reflected in the phenomenology of our knowledge of intentional states of ourselves and others. Gopnik's account of first-person access is modelled on an information-processing view of visual perception as explained by Marr. Even the very simple "direct" perceptions of objects in space actually involve very complex functional relations, top-down influences, implicit inferences and computations (Marr 1982; Rock 1983). Similarly, our supposedly "direct" experience of our own mental states is the result of bottom-up transformation of information received as proximal stimuli as well as top-down effects generated by expectations, preconceptions, other beliefs, expertise and so on. But there is no way to delineate what is directly observed and inferentially imposed as in the case of an expert. The theoretical knowledge affects an expert's perception of a situation, e.g. a chess expert "seeing" the king's strength. As mature adults we are experts in the business of attribution of mental states and this explains the phenomenological feeling that we are "directly" aware of our mental states. Phenomenologically, it may feel as if we see an apple directly; or that the expert sees the king's strength; or that we see a friends' disappointment; but such directness cannot be taken to indicate "direct" or "unmediated" access to the world or one's own mind. Given the analogy with perceptual cases, it is no surprise that our subjective experience does not match the underlying intentional state that is caused by our experiences and also causes our behaviour. Thus, we may safely disregard the phenomenological feeling of "directness" that accompanies the subjective experience as the source of our first-person knowledge and self-ascription of intentional states.

The psychological evidence presented here will convince

many that there is nothing special about first-person access to mental states. However, others think that developmental data that supports the symmetry in out first- and third-person attributions of thought is mistaken. Recently, Cynthia Macdonald argues that the developmental data presented by Gopnik does not pose a problem for the common-sense view that we have direct and thereby privileged access to first-person mental states.[7] Macdonald (2002) develops two objections against Gopnik's claim that the developmental data is incompatible with the common-sense view. Firstly, the developmental data concerns a subject's past beliefs whereas the common-sense view concerns the subject's knowledge of their current psychological states. It will be remembered that the false-belief task with pencils in a candy box requires the children to report on their immediately past beliefs. Macdonald argues that the data may show that subjects are not authoritative about their own psychological states in the past, it does not show that they are not authoritative about their current psychological states. Gopnik claims that our immediate recall of psychological states that occur within a span of a few minutes as in the case of false-belief task *ought to count as a part of a subject's current psychological state* (Gopnik 1993b). I

7. To be fair, Macdonald's project is larger than just this thesis. Macdonald hopes to show that Gopnik's claim that the developmental data shows that theory theory is incompatible with the common-sense view is untenable. Macdonald's strategy is to show this by dealing with two parts separately: (a) whether the developmental data presents a problem for the common-sense view, and (b) whether it constitutes an argument in favour of theory theory. Macdonald argues that the answer to the (a) is "no' irrespective of what the answer to (b) is. This is exactly where I disagree with Macdonald. I think the answer to (a) is yes, but she is right in insisting that there is a further issue whether the developmental data constitutes an argument for a theory theory. I don't think it does constitute a conclusive argument in favour of theory theory, in the strict sense, in which Gopnik uses the term.

think Gopnik is right on this matter, we should not individuate the "current" too finely, i.e. less than a few minutes, the objects of our first-person intentional states will be restricted to something like ephemeral sense data. In the false-belief test children are asked to recall their immediately past belief.

The second argument offered by Macdonald against Gopnik's use of the developmental data raises a conceptual issue. On the basis of the developmental evidence Gopnik claims that children between ages 3-4 years lack a theory of mind and the concept of intentionality. They acquire this understanding only through their understanding of other minds and this explains the symmetry of errors in their ascription of intentional states to others and themselves. Macdonald suggests an alternative interpretation of the data. She suggests that children do appreciate the intentionality of their beliefs to the extent that they appreciate that beliefs are about the world around them. What they lack is complete understanding of the intentionality of psychological states, that is, they do not appreciate the fact that intentional states sometimes *misrepresent* the world. She claims, "In other words, they do not lack a concept of intentionality altogether, they simply have an incomplete concept" (Macdonald 2002: 476). Macdonald claims that three-year-olds' grasp of the concept of belief is partial: they understand that belief aims at truth but fail to realize that beliefs do sometimes fail to reach their target. This discussion of grasp of the incomplete concept of intentionality is misleading. First, it seems that the data only shows that three-year-olds understand the distinction between states of the mind and states of the world (as evidenced by the fact that they report their "imaginings" like making pictures). They also, of course, have a grasp of the fact that some mental states, "serious states" (Wellman) are copies of the world like perceptions. So, it is fair to say, as Macdonald does, that three-year-olds appreciate the fact that some mental states are about the world. But Macdonald's further claim that three-year-olds thereby have an incomplete concept of intentionality is from the mouth of the sophisticated theorist who appreciates what it is to grasp the concept of intentionality "incompletely". The data is not fine-grained enough to support the further claim. The data is equivocal on whether the child has an incomplete concept of intentionality or some other concept. So there is no good reason to endorse Macdonald's claim. Furthermore, I am inclined to favour Gopnik's claim that three-year-olds lack the concept of intentionality because the data shows and both Macdonald and Gopnik agree, that three-year-olds do not grasp the idea that intentional states can sometimes misrepresent the way the world is. This feature is essential to the concept of intentionality as discussed by recent philosophers.[8] Tim Crane notes that the familiar idea that consciousness is always consciousness *of* or *about* something is captured by the notion of *apparently* relational structure of intentionality. It is important to stress the qualifier "apparently" because although intentional states *appear* to be relations between thinkers and the objects of thought, this cannot be true in general, since intentional states can be directed towards things which do not exist and relations entail the existence of their relata. Macdonald's discussion shows that she misses the *apparently* relational structure of intentionality. She says, ". . . three-year-olds, appreciate the intentionality of their beliefs to the extent that they appreciate that they are *about* the world around them" (ibid.). Treating intentionality as a relational concept just misses the essential feature of the concept of intentionality. In an Appendix to his *Psychology from the Empirical Standpoint* puts the point thus,

8. Tim Crane (1998), "Intentionality as the Mark of the Mental", in *Contemporary Issues in Philosophy of Mind*, ed. Anthony O'Hear, Cambridge University Press, pp. 229-53.

> If someone thinks of something, the one who is thinking must certainly exist, but the object of thinking need not exist at all. . . . We might doubt whether we are dealing with something relational here, and not, rather, with something similar to something relational in a certain respect, which might therefore better be called "quasi-relational"
>
> — Brentano, op. cit.: 272

The idea that the objects of thought may not exist or equivalently that beliefs may be false is a necessary condition for the possession of the concept of intentionality and that of belief. Three-year-olds do not grasp this necessary condition thus it is improper to say that they have an incomplete grasp of the concept of intentionality or belief, it is better to admit that they lack the concept of intentionality or belief altogether. They may have some other concept like that of a "serious state" (Wellman 1990) which incorporates true beliefs, veridical perceptions, real memories, and so on. But it is misleading to equate a grasp of such a concept with the grasp of an incomplete concept of intentionality.

Furthermore, Macdonald's reinterpretation of the data does not help in explaining away the fact that there is *symmetry* in errors in self-ascription and other ascription in the false-belief task. It only explains the fact why children give the wrong answers in the false-belief task. The fact that there is symmetry in errors is crucial to Gopnik's argument that children's understanding of intentional states requires a grasp of a "theory of mind" which in turn evolves by parallel engagement with first- and third-person cases. We may agree with Macdonald and say that the *complete* understanding of the concept of belief or intentionality requires a grasp of a "theory of mind" which evolves by parallel engagement with first- and third-person cases. This reinterpretation will only be further support Gopnik's claim that the concept of an intentional mental state, like belief or desire, requires a grasp of a "theory of mind" and appreciation of other minds.[9]

## Conclusion

The epistemic continuity fits nicely with the developmental evidence and it also explains the symmetry and the systematicity of errors between first- and third-person ascriptions. Once we deny direct and immediate access to our own mental states as Davidson does, it is not easy, as we saw, to account for the epistemic asymmetry in first and third-person ascriptions underlying FPA. The psychological literature suggests that there is no such asymmetry. The asymmetry is an epistemic illusion, perhaps one that is required to sustain interpretative practices, but an illusion none the less. We are designed to entertain the transcendental presupposition of FPA, just as we are designed to respond to refraction of light and see that a stick dipped in water bends.

9. Gopnik treats the theory of mind as a cognitive construction that shares many features of a scientific theory although the theory of mind is implicit. Beliefs and desires have to be understood as theoretical constructs connected by laws, such as practical syllogisms, which account for their predictive power. In addition, she insists that the acquisition of the ideas of beliefs, desires and particularly the idea of intentionality, is a process of knowledge construction rather than enculturation. We do not learn how to psychologize appropriately, like we dress and eat politely. She admits this may be true for some sophisticated emotional states but not for the simple states that are a part of common-sense psychology. I think, Gopnik has overstated the case that the theory of mind is a cognitive construction. In so far as the interpretation theory provides a framework for common-sense psychology, it highlights the normative elements which are an essential part of the theory. And not all norms are global, to some extent they are infected by local interests of agents and the social and political communities they are a part of. So it is quite possible that our theory of mind and thus our understanding of the simple psychological states is infected by enculturation and cannot be thought of purely as a cognitive construction.

## References

Brown, J. (2004), *Anti-Indvidualism and Knowledge*, Cambridge, Mass: MIT Press/Bradford Books.

Bilgrami, A. (1998), "Self-Knowledge and Resentment", in C. Wright, B. Smith, and C. MacDonald (eds.), *Knowing Our Own Minds* Oxford: Oxford University Press, pp. 207-41.

Byrne, A. (2005), "Introspection", *Philosophical Topics*, 33, forthcoming.

Crane, T. (1998), "Intentionality as the Mark of the Mental" in Anthony O'Hear (ed.), *Contemporary Issues in Philosophy of Mind*, Cambridge University Press, pp. 229-53.

Davidson, D. (1984), "First Person Authority", *Dialectica* 38, 101-11.

Davidson, D. (1986), "Knowing one's Own Mind", *Proceedings and Addresses of the American Philosophical Association*, 441-58.

Davidson, D. (1982), "Rational animals", *Dialectica*, 36: 318-27.

Davidson, D. (1973), "Radical Interpretation" reprinted in *Inquiries into Truth and Interpretation*, 2nd edn. Oxford, 2001.

Gopnik, A. (1993), "How we Know our Own Minds: The Illusion of First-person Knowledge of Intentionality", *Brain and Behavioural Sciences*, 16, 1-14.

Gopnik, A. (1993), "Psychopsychology", *Consciousness and Cognition*, II, 264-80.

Grandy, R.E. (1973), "Reference, Meaning and Belief", *Journal of Philosophy*, 439-52.

Hacker, P.M.S. (1997), "Davidson on First-Person Authority", *The Philosophical Quarterly* 47 (188), 285-304.

Macdonald C. (2002), "Theories of Mind and The Commonsense View", *Mind & Language*, 17, 467-88.

Makinson, D. (1965), "The Paradox of the Preface", *Analysis*, 25: 205-07.

Medina, J. (2006), "What's So Special about Self-Knowledge", *Philosophical Studies*, 129: 575-603.

Medina J. (2006), "What's So Special about Self-Knowledge?", *Philosophical Studies* 129: 575-603.

Meltzoff, A.N., & A. Gopnik (1993), "The Role of Imitation in Understanding Persons and Developing a Theory of Mind", in S. Baron-Cohen, H. Tager-Flusberg, & D.J. Cohen (eds.), *Understanding Other Minds: Perspectives from Autism*, New York: Oxford University Press, pp. 335-66.

Meltzoff, A.N., & M.K. Moore (1983), "Newborn Infants Imitate Adult Facial Gestures", *Child Development*, 54, 702-09.

——— (1989), "Imitation in Newborn Infants: Exploring the Range of Gestures Imitated and the Underlying Mechanisms", *Developmental Psychology*, 25, 954-62.

Meltzoff, A.N. (1990), "Foundations for Developing a Concept of Self: The Role of Imitation in Relating Self to Other and the Value of Social Mirroring, Social Modelling, and Self-Practice in Infancy", in D. Cicchetti & M. Beeghly (eds.), *The Self in Transition: Infancy to Childhood*, Chicago: University of Chicago Press, 139-64.

Moran, R. (1994), "Interpretation Theory and the First Person", *Philosophical Quarterly*, 44, 154-74.

Nisbett, R. and Wilson, T.D. (1977), "Telling More Than we can Know: Verbal Reports on Mental Processes", *Psychological Review*, 84: 231-59.

Nuccetelli, S. (2003) (ed.), *New Essays on Semantic Externalism and Self-Knowledge*, Cambridge, Massachusetts: MIT Press.

Parker, S.T., R.W. Mitchell and M.L. Boccia (1994), *Self-awareness in Animals and Humans: Developmental Perspectives*, Cambridge New York, NY: Cambridge University Press.

Rock, I. (1983), *The Logic of Perception*, Cambridge MA: MIT Press.

Root, M. (1986), "Davidson and Social Science", in E. Lepore (ed.) *Truth and Interpretation: Essays in the Philosophy of Donald Davidson*, Oxford: Basil Blackwell, 165-89.

Shoemaker, S. (1990), "First-Person Access", *Philosophical Perspectives*, 4, Special Issue *Action Theory and Philosophy of Mind*, 187-214.

Strawson, P. (1959), *Individuals: An Essay in Descriptive Metaphysics*. London: Meuthen.

Swoyer C. (2003), "Preface Paradox", *The Stanford Encyclopedia of Philosophy* (Winter Edition), ed. Edward N. Zalta, URL: http://setis.library.usyd.edu.au/stanford/entries/relativism/supplement5.html#preface

Wellman, H.M. (1990), *A Child's Theory of Mind*, Cambridge: MIT Press.

Wimmer, H. and M. Hartl (1991), "Against the Cartesian View of Mind: Young Children's Difficulty with Own False Beliefs", *British Journal of Developmental Psychology*, IX, 125-28.

Wright, Edmund (1983), "Inspecting Images", *Philosophy*, 58: 57-72.

# 4

# Intentionality and First-person Authority

*Manidipa Sen*

## Preliminaries

KNOWLEDGE of our own minds and the notion of first-person authority that seem to accompany an account of such knowledge have once again become an important domain of enquiry in philosophy, particularly in Philosophy of Mind. One may wonder why this issue has received such an enormous amount of attention in recent philosophical literature. The reasons are many. But one can try and articulate a couple of such reasons which may have prompted philosophers to engage with this debate anew. One set of reasons, which provides a negative impetus to philosophers to try and understand, as well as appreciate, the importance of self-knowledge and the underlying notion of first-person authority is to try and grapple with various forms of naturalism in philosophy of mind as well as various forms of reductionist tendencies which are offshoots of the naturalization tendencies. Another set of reasons that one may articulate is linked with the common-sense idea that knowing our own minds is in some way different from and superior to knowing the minds of others. What this difference and, maybe, superiority consists in is an issue where philosophers have come up with important alternative accounts.[1]

Let us try to elaborate on the nature of the asymmetry between the first-person and third-person perspectives. The basis of this asymmetry lies in the fact that when it comes to making reliable psychological ascriptions to oneself (e.g. "I have a severe toothache" or "I believe in God") one does it without any evidence, whereas when one ascribes them to others, one requires some evidential support. In characterizing such first-person ascriptions, Davidson remarks:

> the self-attributer does not normally base his claims on evidence or observation, nor does it normally make sense to ask the self-attributer why he believes he has the beliefs, desires, or intentions he claims to have.[2]

Davidson goes on to say that the problem of self-knowledge consists in explaining this authority, trying to see where this authority comes from, not just in describing it. A similar point has been emphasized by Richard Moran in his book *Authority and Estrangement* (Princeton and Oxford: Princeton University Press, 2001). According to both Davidson and Moran, this is a rather modest characterization of first-person authority since it does not make a claim to completeness, reliability and infallibility as traditional introspective accounts do. Moran goes on to saying, in the line of Davidson,

> But perhaps more pressing than the question about the epistemic completeness or reliability of introspection are

1. As we know, there are different cognitive; accounts, like the Cartesian dualistic account, as well as non-cognitive accounts of self-knowledge, like a Wittgensteinian expressivist account, which have tried to grapple with the asymmetry that exists between self-knowledge and knowledge of other minds.
2. See his "First Person Authority", in *Subjective, Intersubjective, Objective*, Oxford: Clarendon Press, 2001, p. 4.

> philosophical questions concerning how there could even be such a thing as this capacity, however imperfect its deliverances? How is it possible for there to be knowledge of contingent matter of fact (e.g., the fact about what I believe or hope for) that is not based on observation of some kind? And in what sense is this knowledge to be essentially or exclusively first-personal?[3]

Before we embark on a discussion of the main issue, let us note that when we talk about having first-person authority *vis-à-vis* our mental life we can be referring to two sorts of things: one is the phenomenal experiences, the other are the intentional states that we have. The first kind of states are ascribed to ourselves with the help of "phenomenal avowals" (like "I am in pain") while the others are ascribed with the help of "attitudinal avowals" (like, "I wish that I didn't have to write this paper").[4] The difference between these two kinds of mental phenomena lies in the fact that while the so-called intentional states have directionality, that is, they are directed towards some object outside of the mind, phenomenal states are characterized by experientiality, that is, what it is like to be in a state of this kind. In this sense we can, according to the philosopher psychologist Gopnik, distinguish between psychological experiences as opposed to psychological states.[5] As she says,

---

3. Davidson, "First Person Authority", in *Subjective, Intersubjective, Objective*, Oxford: Clarendon Press, 2001, p. 13.
4. For an account of the distinction between phenomenal and attitudinal avowal, see Crispin Wright, "Self-knowledge: A Wittgensteinian Legacy", in Crispin Wright, Cyntia Macdonald and Barry Smith (eds.), *Knowing Our Own Minds*, Oxford: Clarendon Press, 1998, pp. 14-15.
5. See her "How We Know Our Minds: The Illusion of First-person Knowledge of Intentionality", in Alvin I. Goldman (ed.), *Readings in Philosophy and Cognitive Science*, Cambridge (Mass), London (England): The MIT Press, All the reference in this paper will be from this edition.

> . . . we use mentalistic vocabulary to talk about conscious experiences with a Woolfian stream of consciousness. I will call these "psychological experiences". These experiences are phenomenologically distinct from other types of experience, such as our experiences of trees or rocks or colours.[6]

In contrast we can have psychological states like beliefs and desires which are "underlying entities that explain our behaviour and experience. Describing such states is the goal of scientific psychology".[7] This is an important distinction which plays a crucial role in the discussion which is to follow. But one of the implications of this distinction is that due to the subjective character of these phenomenological experiences they are available directly to the person who has those experiences, while that may not be the case with the intentional states.[8]

We stop here with these preliminary remarks in place. Our aim in the next section is to elaborate in detail, how Gopnik argues that first-person knowledge of intentional states is illusory.

**First-person Authority versus Intentionality**

In answer to the question: Is first-person knowledge of intentional states "profoundly different" (p. 317) from our third-person knowledge of such states? Gopnik says that it is really not so. In her influential paper "How we know our minds: The illusion of first-person knowledge of

6. Gopnik "How We Know Our Minds: The Illusion of First-person Knowledge of Intentionality", in Alvin I. Goldman (ed.) *Readings in Philosophy and Cognitive Science*, p. 315.
7. Ibid.
8. Note that externalists like Putnam also holds that we do not and cannot have a direct access to our intentional states like belief because it is individuated partly by what is outside of the experience as such. Therefore, authoritative self-knowledge with regard to psychological states is not possible.

intentionality" (first pulished as a target paper in *Behavioral and Brain Sciences* 16, 1993) she argues in favour of her position by considering developmental data of three-year and four-year-old children, particularly about their attitude towards their intentional states. Contrary to the common-sense belief "that our knowledge of intentionality, like knowledge of sensations, comes directly and reliably from our psychological experience" (p. 317), Gopnik proposes the following:

> Empirical findings show that the idea of intentionality is a theoretical construct, one we invent in our early lives to explain a wide variety of evidence about ourselves and others. The theoretical construct is equally applicable to ourselves and others and depends equally on our experience of ourselves and others.
> — p. 317

The argument that she proposes runs as follows:

> If our knowledge of our own intentional states is direct then it cannot depend upon any other knowledge.
>
> Our knowledge of our own intentional states have to depend upon knowledge of intentionality as a theoretical construct, which is a distinct form of knowledge.
>
> Therefore, our knowledge of our own intentional states is not direct.

According to Gopnik, the directness that we experience with regard to the knowledge of our own intentional state is a mere illusion, an illusion which is a result of our being experts in common-sense psychology. It can be compared to an expert in any field, say an expert swimmer, and so she says:

> Experts experience their knowledge as immediate and perceptually based; in reality, however, it depends on a long theoretical history. Similarly, we as experts in common-sense psychology, may experience our theoretical knowledge of the intentionality of our psychological states as if it were the result of direct perception. . . .
> — p. 318

She further argues against first-person authority in the following way: If our knowledge of our intentional states is not direct then we cannot have first person authority with regard to those states.

Our knowledge of our own intentional states is not direct. Therefore, we cannot have first-person authority with regard to those states.

What she tries to prove in this seminal paper is the second premise of the argument mentioned above, that is, the claim that our knowledge of our own intentional states as being intentional has to depend upon our prior knowledge of a theory of intentionality, or broadly on a theory of mind. This she tries to prove by considering experimental studies involving the behaviour of three-year and four-year-old children regarding their knowledge of intentional states and ascriptions of those states. Gopnik does this in two stages: First, she looks at how they ascribe intentional states to others, and, second, how they ascribe intentional states to themselves. She compares the third-person perspective with the first-person perspective of children of this particular age-group and comes to the following conclusion:

> We have compared children's performance on "other minds" tasks like those we have just described with their performance on tasks that require them to report their own immediately past mental states. We find that children make errors about their own immediately past states that are similar to the errors they make about the states of others.
>
> — p. 326

At this stage, it is important to take a look at the evidence that leads to the above conclusion. Gopnik informs us that most of the investigation centres around children who are between two and half and five years of age. She acknowledges a whole lot of abilities that these groups of children have with regard to mental states, recognizing them, linguistically referring to them, understanding the difference between their own mental states and the states of others, that develop in children during these years, and they are certainly "impressive". But, she goes on to remark,

> . . . the failures of these children are equally impressive. Three-year-old children consistently fail to understand certain other problems, or rather understand them in a way that is profoundly different from adult understanding.
>
> — p. 319

A particular kind of failure, one that Gopnik takes to be an important piece of evidence for the conclusion that she derives, consists in the failure on the part of a three-year-old child to understand what it is to have false beliefs both in the context of others as well as in their own context. In one such case children are shown a candy box which turns out to be full of pencils when they open it. However, when the same group of children are asked what someone else would think or believe to be inside the box when they first see the box, three-year-old children, more or less consistently reply that the other person will think that there are pencils in the box. What this reply indicates is that children belonging to this age-group are *unable to understand that other person's belief may be false*. They fail to understand that the other person has a false belief even when they see the other person responding to the finding inside the box in surprise, or even when they are explicitly told that the other person has a false belief.

The same experiment is now repeated only with the difference that what the child is asked now is, "what did you think was inside the box when you saw the unopened box?" And the reply, even in this case, was that she thought that there were pencils inside the box, which indicates that children fail to recognize their immediately previous belief as a false belief.

This developmental evidence, according to Gopnik, proves the following points:

1. There is a parallel between a child's understanding of the psychological states of others, and her understanding of her own psychological states.
2. The common-sense psychological account of intentionality, as innately given, needs to be replaced by an account of intentionality which appears to be constructed between the age of three and four.
3. There is dissociation between the psychological states that cause the children's behaviour and their conscious and sincere report such that intentionality of psychological states cannot be discovered through first-person experience.
4. Children therefore, have to construct a theory of mind, "a coherent abstract account of the mind" (p. 333) which enables them to explain, and psychological phenomena both of others as well as their own.

Therefore Gopnik says:

> The important point is that the theoretical constructs themselves, and particularly the idea of intentionality, are not the result of some direct first-person apprehension that is then applied to others. Rather they are the results of cognitive construction. The child constructs a theory that explains a wide variety of facts about the child's experience and behaviour and about the behaviour and language of others. — p. 334

This theoretical knowledge about intentionality does not come from and, in fact, cannot come from experience, even if we do feel that it does. This further claims that theoretical knowledge in general is devoid of any experientiality.

One must here also highlight that Gopnik does not deny that we have first-person authority with regard to our psychological experiences like feeling a pain, but first-person authority is not there and is a mere illusion when it comes to our knowledge of intentional states.

## Reconciling Intentionality with First-person Authority: Macdonald against Gopnik

Cynthia Macdonald in her article "Theories of Mind and 'The Common-sense View'" (*Mind and Language*, vol. 17, no. 5, 2002) raises several objections to the arguments posed by Alison Gopnik. Her objections revolve around two sets of points. One set of points questions whether the developmental evidence proves the falsity of common-sense view, and another set of argument questions the position that common-sense view is against or contrary to theory theory. We will concentrate mainly on the first set of points and buttress her arguments against Gopnik with some additional arguments. We will also take up one particular issue pertaining to the second set of arguments and try to see wherein Gopnik might have gone wrong regarding her notion of intentionality.

According to Macdonald, the developmental evidence that Gopnik provides us with in order to challenge the common-sense view shows that *we have no direct access to our psychological states*. We may understand this point by comparing it with the case of perception. In case of perceptual experience there is a direct relation between the experience and the object of that perceptual experience. But that is not the case with the relationship between experiences of psychological states and psychological states themselves. The main point that Gopnik wants to establish with the help of the evidence is the following:

> Subjects do not perceive, in any sense of "perceive" that involves the idea of direct experience, the intentionality of their own psychological states — their representational nature. Further, since intentional psychological states have no particular phenomenology associated with them, subjects do not perceive these states. — Macdonald, p. 472

One may ask two questions here:

1. Does the developmental evidence really show that there is a gap between the experience of psychological states and psychological states themselves? and,
2. Is it really true to say that intentional psychological states have no particular phenomenology associated with them?

We will take up these questions one at a time.

The first question becomes important, according to Macdonald, if we recognize what happens between the age of three and four. A three-year-old child lacks self-knowledge of her own intentional states because she lacks the concept of intentionality, or a theory of intentionality. By the time the child reaches the age of four she acquires a concept of intentionality, and thus has knowledge of her own mental states as intentional state. So, the difference between a three-year and a four-year-old child consists in the fact that the four-year-old has a theory of mind which helps her to identify her psychological states as being intentional. And, since it is only after the construction of a theory of mind that a child can have self-knowledge of the intentionality of her psychological states, it is further argued that this self-knowledge is neither direct nor authoritative and hence on a par with knowledge of the intentionality of another person's psychological state.

Let us try to unpack one important assumption on which the above argument is based. The assumption is that there is a qualitative difference between the knowledge that a three-year-old has with regard to her intentional states and the knowledge that the *same* child who turns four has with regard to the same intentional state. If that is the case then what we have to say, according to Macdonald, is that construction of the concept of intentionality is an all or nothing affair, which suddenly emerges in the developmental process of a child. As opposed to this rather implausible account, where knowledge of intentionality crops up at a particular point in life, a much more plausible account could be that,

> . . . three-year-olds do appreciate the intentionality of their beliefs to the extent that they appreciate that they are about the world around them. What they lack is a *complete* understanding of the intentionality of their psychological states. In particular, they do not appreciate that their psychological states may *mis*represent the world as it is. In other words they do not lack a concept of intentionality altogether, they simply have an incomplete concept.
>
> — Ibid., p. 476

This certainly seems to be a more plausible account since it takes our psychological development to be a continuous process involving the acquisition of higher levels of conceptual repertoire.

We can understand this point by looking at the characterization of intentionality. As we know the concept of intentionality was a medieval concept reinstated into philosophy by Brentano to characterize mental states as such, intentionality being the mark of the mental, and all and only mental states can be intentional. What do we mean when we say that mental states are intentional? — Without going into the detail we can say that it is directionality which is the characterizing feature of intentionality. Directionality suggests world-involvingness[9] of our mental states. So, one can have a notion of intentionality of this basic kind without "having yet acquired a firm grasp of the fact that belief aims at truth but sometimes fails to reach its target" (ibid., p. 477). Having a theory of intentionality as advocated by Gopnik involves this full-fledged conception of intentionality, but that does not

9. See McCulloch, *Life of the Mind: An Essay in Phenomenological Externalism,* London: Routledge, 2003.

mean that there is a complete lack of the concept of intentionality when a child lacks a full-fledged notion of intentionality.

If this is when a child lacke a full-fledged notion of intentionality the way in which we can understand the developmental data, then we can think of authority as something which the subject acquires continuously and not suddenly. Macdonald thinks that this idea is consistent with the common-sense notion of self-knowledge as being direct. Having direct access to one's psychological states does not imply that our knowledge of our own minds is infallible and indubitable. It is only when one equates the notion of directness with the notions of infallibility and indubitability that the problem crops up. Thus Macdonald rightly points out,

> . . . that subjects have direct and privileged knowledge of the contents of their psychological states (of their representations) is compatible with the failure to recognize that sometimes these contents can misrepresent. Indeed, the common-sense view about epistemic privilege concerns the contents of such states only; it says nothing about the epistemic status of the subject's knowledge of the truth or falsity of such contents, let alone how that knowledge is acquired. This being so, it does not extend to knowledge that a content *mis*represent. —Ibid., pp. 478-79

Another important point that Macdonald raises against Gopnik's position is concerning the notion of perception that Gopnik presupposes. According to this notion, perception as a direct mode of awareness is like that of sensation, that is, it does not involve the awareness of the object as one thing or the other. Hence, she says that as our knowledge of our own intentional state requires that we be aware of those states as intentional states, our knowledge is conceptual, and thus non-perceptual, and therefore, indirect. According to Macdonald, Gopnik recognizes two types of perception, "perception can be understood 'transparently' (as simply 'seeing x', for some object or state of affairs x) or '. . . mediated by representations on propositions' (as in perceiving or seeing *that* something is the case" (p. 479).

However, we can think of another model of perception, which Macdonald thinks could fall somewhere in between these two forms of perception: one being purely non-conceptual, while the other being purely conceptual. Following John Mcdowell, we may characterize such a form of perception as "seeing as". The notion of perception as embodied in the idea of "seeing as" may be understood in the following way:

> Perceptual experience is a matter of *seeing as* in the sense that, when a subject has such an experience, she takes an object x to have some property or the other. She does so because the content of her experience represents the world around us as being some way or other. —Ibid., p. 479

There are two important points that may be highlighted regarding this form of perception:

1. Though the subject of such perceptual experience takes the object to have some property, she need not be able to identify the specific property that the object has.
2. In this form of perception one does not deny the fact that there are many things that we see which are not necessarily fully articulated in our conception of it.

Now, if we take into consideration this kind of a model of perception then we can say, that having knowledge of our own mental states consists in knowing intentional states as intentional states without having a conceptual knowledge of intentionality as such. This really means that we see these intentional states as having directionality, as concerning things and objects in the world without necessarily being aware of what exactly these objects are, and how the relation is to be understood fully. In this sense, we can maintain that our self-knowledge is direct without being necessarily indubitable or incorrigible.

These are some of the main arguments that Macdonald raises against Gopnik. I am mostly sympathetic towards Macdonald's position, but think that it can be substantiated further by taking some further features of intentional states and first-person authority. But it is also important to consider the relationship between intentionality of psychological states and the phenomenology or experientiality of psychological states.

**Experientiality of Intentionality**

One of the main features of intentionality that emerges from Gopnik's arguments against the experience of intentional states is that intentionality needs to be separated from the phenomenal features of conscious experience. This is evident from her distinction between psychological experiences as opposed to psychological states. She also suggests that there is no major problem in accepting first-person authority of psychological experiences as knowledge of sensations comes directly from our psychological experience due to its distinctive phenomenological feel. So, there is a clear distinction to be drawn between cognitive intentional states and phenomenal states, and further our knowledge of our cognitive states is indirect and hence non-authoritative, while our knowledge of our own phenomenal states is direct and thus authoritative.

This compartmentalization of our mental life seems to be highly unwarranted. What we would like to suggest here is that intentionality is not completely devoid of phenomenality. We can strengthen the point that intentionality may not be devoid of phenomenality with the help of a series of interesting points that Galen Strawson makes in his article, "Intentionality and Experience" (in Amie Thomasson and David W. Smith (eds.), *Phenomenology and Philosophy of Mind*, Oxford: Clarendon Press, 2005). A lot of unnecessary debates in recent analytic philosophy of mind, according to Strawson, emanate from:

> First, separating the phenomenal from the intentional,
>
> Second, equating phenomenality with subjectivity, and thus claiming that phenomenal experiences belong to the inner domain of consciousness, while equating intentionality with objectivity, and thus claiming that intentional states essentially relate to the outer,
>
> Third, suggesting that we can take a first-person stance *vis-à-vis* the domain of phenomenality, and not *vis-à-vis* the domain of intentionality.

The problem that a view of intentionality of this kind has led to has been highlighted by Galen Strawson in his article "Intentionality and Experience: Terminological Preliminaries". He starts the article by noting:

> Much of the recent history of analytic philosophy of mind could be rewritten as the sort of what happened when intentionality was allowed to exist without experience (consciousness) — the story of how far philosophers were prepared to go in their uses of words like "mental", "mind", "think", and so on, in order to accommodate the chain reaction set off by this particular terminological decision. Another connected part of the story is about what happened when it became common to talk in a strongly reificatory way about mental states as if they were things in us, rather than things — states — we are in. — Ibid., pp. 45-46

This is certainly not the way in which phenomenological tradition starting with Brentano understood the notion of intentionality. For them intentionality is the mark of mental states — and by mental state they would mean both phenomenal as well as cognitive. According to Strawson, this division has led to the further unfortunate consequence of reification of cognitive states leading to the abandonment of what he likes to call "cognitive experience". Contrary to Gopnik's account of intentional states, we can say, following Strawson, that belief and other propositional attitude states, are marked by their phenomenality, that is, what it is like to be in a belief state. Strawson provides three arguments in favour of this notion of "cognitive experience":

1. It would be impossible to explain how we could be gripped by a talk or moved by a piece of music, if we did not accept the fact of experientiality in our cognitive enterprises of various kinds. As a result, Strawson rightly points out, "many things which are not utterly mysterious would be utterly mysterious" (p. 47). It would be impossible to explain these phenomena of our daily life if we separate the phenomenal from the cognitive and hence intentional.
2. The second argument, which is even more fascinating and integrally connected with the above argument is that, if we reject the existence of cognitive experience (or may be, we can call it "cognitive feeling"), "life would be fabulously boring. . . . Life is not fabulously boring" (ibid., p. 47).
3. The very fact that one is understanding or not understanding the sentence that I am uttering now is very much a part of the character of our experience, so it is difficult, in fact impossible, to differentiate between experience of understanding and the understanding itself.

If these arguments are convincing enough then it becomes obvious that intentionality, which belongs to the cognitive domain of our mental life, is also characterized by phenomenality, and to that extent, we cannot altogether deny subjectivity associated with intentionality. If we accept this then it becomes easier for us to appreciate the idea that Macdonald proposes with regard to having a concept of intentionality without involving the knowledge of a theory of intentionality, and that this concept may very well be an incomplete concept for humans of a particular age. We have a concept of intentionality because we are experientially aware of these states. This could be regarded as knowing intentional states as states which suggest the existence of the world around us, though it may not be the awareness of our full representational content.

So, we may conclude this discussion by making these general points about the nature of intentional states as being continuous with experience:

- The first, and the negative conclusion that can be drawn from a rejection of the phenomenal-intentional distinction is that we cannot really talk about a purely subjective domain of our consciousness and a purely objective domain of consciousness, or a subjective consciousness and an objective consciousness.
- It follows from the above point that the subjective and the objective contents belong to the same conscious domain. So, there is an intimate connection between the world-as-experienced and the experience of it. The connection is not between an objective world and our internal private experiences of that world.
- It further follows that we cannot understand the subjective as that which is wholly "in the head", nor can we understand the objective as just being "out there" before the mind to be grasped/conceived.
- The mental is not relational in the sense that there is some intrinsic feature of the mental that is in some way related to some extrinsic feature of the non-mental domain.

**First-person Authority**

Self-knowledge has been understood in terms of having authoritativeness which is,

1. Derived from the first-person perspective from which the subject comes to know her own psychological states, be it phenomenal or intentional, and
2. It is further maintained that due to this first-person perspective the kind of direct knowledge that we have is a form of perception of our own mental states.
3. And, finally it is claimed that this perception is a form of inner observation or introspection.

This obviously takes us to be passive spectators of what is going on in our own minds without being actively involved in the experiencing of our mental life. This is what Amie Thomasson, while describing Amstrong's inner observation model of self-knowledge remarks in her article "First-person Knowledge in Phenomenolgy" (in Amie Thomasson & David Woodroff Smith eds., *Phenomenology and Philosophy of Mind*, Oxford: Clarendon Press, 2005):

> Such inwardly directed observations are higher order states, since they take our first-order mental states (perception, thought, desire, etc.) as their objects. This idea that our knowledge of our own mental states is based on inwardly directed observation can then explain the distinctive first-person character of knowledge of our mental states, since in each case this form of observation is possible only for one's own mental state. —p. 117

However, such a higher-order view of consciousness faces various problems, among them two may be mentioned here without going into a detailed discussion.

1. If a state is conscious only if there is a higher-order state that takes it to be conscious then we are left with an infinite regress of higher-order mental state, or
2. We have to say that there is a huge number of unconscious and non-conceptualized mental states which make conscious conceptualized states possible.

Both these positions seem to be equally implausible. Hence Thomasson suggests that instead of an inner observation model of self-knowledge, what we may think about and develop is an outer observation account of knowledge of our own mind. This is an account which can be derived from Wilfred Sellers's account of perception, contrary to the traditional sense-data theory of perception, and can be taken as an example of an one-level view of consciousness. So, Thomasson says:

> An entirely different approach to self-knowledge has occasionally been proposed: that our apparent knowledge of our own mental states is based not in a special observation of our mental states, but in awareness at least apparently directed *outwards,* towards the world (not towards our own minds). Such is the basic insight of what I will call "outer awareness" views, . . . . — Ibid., pp. 119-20

According to this view, instead of basing the knowledge of our world on the knowledge of sense-data, what we need to do is to base our knowledge of sense-data on the knowledge of our world. We won't have time to develop this interesting suggestion fully here, but we can mention one important insight on which this "outer observation" model is based, one which may be exploited in order to understand the idea of first-person authority in self-knowledge without bringing in an occult view of inner observation. It is the idea that self-knowledge is based on the commitment that we have about the world and the other human beings around us. This commitment may come in degrees and would never be fully complete, still it is this which makes my perspective towards my mental states first personal.

Here, we may end our discussion by connecting this idea with what Richard Moran, in his book *Authority and Estrangement: An Essay in Self-knowledge,* Princeton: Princeton University Press, 2001, says about the first-person perspective.

According to Moran, the criticisms that Wittgenstein and Sartre raise against the inner observational model and hence of privacy, are that this kind of a picture of knowledge of our own minds,

> ... present(s) an essentially superficial view of the differences between my relation to myself and my possible relations to others. For, in essence what we have here is a picture of self-knowledge as a kind of mind-reading as applied to oneself, a faculty to be aimed in one direction rather than another. Hence in filling out the picture of such a person's self-knowledge we may even dispense with any work of interpretation on her part altogether. —p. 91

In going from the world to the mind, as outer observation suggests, we retain knowledge from the first-person position without claiming it to be purely inner and hence transparent. It is part of our common-sense understanding of an intentional state, like belief, that belief carries with it the commitment to truth, though we may not be completely aware of it. It is this commitment that helps a person,

> to make up his mind, change his mind, endorse some attitude or disavow it. This is a form of authority tied to the presuppositions of rational agency and is different in kind from the more purely epistemic authority that may attach to the special immediacy of the person's access to his mental life. —Ibid., p. 92

If we can extend our notion of first-person authority from being a purely cognitive achievement to an ethical and agential commitment, then we may try to understand its cognitive base on the outer observational model proposed by Thomasson in line with Sellers and Husserl. So the task at hand is to expand or loosen the notion of intentionality, as well as the notion of first-person authority, in order to understand how an authoritative self-knowledge could be a continuous process from the experiences of a child to that of an adult.

# 5

# Self and Its Knowledge*

*Madhucchanda Sen*

WHO AM I?

> The Greeks believed they were playthings of fate. Christians saw themselves as miserable sinners, Descartes thought that man was a thinker, liberals stressed self-determination, Romantics self expression, while Freud invited you to go and lie upon the coach.[1]

THERE seems to be no "the" problem of the Self and no "the" problem of self-knowledge, but only a variety of conundrum that we encounter as we try to reflect upon the self and its knowledge. In Sāṁkhya theory of perception we find a list of reasons for error in perception, one of which is proximity. Proximity is definitely the reason for which there is no end to confusion and no end to disputes regarding the two things that we intend to discuss in this paper, i.e. self and self-knowledge. The self, which is quintessentially proximate to us, and the awareness of it, which is regarded as ever present in our consciousness, are ironically both evident and remote. What I seek to do in this paper is to show that how we conceive

* I am deeply indebted to the Centre for Philosophy, Jawaharlal Nehru University for inviting me to this seminar and for giving me this opportunity to share my thoughts with them. I am especially grateful to my friend Maushumi Guha for providing me with invaluable reading material.

1. R. Porter, ed., *Rewriting the Self*, London: Routledge, 1997.

the self is not only important but also is in certain sense constitutive of how we conceive self-knowledge. This might seem a triviality, but it isn't, as there is a strong tradition in which these two things have been kept apart. The focus of this paper is primarily on the ways in which the self might be conceived and how the different views of self have determined the different views of self-knowledge. I shall, however, start off with at least three ways in which we can speak of self-knowledge.

## Knowledge of Self, Self-knowledge, Sense of Self: Some Preliminaries

There are ever so many ways in which we can speak of self-knowledge. In classical Indian philosophy itself we find at least three ways in which self-knowledge is discussed: self-knowledge in the sense of self-consciousness (which we will call "sense of self" following Galen Strawson), theoretical knowledge regarding the true nature of the self (which we will call "knowledge of self"), and self-knowledge in the sense of self-realization.[2]

The knowledge of self, which is said to have an emancipatory power, is said to be the knowledge about the true nature of the self, i.e., knowledge of the kind of thing that we truly are. We may call this knowledge of the metaphysical self. That this true nature of the self is not always revealed to us, but rather is ever elusive, and that only the wise and the tenacious can achieve its knowledge through philosophical wisdom or divine vision, is something that gained acceptance in all ancient traditions. In the classical Indian philosophy misconceptions about the self was regarded as the root cause of suffering which can only be terminated in liberation by attaining knowledge of the true nature of the self.

Even when philosophical enquiry started to lose its identity

2. For a marvellous introduction see Srilekha Dutta's, "The Self and Self-Knowledge in Indian Tradition", in *Rabindra Bharati Journal of Philosophy*, vol. X, 2004.

as an emancipatory discourse, philosophers still were keen on knowing the true nature of self. The questions which became more pressing for them were: What kind of an entity (ontologically speaking) is the self? Do we need to admit such an entity in our ontology at all? We shall not concern ourselves in the discussion of self-knowledge seen as self-realization but we shall definitely speak about the knowledge of the kind of thing we are, or knowledge of the metaphysical self. Philosophical literature is replete with theories of the true nature of the self. While some philosophers thought that the *raison d'être* of their philosophical enterprise was the revelation of the true nature of the metaphysical self, others took the self as a shifter. Hume for instance believed that whenever he investigated into the self it disappeared. This empiricist doctrine is very near to what postmodernists thought about the self. But even philosophies that announce such a disappearance of the self face the question: what is it that disappears? The paradigmatic no-self theorists are the Buddhists. On the other side, there are philosophers who believe self to be something that is given and who believe that only deep metaphysical enquiry can reveal the true nature of this given. There are others who take the self to be neither given, nor brought into being, but as something that is modified in various ways by social or interpersonal processes and structures. It is not only metaphysically important to understand the nature of the self but also important otherwise because it is the self or selves that is/are the bearer of legal, social and religious rights and responsibilities. What then is the self whose knowledge we seek?

What is perplexing is that whereas the knowledge of the metaphysical self requires great effort, we seem to believe that we are blessed with a kind of immediate variety of self-knowledge. This is nothing but the knowledge of particular states of our own minds. We are said to have an immediate incorrigible access to our mental states, as they are self-presenting (in the sense that there cannot be any particular mental state that I might have which can go undetected, or even be detected improperly). And this is why we speak of first-person authority. Theories of mind are keen on discussing the nature of particular self-knowledge at the wake of challenges brought up by certain theories that question first-person authority.

There is yet another way in which we speak of self-knowledge. We may be said to have a sense of self[3] — each one of us (no matter how radical a view about the self we may harbour) has a sense of ourselves as being a self-same enduring mental something who has certain traits or characteristics and who is the "owner" of certain specific mental states. What is the nature of this sense of self? Why do we have it at all? How do we come to have it? — These are the questions that philosophers have been asking about the sense of self that we have.

Though we can speak of these various kinds of self-knowledge we cannot speak about any particular kind without speaking about the other. This is a point that needs to be emphasized as I feel much of the confusion about the nature of any of these kinds of self-knowledge is created because the discussions about one kind seem to ignore discussions about the other. This is what is distinctive of the works of Descartes, Hume, Kant. They have kept "particular self-knowledge" and "knowledge of self"[4] apart. They have believed that the knowledge of the kind of thing we are and our knowledge of our particular mental states are so distinct that we can discuss one without going into the discussion of the other. I believe that they adopt such a view because they adopt a particular

3. Which is called the I-consciousness or *aham pratyaya* in the classical Indian systems of philosophy.

4. See Quassim Cassam's introduction to *Self Knowledge*, Oxford University Press, 1994.

view about the nature of self. I take them to be believing that the self (if there is such a thing) has to be a metaphysically given object whose knowledge would consist in unravelling its true ontological nature. This belief has led Hume to believe that there is no such self and has led Kant to believe that nature of such a self is unknown and unknowable. This idea of the self as a metaphysically given entity has also led these philosophers believe that knowledge of self and particular self-knowledge and sense of self should be kept apart. The self that is presented in our self-consciousness for many of them cannot be the true metaphysical self, at best it might be called as the phenomenological self. And while having an immediate access to our particular mental states we are not aware of the self who is supposed to be the owner of those states.

I would like to very briefly make one observation here. Philosophers who have believed in the authoritative nature of particular self-knowledge have been deeply influenced by Descartes. I have in mind, in particular, Descartes' positive view about the self or the ego as being a substance, which is self-contained with respect to the world. What is meant by this thesis is that the life of the self or the ego is independent in every respect from the world and its happenings. This has given rise to what may be called the notion of a self as a purely subjective entity. If one adopts this view about the self then the idea of first person authority with respect to particular states of the mind (self/ego) will automatically follow. This is discussed in great detail by philosophers like Donald Davidson in his *Knowing One's Own Mind*[5] and *Myth of the Subjective*[6] and Greg McCulloch in his *The Mind and Its World*.[7] I would like to

5. See Quassim Cassam's introduction to *Self Knowledge*, Oxford: Oxford University Press, 1994.
6. In his *Subjective, Intersubjective, Objective*, Oxford: Clarendon Press, 2001.
7. London: Routledge, 1995.

say (following Davidson and to certain extent Wittgenstein's *Philosophical Investigation*) that if we give up this idea of the self as a purely subjective entity then our conception of particular self-knowledge would change significantly. So we see that our view of what the mind is or the self is definitely determines our stand on particular self-knowledge.

In this paper I make my task extremely difficult (and possibly get myself into all kinds of problems and disputes) as I acknowledge the varieties of self-knowledge as well as varieties of ways of conceiving the self and as I also acknowledge that we can never make a headway in these matters unless we relate the different kinds of self-knowledge and relate the different ways in which the self is conceived and relate the ways in which we conceive of the self with the different senses of self-knowledge. Possibly all I succeed in doing here is getting myself into deep trouble and wait for others to get me out of it. I must confess that I do not have an argument that shows that there must be a deep almost logical relation between how we conceive of the self and how we conceive of particular self-knowledge or sense of self. Instead, I try to pick up instances where a philosophical view about the nature of self has determined the nature of particular self-knowledge and sense of self, and sometimes the other way round. In doing this, I am doing a lot of time travelling and culture-jumping and possibly this will make my paper seem a little disorganized.

**Selves**

There is a tradition of theoretical enquiry into the nature of the self, which stretches between the ancient Greek tradition to the modern-day neuroscience and cognitive science. The dispute regarding the nature of the self, it was believed, could be resolved by unravelling the composite nature of human existence. Aristotle, for instance, believed that who we are, is closely tied to our embodied existence but strangely it transcends this embodiment. There is perhaps no single way of characterizing human existence and no single way of characterizing the self, which lies in the centre of this human existence.

We now come to talk about the different ways that the self may be conceived. All this talk would seem fruitless on a no-self theory but it is not so as what we are trying to understand here is what are different ways of understanding "the self-phenomenon" (to borrow a phrase from Galen Strawson[8]). So even if we are to opt for a no-self theory (of any brand you say, Buddhist, Humean, No-ownership theories or others) we still need to explain the self-phenomenon. Even a no-self theory would count as a theory that explains the self-phenomenon.

There are many ways of conceiving the self. It is not my task here to go into a detailed exposition of all the ways in which the self may be conceived. What I shall do instead is to pick up certain instances of ways in which the self is conceived and show how such a conception has led to a particular conception of self-knowledge (which would include both particular self-knowledge and also sense of self). I start off with the most predominant assumption about the self, which takes the self (if it at all existed) as a metaphysically real entity.

## THE SELF AS GIVEN : DETACHING THE SELF FROM SELF-KNOWLEDGE

Philosophers who have kept substantive knowledge of self and particular self-knowledge apart, I would like to argue, have all believed that if there is a self at all then it must be an ontologically given entity. We may again start with Descartes, from whom the discussion of particular self-knowledge gained a distinctive prominence in comparison with substantive

8. See his "The Self", in S. Gallagher and J. Shear (ed.), *Models of Self*, Exeter, UK: Imprint Academic, 1999.

knowledge of self. His dualism speaks of an ontologically distinct conscious substance which is the self, whose existence is proved by each conscious mental state — states which are sel-presenting. Descartes' emphasis is on these self-presenting undeniable conscious states on which he builds his entire epistemology. In the Cartesian tradition, we find that there is a kind of scepticism about the very possibility of knowledge of self, though a lot is being said about particular self-knowledge. When Descartes came to the conclusion that we are immaterial substances and that our essential characteristics was thought, he was not actually talking about knowledge of self. This was pointed out by Gassendi. Gassendi said that although Descartes succeeded in showing that we cannot doubt that we are thinking, Descartes was unable to show what kind of things, we, who are thinking, are. What Gassendi wanted to point out was that knowing that we think or we doubt or we understand, does not constitute *substantive* knowledge of the self. So, what Descartes really managed to prove is particular self-knowledge, i.e. knowledge of particular episodes of thinking, doubting, understanding, seeing, etc.

What is being suggested by later philosophers like Hume and Kant, is that particular self-knowledge can be detached from knowledge of the self. For one thing, these philosophers could say that particular episodes of the mind are immediately accessible to consciousness. Our particular mental states, on this view, are entirely transparent, in the sense that, they cannot occur without being detected. Hume says in his, *A Treatise of Human Nature*,[9] that actions and sensations of the mind are transparent, in the sense that "they must necessarily appear in every particular what they are, and be what they appear". But Hume is thoroughly sceptical about the possibility of knowledge of the self as an abiding substance. He also says

9. Ed. L.A. Selby-Bigge Oxford: Clarendon Press, 1978, 2nd edn., p. 190.

that one has to enter into "most profound metaphysics" in order to seek knowledge of the self and we know that Hume was sceptical about the possibility of metaphysics and also about the reality of an abiding self. This is how in Hume's philosophy, the two levels of self-knowledge became disjoined. On his empiricistic theory, the abiding self is never presented in our experience and hence it is doubtful as to whether such an abiding self really exists. We might say that what Hume says amounts to accepting that if there has to be self it has to be like a body whose abiding existence is presented in our experience.

In Kant's writing we find a different way in which the two levels of self-knowledge becomes detached. Kant came up with an argument showing that the nature of self, as it is, in itself was in fact unknown and unknowable. But he too believes that we can know the particular states of our mind. This marks a serious divergence between the two levels of self-knowledge.

In order to understand Kant's thesis that self in its true nature is unknown and unknowable we have to remember one of Kant's fundamental claims about the generation of knowledge. According to Kant our knowledge is generated from concepts and intuitions. If we apply this model to the knowledge of self then it will be clear why Kant is saying that knowledge of the kind of thing that we are is impossible. Let us explain this: To begin with, if we think that our knowledge of what we are comes through the union of senses and understanding then the question would be, what is the sense that is involved in knowledge of self? It is customary to believe that it is introspection that gives us knowledge of self rather than an employment of some outer sense. Consequently, introspection is regarded as a form of inner perception. And this kind of inner perception involves not the exercise of some outer sense but the exercise of an inner sense. He goes on further to say that all that the mind can intuit through inner sense are our particular states of the mind, and no "fixed and abiding self can present itself in this flux of inner appearances".[10]

Both Hume and Kant subscribed to what is known in the literature the Elusiveness Thesis as they both thought that whenever "one is introspectively aware of one's thoughts, experiences and sensations, one is never aware of a persisting self which has them".[11] It is clear from the Elusiveness Thesis that these philosophers indeed took the self to be an ontologically given entity which had to be known in the way bodies or other ontologically given entities are known. So if we fail to know the self in this way either we have to say, like Hume, that there is no such thing, or we have to say, like Kant, that the self is unknown and unknowable.

The point that I want to make here is that Hume's rejection of possibility of substantive knowledge of self and rejection of the abiding self is motivated by the notion of the self as a given entity rather than an evolved or constructed entity. It is because of this he thinks that he requires to know the existence of a persistent self in the way that he knows bodies, sticks and stones. His complete faith in the immediacy, transparency and incorrigibility of particular self-knowledge would be questioned by those who did not take the self as given but rather constructed or evolved.

We now take Kant. What arguments does Kant give for the Elusiveness thesis? The argument that Kant gives may be called the sceptical argument against the possibility of knowledge of self. Let us now try to understand this sceptical argument. This argument has five assumptions:

---

10. *Critique of Pure Reason*, trs. N. Kemp Smith, London: Macmillan, 1929, A 107.

11. Quassim Cassam (ed.), *Self Knowledge*, Oxford: Oxford University Press, 1994. p. 3.

1. Knowledge requires intuitions and concepts.
2. Introspection is the source of much of our knowledge of self.
3. Introspective awareness is a form of perceptual awareness, involving the exercise of "inner sense".
4. For a persisting self to acquire knowledge of her own nature through introspection she would need to be aware of herself through inner sense.
5. No persisting self could present itself in inner sense (the Elusiveness Thesis).[12]

Most of the attempts that have been made by contemporary philosophers to criticize the sceptical argument have been in form of a critique of one or more of these assumptions. The whole post-Kantian tradition will have difficulty in rejecting the first presupposition that knowledge requires intuitions and concepts. But all the other assumptions have faced severe criticism.

We can start with the second assumption. Elizabeth Anscombe in her essay "The First Person"[13] tries to say that much of our knowledge of the kind of thing that we are, is a result of out interaction with other people who provide us with information and insights about our own nature. And this is why Anscombe refuses to accept that introspection is the main source of our self-knowledge.

Philosophers have also found it difficult to accept that introspective awareness is a form of perceptual awareness involving the exercise of an "inner sense". Gareth Evans in his article "Self Identification"[14] points out that the "inner

---

12. Quassim Cassam (ed.), *Self Knowledge*, see the Introduction.
13. Ibid., pp. 140-60.
14. Ibid., pp. 184-210.

sense" model of introspection is wrong. He gives us an extremely technical argument, which can be presented in a simplistic manner. First of all we have to understand that when supporters of elusiveness thesis were talking about the "inner sense" model of introspection they were taking introspection as inner perception involving an "inner sense" which was analogous to outer perception with the help of outer senses. Evans says that though there is a way in which the outer objects of the world can be presented to the outer senses, the inner states of the mind could not be presented to the inner sense in the same way. Scepticism about the "inner sense" model of introspection has led to scepticism about the fourth assumption that if we are to know the persisting self then the persisting self has to be presented to us through "inner sense". One way of trying to criticize the elusiveness thesis and yet accepting the Kantian thesis that knowledge requires intuition and concept is to give up the "inner sense" model of introspection.

What the Kant and Hume cases demonstrate is that their specific view about the nature of self, has, in a way, shaped their position on the possibility of substantive knowledge of self. I have also hinted that if one were to opt for a different view about the self, i.e. a view which denies that the self is an ontologically given entity, then one could have the possibility of doubting first-person authority, i.e. doubt that our particular self-knowledge has the authoritative, immediate, incorrigible character. What I haven't done here but what needs to be done is taking into such alternative conceptions of self and see what the nature of particular self-knowledge becomes under that conception.

One interesting line of thought is what would happen if we were to give up the idea of the self as a given. I shall not be embarking on this issue here as it needs a full-length paper to discuss just this. One idea that I want to suggest is that those who are opting for an idea of the self, a social construction would not be to bother about first person authority at all.

## FROM THE NATURE OF THE METAPHYSICAL SELF TO THE NATURE OF SELF-CONSCIOUSNESS: CASES FROM CLASSICAL INDIAN PHILOSOPHY

We now will take up an instance of how a particular conception of the nature of the metaphysical self determines the nature of the sense of self that we have. And we take up the instance from classical Indian philosophy. Every school of classical Indian philosophy admits the existence of something corresponding to the notion of "I" that is present in each and every individual, something that is the reference of the pronoun *aham* or "I". We have to remember that we have two different conceptions of this self (in the metaphysical sense) in the classical Indian philosophy: (a) Self as a substance which is endowed with consciousness; and (b) Self as consciousness itself. Nyāya, Vaiśeṣika, Mīmāṁsā and Cārvāka schools of thought believe in the first notion of self while Sāṁkhya, Vedānta, Yogācāra Buddhist and Jaina schools believe in the second notion. Those who believe the self to be a substance, which is endowed with consciousness, however, differ about what would be regarded as the nature of this self.

In determining the true nature of the self, philosophers have started with the simple and common notion that the self is the thing that is referred to by the pronoun "I" (*aham padārtha*).[15] So the main task of philosophers would be to determine the true nature of the thing that is denoted by the term "I". In doing so one could take the help of common usage in language, which involves the use of the pronoun "I". But such common usages have often been misleading. This is so because just as we find uses like "I know", "I am happy", "I desire this", etc. we also have uses like "I am tall", or "I am

15. I shall discuss only this in the paper.

short", "I am fat", "I am thin", etc. So the question arises that what kind of an object can be ascribed to both physical and mental properties at the same time. This is a problem that we have found most directly addressed in P.F. Strawson's chapter on "Persons" in his *Individuals*. This mystery has been attempted to be solved in different ways by different philosophers in India. The materialist Cārvākas would claim that a mind-body identity thesis would solve this mystery quite easily. This was also the physicalist's ploy in recent times. The Nyāya-Vaiśeṣika and Mīmāṁsā schools would take all ascriptions of physical properties to the self as erroneous. They believe that the self is distinct from the body or the sense organs, and it can only have properties like consciousness, happiness, etc. One could say that this is a kind of dualistic thesis. The Advaita Vedāntins would say that the term "I" or *aham* actually does not refer to the real self or pure consciousness. For them "I" signifies consciousness falsely identified with inner organ (*antaḥkaraṇa*). Buddhists, on the other hand, take the pronoun "I" as a shifter and not as a term referring to a persisting substance. In a way they would say that the substantive persisting "I" is a construction. So we could say that they would adhere to the discrete states of self-consciousness as distinct from the constructed concept of a persistent self. We will see how these two distinctive ways of seeing the self have influenced the idea of knowledge of this self. For instance, for the Naiyāyikas the self can be inferred from its *guṇa*s (properties), like *sukha* and *duḥkha* (pleasure and pain). The Vedāntins say that we attain knoweldge of the real self only when the *adhyāsa* (all the superimpositions) that led us to take the *antaḥkaraṇa* as the self, are dispelled. So we shall see how the metaphysical concept that one has of the self, would determine the idea that one has of the way in which the knowledge of such a self may be attained.

As we have already noted, in the classical Indian

philosophical tradition, self-knowledge may signify three things:

1. Self-consciousness;
2. Theoretical knowledge regarding the real nature of the self; and,
3. Self-realization.

For the purpose of this paper we are concerned with the first kind of knowledge, i.e. self-consciousness. Every person has a kind of self-awareness. And it is in the context of this self-awareness that the relation between what we take the self to be and how we conceive of self-consciousness is revealed in a very interesting way. And, I take this as an example that instantiates my claim, and also because this history reveals a great deal more.

We find classical Indian philosophers asking a particular question regarding self-knowledge: Which is the *pramāṇa* (source of valid cognition) that is required to have self-knowledge in the sense of self-consciousness? (another interesting question they discuss elaborately is whether the self can be an *object* of knowledge at all). We find at least three kinds of views about self-consciousness or, as we have been calling it in our discussion so far, sense of self, which are all closely connected with corresponding views about the true nature of the self. These are:

1. The self is self-luminous (*svaprakāśa*) or self-revealing.
2. The self is revealed by the self-luminous consciousness.
3. The self is known by internal perceptions of the form "I am happy" (*aham sukhī*).

Here I will be looking into all the different conceptions of self-consciousness and all the different theories of the self that have influenced them.

The first view, which says that self is self-luminous or self-revealing, is a view that was accepted by the Advaita Vedāntins. Now the Advaita school believed that "I" or *aham* does not actually stand for the real self as the real self is for them pure consciousness. In elucidating the true nature of the self the Vedāntins also try to sketch out a solution to the mystery regarding the ascription of antithetical properties to the self-same object. "I" for them means consciousness that is falsely identified with the *antaḥkaraṇa*. This complex identity is actually the individual or empirical self. And it is this self which is denoted by the term "I" or *aham* and it is this *I* which is qualified by properties like knowerhood (*jñātr̥tva*) and agenthood (*kartr̥tva*). According to the Advaita thought the *antaḥkaraṇa* is super-imposed on the self due to ignorance (*avidyā*), which results in the false ascription of properties of knowerhood and agenthood to the self, and there is a superimposition of the body and sense organs on the self which results in the ascription of corporeal properties to the self as well. This is why there is ascription of antithetical properties to the self. But this is not the real self. The real self is consciousness itself and so is devoid of any of these properties. Now we come to the qustion how is the self revealed in self-consciousness? Consciousness reveals everything including itself. The Vedāntin logic runs in this way: Self could not reveal other things if it waited for something else to reveal itself. So we need no extra means (i.e. *pramāṇa*) by which we acquire self-knowledge.

The second view is the view of the Prābhākara Mīmāṁsaka philosophers. The Mīmāṁsakas, unlike the Advaita Vedāntins, and like the Naiyāyikas, believed that self can truly be ascribed properties of *jñātr̥tva* and *kartr̥tva* and enjoyerhood (*bhoktr̥tva*). These properties though are the real properties of the self, yet are only contingent ones. So the self has these properties but only as long as the self is attached to a body, sense organs (including the inner sense organ or *manas*). The Mīmāṁsā and Nyāya philosophers make a distinction between the empirical self and the self in its true essence. In liberation the self regains its true nature and so in liberation it is devoid of consciousness. This being the Prābhākara Mīmāṁsaka view of the nature of self, let us now try to understand how it has influenced the Prābhākara Mīmāṁsaka conception of self-consciousness. The Prābhākara view is that the self, which is the owner or the subject of consciousness, is revealed in each and every state of consciousness. For them consciousness which is a contingent property of the self is self-revealing in nature. In every conscious state this consciouseness reveals its object, the subject and itself. For the Prābhākara Mīmāṁsaka, knowledge of any kind takes the form "I know . . .". So in each case the self, the consciousness, and the object of consciousness are all and equally presented.

The third view can be ascribed to the Bhāṭṭa Mīmāṁsā and Nyāya schools. On this view, in the internal perception of the specific properties of the self, the self too is revealed. It is not as though we have an awareness of the form "this is pleasure" when we experience pleasure or "this is desire" when we desire something, rather it takes the form "*I* am happy" or "*I* desire this". In this inner perception, self becomes an object of knowledge. But we have to remember that for the Naiyāyikas we infer the existence of the self as the subtance which is characterized by the *guṇa*s of *icchā* (desire), *dveṣa* (aversion), *prayatna* (intention), *sukha* (pleasure), *duḥkha* (pain), *dharma* (merit or virtue), *adharma* (demerit or vice). So, for the Naiyāyika, the knowledge of self is an inferential knowledge.

### *Can the Self Be an Object of Knowledge at All?*

There is an extremely interesting debate between Vedāntins and Prābhākara Mīmāṁsakas on the one hand and the Bhāṭṭa Mimāṁsakas and the Naiyāyikas on the other. The former two deny that self can be a *bona fide* object of knowledge, while the latter two take the self to be one such object. Let us just briefly go into this debate. Though there is a significant difference in opinion between the Prābhākara Mīmāṁsaka and the Vedāntins, yet both would refuse to accept that the self could be a *bona fide* object of knowledge. The reservation against the view that the self can be a *bona fide* object of knowledge, that these two schools of philosophy have, is that to say that the self is both the knower and the object of knowledge, is to say something rather absurd. The reason that they feel that this is absurd is that there is a significant incompatibility between agency and objectness. If knowledge is looked up as a *kriyā* or an act then there is a *kartā* (more specifically a *jñātā* in this case) or agent of the act then there will also be an object or *viṣaya* of the act. What the Prābhākara Mīmāṁsaka and the Vedāntins are trying to say is that the same thing could not possibly be the seat of the properties of *kartṛtva/jñātṛtva* and *viṣayatva* (objecthood).

> An act of the subject is directed towards something else, in the sense that the result of an act done by the agent is the production of another thing which is called the object. For example, when somebody cooks rice, the result of the act of cooking, namely the softening of the rice is produced in the rice. So the agent who cooks and the thing that is cooked are different. So the self who is the knower knows something else. It itself cannot be the object of its own act. One motivation is clear from this argument, and it reflects the Vedāntin intuition that the self is *subject par excellence.*[16]

Let us now see what the opponents have to say. We first discuss the Bhaṭṭa reply to the Prābhākara point that to say that the self can be an object, amounts to saying that the act of knowing produced its result in the knower, who is actually the agent

16. Srilekha Datta, *The Self and Self-Knowledge in Indian Tradition*, p. 7, italics mine.

of the act. Parthasarathi Misra of the Bhaṭṭa school, in his *Śāstradīpikā* strongly argues that the Bhaṭṭa assumption that the self can indeed be an object of knowledge does not amount to saying that the act of knowing produced its result in the knower. He tries to argue that the purpose of the knowledge-act is manifestation or revelation. And it is the self, which is revealed. The Bhāṭṭa Mīmāṁsaka would say that there is no other way that the self can be revealed, but by its own act of knowing. A subtle point is made here and it is about revelation of the self in knowledge which always takes the form "I know . . .". This is something that even the Prābhākaras would admit. But the question is whether this would necessarily mean that this "I" thereby becomes the object of the knowledge-act.

The Prābhākara defence comes in two ways. First of all, the Prābhākara says that in spite of the fact that the self is revealed yet "neither the definition of *karma* is satisfied by the self nor is the inflexion for objective case applied to the self or the object is defined as *parasamavetakriyāphalabhagitva*, that is, an object is that which possesses the result of an act that belongs to someone else".[17] The second response of the Prābhākara comes in the form of a linguistic argument from the analysis of a sentence expressing knowledge. What they think is most important in the analysis of sentences of the form "I know so and so" is that in spite of the fact that the self is revealed here, it is not revealed as an object as the inflection for objective case is never applied in the case of the word signifying the self. For example, in the sentence *aham ghaṭam jānāmi* (I know pot), the objective inflexion *am* is applied not on the pronoun *aham* (I) but on the term *ghaṭa* (pot). Of course, the Bhāṭṭa Mīmāṁsaka readily comes up with examples of knowledge-sentences where the self is indeed characterized by the objective inflexion. The examples are *ātmanam veda*, or

17. Srilekha Datta, *The Self and Self-Knowledge in Indian Tradition*, p. 8.

*svasamvedya sa bhavati*, or *ātma jñātavya*. For the Bhāṭṭa Mīmāṁsaka, the self is not always the object of knowledge, but is so only when linguistic usage justifies it. For instance, the Vedic sentence *sa manasina ātma jananam* justifies the claim that the self is internally perceived as the object of I-consciousness. There is another interesting argument that the Bhāṭṭa Mīmāṁsakas put forward. They say that we could not explain *recognition* or *pratyabhijña* unless we accepted that the self could be an object of knowledge. The form that any recognition takes is *I am seeing something that I have seen before*. Notice that here the self is presented as the person who saw something in the past and is encountering the same thing later on. So the self is an object of recognition or *pratyabhijña*.

The Vedāntins regard the self as self-luminous but the Bhāṭṭa Mīmāṁsakas deny this, by saying that if this was so, then we would always be self-conscious. This is unacceptable because then dreamless sleep would not be possible.

The way in which Naiyāyikas retort of the Prābhākara and Vedāntin charge of *karma-kartṛvirodha*, is different from the way in which the Bhāṭṭa Mīmāṁsakas retort. The Naiyāyika philosopher, Jayanta Bhaṭṭa says that since we do indeed have perceptual as well as inferential knowledge of the self by the self, we have to say in this case there is no *karma-kartṛvirodha*. He says that the self can be both a subject and an object. But when the self is a subject the relation that it has with the knowledge is inherence (*samavāya*) as the knowledge inheres in the subject, whereas when the self is an object the relation it has with the knowledge is not inherence but is objecthood (*viṣayatā*).

We have now seen how this debate regarding the possibility of the self's being a genuine object of knowledge has taken its peculiar course, in consonance with the variant views, regarding self that the contending parties in the debate have taken.

## FROM PHENOMENOLOGICAL SELF TO METAPHYSICAL SELF: GALEN STRAWSON

I now take up Galen Strawson's work as I think that it is interesting to see how he shows that we can find a logical route from the phenomenal self to the metaphysical self. I shall be discussing mainly his article, "The Self". For me, the most crucial point that Strawson makes is that we have a sense of self and this itself has a deep metaphysical implication. Strawson is convinced that

> The problem of self doesn't arise from an unnatural use of language which arises from nowhere. On the contrary: use of a phrase like 'the self' arises from a prior and independent sense that there is such a thing as the self.[18]
>
> Strawson believes that the problem of the self is a metaphysical problem but that metaphysics must wait on phenomenology.[19]

Most of us believe in the self as an entity, and though most of us have no clear idea about what that self, is yet we are not ready to take the self as an illusion. We have what may be called a sense of self, which, in a way, phenomenologically precedes most other things. Strawson asks primarily two phenomenological questions; one local and the other general. The local one is regarding the nature of the human sense of the self, and the general one is regarding the possibility of articulating the minimal case of genuine possession of the sense of the self. These two questions lead to a question regarding the grounds or pre-conditions of the possession of a sense of the self. And all these give rise to the most crucial metaphysical question: Could there be such a thing as the self?

To start with, Strawson believes that we can generalize about the human sense of self as it lies at a level that is

18. "The Self", p. 1.

19. Ibid.

unaffected and in a way prior to any cultural variations. And when we are asking what the human sense of the self is, we are asking a conceptual rather than an affective question. Strawson says that we experience ourselves as:

(1) a *thing*, in some robust sense
(2) a *mental* thing, in some sense
(3, 4) a *single* thing that is single both *synchronically* considered and *diachronically* considered
(5) *ontically distinct* from all other things
(6) a *subject of experience*, a conscious feeler and thinker
(7) an *agent*
(8) a thing that has a character or *personality*.[20]

While trying to answer the more general question about whether there is a minimal case of genuine possession of sense of self one has to consider if we need to mention all of these or if there was a core of conditions that might together constitute our minimal sense of self.

Strawson, here, claims that the phenomenological investigation into the self is in a significant way independent of metaphysical investigation, but metaphysical investigation of self is in a significant sense subordinate to the phenomenological investigation of the self. Strawson seems to think that there might be extremely strong phenomenological constraints on any acceptable metaphysical theory of the self. He says that there is an equivalence between the two questions "Is there such a thing as the (mental) self?" and "Is any (genuine) sense of the self an accurate representation of anything that exists?"[21]

20. "The Self", pp. 3-4.

21. There seems to be a Kantian reservation against the acceptance of this equivalence (as we have already seen in the section on Self as Given). Kant would resist the position that if there such a thing as the self there must be some accurate representation of it in a sense of self. This Kant would resist because he would insist that the true nature of the self is never given in experience.

What is interesting for us is this equivalence. Let us try to understand this equivalence. This equivalence can be understood as a conjunction of two implications:

(E1) If there is such a thing as the self, then some SMS is an accurate representation of something that exists,

(E2) If some SMS is an accurate representation of something that exists, there is such a thing as the self.[22]

Each of these may be challenged. On a thesis that the self is ineffable or unknowable, E1 will be false. A philosopher challenging E2 might say that even if there is a sense of self that accurately represents something that exists, that something might not be the (mental) self because it does not have some feature that the mental self must have.

Strawson says that what is distinctive of E1 and E2 is that they rule out the possibility of such challenges. If we carefully take note of E1, then we will see that it says that "nothing can count as a mental self unless it possesses all the properties attributed to the self by some genuine SMS". This equivalence actually rules out the validity of any metaphysical claim about the self, which does not "respect limits on the concept of self revealed by the phenomenological investigation". This is actually giving us the necessary conditions for something to count as a self. E2, on the other hand, specifies the sufficient condition for something to count as a self, as it says that nothing which possesses all the properties we find in a SMS can fail to be the self. And this equivalence excludes two things: The possibility of there being a self whose nature will always elude

22. There seems to be a Kantian reservation against the acceptance of this equivalence (as we have already seen in the section on Self as Given). Kant would resist the position that if there such a thing as the self there must be some accurate representation of it in a sense of self. This Kant would resist because he would insist that the true nature of the self is never given in experience. See page 6 of Quassim Cassam's Introduction to *Self Knowledge*.

us and the possibility that we might have a sense of self which is an accurate representation of something which is in fact not the self at all. Strawson says "Any metaphysical speculations that are not properly subordinate to phenomenology can be cheerfully 'commit[ted] to the flames'".

What seems striking to me about Strawson's approach, is that he is trying to show whatever the metaphysics of the self maybe, it must respect the phenomenology of self. This is so because the reason that we admit of the self is that we want to make sense of the self-phenomenon, that is revealed in our sense of the self. We are as if asking what is that entity that can give rise to this sense of the self. Whatever we answer, should be in consonance with all that we gather about that entity in our sense of the self.

## Conclusion

We have now seen at least four distinct trends in philosophy where how one conceives of the self has determined one's conception of self-knowledge — be it particular self-knowledge, or, be it sense of self, or, be it the knowledge of the kind of thing that we are. What I intend to claim is that it would be wrong and unwise to keep the two questions, "What is the self like?" and "What is the nature of self-knowledge?" apart. It would be wrong to assume that one could attempt at an answer to one without attempting an answer to the other. The Cartesian tradition definitely committed a mistake in keeping these two questions apart, and in fact, their views about particular self-knowledge *are* determined by their view that the self is a subjective entity or, is a substance that is self-contained with respect to the world. We can possibly make some progress by considering these two questions together. In fact, we have always done it, without quite admitting that we have.

# 6

# Self-knowledge and the Problem of Experience

*Paul Fletcher*†

LAST summer, it was my privilege and pleasure to spend two months as a visiting fellow in Jawaharlal Nehru University, New Delhi. During my time here I had a host of wonderful experiences. One experience that stands out, was a visit to the old city of Delhi with a group of friends. After a visit to Karim's restaurant, a mecca for meat-eaters, and having a *tandūri rān* — a whole leg of goat — my friends suggested that we visit the Jama Majid, a historical landmark, a short walk from Karim's. While we savoured the sights, we were approached by two women who asked if I would accompany them on the climb up the tower in the mosque, from which the views of the city are quite astounding. When we reached the viewing platform, one of the women asked me what I did and I made the fatal mistake of telling her the truth, that I teach in the Department of Religious Studies at Lancaster University. She then regaled me with stories of spiritual experiences and informed me that she had travelled to India from Australia to write up her PhD on Yoga. During our conversation, I was struck by the way she celebrated the spiritual heritage and

† Paul Fletcher's untimely death occurred in July 2008, shortly after presenting a paper at the *Derrida Today* Conference in Sydney. I thank Deborah Sutton, Paul's partner, for providing me with the text of the paper he read in our conference on Self-knowledge and Agency.

legacy of the subcontinent, but continually criticized Indians for not realizing or understanding the significance of this abundant deposit of spiritual experience.

Initially, I was rather appalled by this person's insipid orientalism and the manner in which India was construed as an exotic playground for the spiritually desolate. But when I later reflected on what she had said to me I thought it interesting that in terms of her view of experience she had actually made a strikingly simple point, one which, whether true or false, in this case deserves some attention and reflection. Put succinctly, one could say that her understanding of contexts of experience boiled down to the fact that in India people *have* a huge range of experience — colour, myth, communal celebration and strong social bonds — but do not really *undergo* it, while in the West we *undergo* a wide range of experiences, but do not *have* experience as such. Now, I do not believe that it is as simple as that but the anecdote does disclose at least a couple of possible reasons why experience along with its consequence and weight is a domain of confusion and even mystification. First, we might consider the words of Hans Falkenberg (See his *History of Modern Philosophy*, Public Domain Books, 2006) who, at the mid-point of the nineteenth century, had reason to reflect on the multiple quests for experiential authenticity in late romanticism, religion and what we now call "popular culture" across the continent of Europe. Falkenberg claimed that "In periods which have given birth to a sceptical philosophy, a philosophy that refuses dogmatic metaphysics, one never looks in vain for the complementary phenomenon of mysticism" (ibid.). The pursuit of an experience or experiences which transgress the bounds of knowledge and sense appears, as it were, as the undesirable and offensive "other" of the critical enterprise, threatens its integrity and risks the flight into irrationalism and enthusiasm. Yet, what is significant about Falkenberg's assessment is that while such episodes are by no means a necessary coexistent of the critical project, his analysis of both their persistence and the fact that their emergence is concurrent with a modern form of philosophy suggests that they are inevitable, even if undesirable occurrences. The second, and concomitant possibility, arises from the peculiarly modern character of this quest for experience. It does not require a highly original analysis to indicate that the dominance of an instrumental, technical or calculable reason as the measure of substance and significance within modern life has produced a range of discourses and practices that arise in protest at the manner in which the meaning and magnitude of life is, as a consequence, squeezed and even asphyxiated. To put the issue more bluntly, it is a common and unshakable claim that modernity has produced the very conditions in which "experience" itself is in deep crisis.

What I wish to attempt in this paper is an exploration of these problems which surround the figure of experience and an assessment of the extent to which their basis might be found in the critical method, where the finitude of understanding is secured via a mathematical or scientific model and a metaphysics defined as the "search for hidden things" is programmatically rejected. [Although it is important to point out that much of the philosophy which counts Kant's work as its source and inspiration has forgotten that his aim in the *Critique of Pure Reason* was not only to map the finitude of the understanding but also to provide the groundwork for an adequate response to the infinite desire to know, that is, for an appropriate metaphysics.] At this stage it seems politic to point out that my aim here is neither to lament the loss of some other form of experience that might be construed as reflecting a truly authentic spirit or disposition nor is it to seek some golden age where the plenitude of experience was possible: as far as the latter is concerned, there never existed, at least in my view, such an age in any case. My desire is, though, to propose, however tentatively, that there are grounds for exploring a form of experience or a form of life that is not so strictly curtailed by canonical epistemological limits (although in doing so I realize that I am, as they say, leading with my chin).

Let us begin this exploration, then, with an overview of the status and significance of Kant's reconfiguration of experience and its role. As early as 1770 in his inaugural dissertation, entitled *The Form and Principles of the Sensible and Intelligible World,* Kant had attempted to reconcile Locke's limitation of knowledge to the bounds of experience — a markedly empirical understanding of what constitutes experience — with Leibniz's insistence on the productive and conditioning character of the "innate truths" of inner experience — a perspective that is distinctively rationalist in its constitution of experienced reality. But as we know, Kant's subsequent epistemological framework was no simple combination of pre-existing versions but constitutes a particularly innovative response to the problems posed by his predecessors and a unique attempt to circumvent their weaknesses.

The novelty of Kant's approach to the problem of experience is apparent at the very opening of the dissertation when Locke's contention that ideas (in his case concepts and intuitions) may be derived from outer experience is thoroughly examined. In response to his uneasiness with the empiricist implications of Locke's stance, Kant moves much closer to Leibniz's argument that they are presupposed by experience, which is to say, that experience itself is dependent upon concepts and intuitions. Then, rather surprisingly, Kant moves on to a definition of experience that sounds almost Lockean in character. Experience is "the reflective cognition, which arises when several appearances are compared by the understanding" (ibid.). He then quickly qualifies this position by saying that "there is no way from appearance [and here by appearance he means perception] to experience except by reflection in accordance with the logical use of the understanding"(ibid.). Thus the organizing principle of reflection is subordinated to and pre-determined by the logical use of the understanding. Here then we have the steps that will enable the inauguration of a critical method by which the cognitive subject actively constitutes experience and the perceived world.

When we consider the later critical body of work, we can witness the implications of Kant's pioneering assessment of experience as such. In the *Prolegomena, to any Future Metaphysics,* (Manchester University Press, 1962), Kant defines experience as "the synthetic connection of appearances (perceptions) in consciousness, so far as this connection is necessary" (ibid., p. 64). Experience is accordingly described as "this product of the senses and the understanding" (ibid., p. 58) which may be analysed into elements. There are first of all "intuition[s] of which I become conscious, i.e. perception (*perceptio*), which pertains merely to the senses" (ibid.). These provide the element of external perception, but do not add up to a full experience. There is the synthesis in a judgement, but this synthesis has particular properties; it does not "merely compare perceptions and connect them in a consciousness of my state" (ibid.) as was claimed by empiricist accounts of perception, but subsumes intuitions under a concept "which determines the form of judging in general with regard to the intuition" (ibid.). These, of course, are the a priori concepts of the understanding, such as cause, which are not derived from experience but which give it its character of necessity.

In the fuller and more nuanced elucidation of the status of experience in the *Critique of Pure Reason*, the synthesis which constitutes experience is not the simple conceptual unification of an intuited manifold, the world of things, but takes place on the basis of a mutual adaptation of concept and sensory intuition. Kant maintains that all synthesis, "even that which renders perception possible, is subject to the categories; and since experience is cognition by means of connected perceptions, the categories are the conditions of the possibility of experience, and therefore valid a priori for all objects of experience". Kant ultimately derives the categories from the spontaneity of the understanding, thus establishing the conditions of the possibility of experience in the mutual adaptation between outer experience (receptivity of sensibility) and inner experience (spontaneity of understanding). The a priori forms of intuition (space and time) — to which we shall return in due course — as well as the pure concepts of the understanding, or categories, establish the conditions of possible experience which determine the limits of legitimate knowledge. As Kant explained with respect to the categories, "everything which the understanding derives from itself is, though not borrowed from experience, at the disposal of the understanding solely for use in experience".

Now on the basis of this rather technical exposition of Kant's peerless construction of an architecture of experiential possibility, a framework that moves beyond both empiricist and idealist accounts, it is important to note three essential features: the relationship between the subject of experience and the subject of knowledge; the manner in which Kant transforms the status of the phenomenon, that which appears in the context of experience; and the significance of time and space as the forms of the possible presentation or reception of experience.

First, we must address the very nature of the subject who arises out of this Kantian schema. While he ascertained the content of possible experience through Euclidean geometry and Newtonian mechanics, at least in the *Prolegomena*, Kant was none the less required to refuse the substantialization of the subject in a discrete and single psychic "I". He is careful to distinguish between a psychological consciousness or an empirical "I" who can be known and a transcendental subject who cannot in any way be cognized. The result is a fundamental reconception of the relation between experience and knowledge (and the subjects of these two diverse terms) and a departure from their relationship as it was generally conceived within the classical philosophical tradition from Antiquity to the last great classical theorist of experience, Montaigne. In Montaigne's celebrated essay "On Experience", certitude is incompatible with experience to the extent that, as Giorgio Agamben (in *Infancy and History: The Destruction of Experience,* London, New York, Verso, 1993) has argued, once an experience has become measurable and certain, it immediately loses its authority. "There is no formulating a maxim or telling a story where scientific law holds sway" (ibid., p. 18). Experience, as it is formulated and delimited by Montaigne, does not offer the requisite substance or character from which certain knowledge might be sought. It is, rather, in Montaigne's definition, "unformed, without a shape to be worked upon". What is being reflected here is the classical separation of a subject of experience and a subject of knowledge, both of whom had what we might call their distinctive places and their separate faculties. The subject of experience in Antiquity and the Middle Ages is related to the *sensus communis* which, as the principle of judgement of the psyché or soul, can be distinguished from the subject of *episteme* or *scientia* which is the *noūs* or the active intellect and is not in any sense a faculty of the soul "but is separate, individuated, impassive", as Aristotle puts it in a formulation which determined medieval epistemology and ontology. Knowledge is brought about through the communication of *psyché* and *noūs,* soul and intellect. For this reason, first philosophy in

Aristotle, that is to say, philosophy which concerns knowledge as such, does not concern the limits and status of possible experience but the question of metaphysics. And Aristotle gives two reasons for this prioritization of what came to be known as the ontological question: first, because the ontological question has the most general (*hon catholou*) as its object; and second, because it enquires into the nature of the highest, the divine being (*theion*). The significance of the Aristotelian formulation is that the central problem concerning knowledge is not the relationship between subject and object but the relationship between the one and the many, a concern which ultimately subsumes the question of experience and which enables, from the outset, only a path from particular individuals (or the many) to the separate intellect and knowledge of the One, or from the sensory to the intelligible, the human to the divine. In contrast, the significance of the Kantian formulation of the experience as knowledge is that while the subject of experience is itself known and experienced, the subject of knowledge is hidden even from me. It exists as little more than an ethereal spectre who might be thought but never known, for it might be an "I", but as a transcendental "I" it is beyond experience. And as a separate subject this "I" does not have even the consolation of seeking and residing within the One.

The second essential feature of Kant's composition of the limits of possible experience also relates to the classical tradition and involves what we might identify as the redemption of nature. As we all know, Kant's subject of experience, he, she or it, who is active in constituting the objects of the world as appearances, transforms the very meaning and ramifications of the term "phenomenon". It is true that the classical tradition had defined a phenomenon as an appearance, an aspect of the sensible world, the a posteriori that was given in experience. But the phenomenon was contrasted with, or even opposed to, the intelligible essence of a thing. This essence was in actual fact the thing such as it is in itself or, and this is crucial, the thing as it is thought. Thus, the phenomenon as such is in no way an appearance that is to be truly trusted as it constitutes a deformation of the thing itself, a partial and ultimately inadequate apprehension of reality. Hence, we have the phenomenon boldly distinguished from the noumenon, a term that actually means "that which is thought". From this perspective, Plato's central theme — leave appearances behind and seek the essence — makes perfect sense.

With Kant a radically new duality is fashioned in which a transformed conception of the phenomenon is produced. The phenomenon, in Kant's philosophical undertaking, is no longer an appearance as it was traditionally understood. As one commentator has argued, the Kantian phenomenon is more accurately described as an apparition in the sense that it is no longer opposed to essence. The apparition is what appears in so far as it appears. Rather than related to essence, as appearance was, the apparition is something which refers, more precisely and exactly, to the condition of what appears. So in the place of the disjunctive pair "appearance and essence", Kant creates a conjunctive duality: "that which appears is paired with the conditions of apparition". This is a remarkable change, not least because the implication of the disjunction between appearance and essence is that the sensible world is basically degraded, fallen and distant from truth. The fact that Kant replaces this formulation with a subject who is constitutive of the conditions under which that which appears to it actually does appear, suggests that the purpose of the subject is no longer to flee the sensible world and this fact invests the world with an entirely different value [Although I have to say, in passing, that I am not too sure how significant this transformation of the status of the sensible world was for Kant himself. Right up until the fragments that amount to the *opus postumum* his occasional statements concerning the importance and status of much of the world as it is known, natural *and* human, are often indifferent if not downright dismissive.]. That said, Kant still leaves us with a subject in-between, a figure who is caught — the classical tradition might have said shipwrecked — between, on the one hand, an intuition that is never in itself an experience as such and, on the other, an inability to experience the sensible world as it is, let alone itself.

The third and, you will be glad to know, final essential feature that I would like to draw attention to is the revolutionary importance of Kant's displacement of time and space from the realm of the natural world and their relocation as the two pure forms of sensible intuition.

Kant's claim here is that while there is most certainly a diversity of what appears in space and time, in other words an empirical diversity, there is also a diversity of space and time themselves, an a priori diversity that is the principle by which all possible experience of empirical diversity is possible. The former, empirical diversity, belongs to what appears, but space and time as forms of intuition constitute the forms of possible presentation or receptivity. Now the revolutionary significance of Kant's position is seldom illustrated, let alone celebrated. And it is with his representation of time that we might appreciate the full force of this "Copernican revolution". Time in Kant is no longer configured in such a way that it is subordinated to the measure of something other than itself which, in the classical philosophical tradition, was astronomical movement. In this radical relocation of its place and purpose, time has ceased to be the number of nature, the measure of periodical movement. Time, in the context of the critical philosophy, becomes time in and for itself, it is transformed into a pure and empty time. In his "Inaugural Dissertation" Kant describes time as "fundamental and originary" and, in the terms of the seventh thesis of the dissertation, he designates it as an "absolutely first *formal principle of the sensible world*" without which our intuition of objects of sense would not be possible. And in the *Critique of Pure Reason* Kant extends his analysis by claiming that it is "Only on the basis of such a presupposition of time that we represent to ourselves a number of things as existing at one and the same time (simultaneously) or at different times (successively)". Time is, as a consequence, formal and therefore empty of content and homogeneous or unchanging no matter whether empirical diversity is simultaneous or successive.

Time, then, no longer measures anything, whether it be movement in the cosmos or movement within the soul, and in the wake of this far-reaching adjustment it takes on an excessive character. The classical dictum: "time is the number of movement" is no longer relevant. In fact, a reversal is at work here because nature is now subordinated to time and, indeed, movement itself must come under the purview of a time that is unaffected by its modifications as empirical time or history.

The most striking illustration that Kant offers of the necessity of time and space as pure forms can be found in section 13 of the *Prolegomena*. In an attempt to demonstrate not that space and time are dependent on any empirical movement but that they are irreducible to the order of concepts, Kant uses the example of the left and right hands, a paradigmatic instance of incongruent counterparts. His intention is to show that it is not possible, on the basis of a conceptual classification, to yield intelligible the difference between similar and equal but nonetheless incongruent things. It is only through intuition, our experience of such things as they appear to us, that we can determine the relation of the order of things. There is, in other words, a spatio-temporal order that is irreducible to the conceptual order. With the left and right hands we can *see* two hands and we can, of course, *think* two hands which are strictly identical in their concept. But there are, nevertheless, two hands and there is something, according to Kant, that is undiminished in their difference. They are matching in their characteristics, symmetrical to the point that each attribute or feature has its identical correlate in the other. And yet there are two of them and they refuse superimposition. They cannot, in other words, be congruent. In short, this is finitude for Kant and it has a distinct and different character to an order of pure concepts. In his attempt to truly and definitively convince us of this fact, Kant then gives his famous example of why the left and right hands are incongruent: notwithstanding all their mutual equality and similarity, the glove of the one hand cannot be used on the other.

But it is at this very point that we might begin to question the limits of experience as they are presented in the critical philosophy both in terms of its mathematical and scientific parameters and its conceptual boundaries. There is something distinctly questionable about Kant's fine example of the glove that will not fit both the left and right hands and it is this very questionability that was interrogated by Ludwig Wittgenstein in a passage towards the end of his *Tractatus Logico-Philosophicus* (Routledge & Kegan Paul Ltd., London, Boston 1981).

In order to think through the implications of the question which, at face value, seems to be a straightforward and unproblematic incongruence, Wittgenstein commences his analysis by simplifying the terms of issue and shifts from the question of three-dimensional hands to assess figures in a one-dimensional space. A cursory glance at the two figures will tell us that the two lines, *a* and *b*, cannot coincide with one another unless they are moved out of their one-dimensional space and turned around in the second dimension (See, ibid., § 6.36111).

The same process is required if we add another dimension.

For example, by analysing two-dimensional scripts, which mirror each other, we can see that a coincidence will only occur if we flip them through a third dimension of depth, as if we were closing a book.

This insight enables Wittgenstein to demonstrate that the right and the left hand that exist in a three-dimensional space are potentially congruent as well: "A right-hand glove could be put on the left hand, if only it could be turned around in a four-dimensional space" (ibid.). But what might constitute this "fourth dimension" of which Wittgenstein speaks? In contrast to a widespread opinion, the fourth dimension is not that of time. Time can and will pass but the right-hand glove will never become a left-hand glove. But if we think again about how a right-hand glove might be turned around in a four-dimensional space, the answer, although not offered by Wittgenstein, will not be found in some kind of improbable or incredible operation but in the simplest of manoeuvres. One can make a right-hand glove into a left-hand glove by turning it inside out. If the first dimension enables us to move right and left, the second dimension up and down and the third dimension forward and back, then it seems that the fourth dimension must allow us to move in and out. From this perspective, the focal point of a fourth dimension is actually a threshold from which one can move inside or outside, inwards or outwards.

In many respects, if the basic gesture of Kant's epistemology is to secure boundaries and limits, then the basic gesture of Wittgenstein's philosophy is that of turning inside out the very membrane or tissue that makes up those limits. Throughout his corpus he shows how the inside is not separated from the outside by some impassable border but by a threshold on a continuum. Like the zero point of an axis, this threshold permits a constant movement from the inside to the outside. Wittgenstein enables us to see how two things that cannot be made to coincide are actually in some sense completely congruent. But rather than offer an overcoming or sublation of difference, as in Hegelian dialectic, he demonstrates how any thesis (the right-hand glove) can easily be transformed into its antithetical counterpart (the left-hand glove). All that needs to be done is to make what is inside an outside and what is outside an inside.

A good example of such a procedure is offered in Wittgenstein's notebooks written during the First World War where he describes what he calls "the way I have travelled" by contending that "idealism leads to realism if it is strictly thought out". Or as he puts it in the *Tractatus*:

> Here it can be seen that solipsism, when its implications are followed out strictly, coincides with pure realism. The self of solipsism shrinks to a point without extension, and there remains the reality coordinates with it. — Ibid., §5.64

In other words, the inner world of the idealist coincides with the external point of the realist by passing through the threshold, this zero point without extension, which Wittgenstein calls the philosophical self. Instead of taking the self to be a mirror of what lies outside or what hides inside, it is conceived as a threshold that makes the seemingly incongruent views of idealism and realism coincide. This gesture will become even more apparent in Wittgenstein's later writings, where we come to understand the problem in seeing language as a simple reflection of the objective world or the expression of our subjective thought. We are invited to consider how what is external and what is internal, what is outside and what is inside, are completely congruent as long as they pass through the conduit of language. But we must remember that there is nothing like "the threshold of language" because language is itself nothing but a threshold. The limits of language, beyond which one cannot speak, shrink to a point without extension, and there remain the internal and external realities coordinate with it.

And yet, as Wittgenstein attempts to illustrate time and again, "to image a language means to imagine a form of life". Like language, form of life is neither the right-hand glove nor the left-hand glove. Form of life is, dare we say it, precisely the experience of the fourth dimension where the glove is turned inside out. It enables things that seem incongruent to coincide.

# 7

# Is "Agency" Embedded in "Consciousness"?

## A Husserlian Critique of Contemporary Naturalism

*Prasenjit Biswas*

SELF-KNOWLEDGE, as a necessary accompaniment of an intentional act, assumes an agency that marks several ways of relating the self and the world. It is this particular relationship between the self and the world that determines whether there is an embedded "agency" in the self or not. Two contrasting points of view are in place: one, the Self-model perspective that conceives of a necessary metaphysical dependence between the self and the body and the world implying a strong sense of agency and the second, a linguistically and discursively constituted notion of agency that makes itself present only as a nominal/pronominal index, with an emptied out sense of agency. Between these contrastive perspectives, the present paper attempts to work out a phenomenologically constitutive notion of "agency" that discloses the world in phenomenal properties of self-knowledge, without a necessary metaphysical theory to back up this piece of knowledge of/by the Self. For this purpose, the paper in section *one* takes into account differing naturalist positions on intentionality between Searle and Galen Strawson, to draw a contrast with Dennett's heterophenomenological position of free will and its agency; section *two* elaborates Dennett's compatibilist notion of agency to reconfigure the notion of intentionality in embodied and enactive notions of Self; section *three* develops a Husserlian notion of enactive contexts of intentionality beyond various models of "self", and section *four* argues out a case for humanization of naturalism for a recovery of agency and consciousness; section *five* considers an enactive debate between Dennett and Husserl on the primacy of consciousness whereas, section *six* explores the possibilities of transcendental consciousness as the source of subjectivity and agency to envisage a recovery of being in the human world.

### Dennett's Free Will: Stuck in the "Puddle" between Searle and Galen Strawson

Within the so-called Analytic tradition, the received understanding of Intentionality falls in the circularity of "representation" and "action", both of which assume Intentionality. In effect, Husserl's understanding of Intentionality as "directedness" is given a peculiarly phenomenalistic turn that reduces the sense-data as "constitutive" to the very notion of the "world" that the self as subject cognizes. Both Searle and Strawson practise a kind of phenomenal externalism in order to defend the possibility of conscious life. The difference between Searle and Strawson lies in the fact that Searle talks of a "fit" between mind and the world, while Strawson talks of "ubiquitousness" of an "underived aboutness" in all non-conscious beings, which has close resemblance with Searle's notion of a determinate structure of unconscious, with causal powers as it obtains in conscious beings.[1] Searle reduces the idea of Intentionality to a causal-connection principle, while Strawson reduces it to an intent to respond to the world that is not derived from the

1. John R. Searle, *Intentionality: An Essay in the Philosophy of Mind*, Cambridge: Cambridge University Press, 1984. Also see, Galen Strawson, "Real Intentionality", in *Phenomenology and the Cognitive Sciences*, vol. 3, 2004, pp. 287-313.

world. If we may call Searle an externalist, then Strawson's is a mix-up between internalized experiential states and the naturally available external states. Both are burdened by the Analytic responsibility of determining "content" of internal-experiential states that can be read from the state of the being. Husserl's emphasis on the universal capability of consciousness to make a move from an already given casually inseparable connection of the Subject with the world *to* temporalized spaces of description in a synthesizing mind is inverted by the Analytic tradition. Even Strawson's phenomenology in the Analytic style does not recover this universalizing capacity of consciousness, neither in the underived aboutness of the non-experiential beings, nor in the experiential qualia of minimally intentional creatures. Searle's heavy subscription to a naturalized notion of Intentionality turns the feature of consciousness into a structure of unconscious that only responds, but does not recreate the world in its own free will. The strategy of emptying out a temporally continuous self as a conscious agency in enacting its intentionality, is a common naturalistic fashion that fails to account for the gravitating and Humean nature of consciousness in a manner that puts the agent "under erasure". *Only a temporalized notion of Consciousness that reflects on its own acts from an immanent presence scores out the externalist position of being Conscious as a Subject standing over and against itself as well as the world.* A kind of cognitivist-logicist dissociation of Consciousness from its subject and object produce the sense-bestowing intentionality of the Searlean kind, while its converse, in the form of logicist-cognitivist association of the external world with Consciousness, grants it an underived agency as Strawson proposes. Searle and Strawson reduce the role of consciousness a posteriori to reflexive acts in the world that reifies the role of consciousness to the minimal in cognition, while it is replaced by the underived intentionality, that is, by the causally given contents of the world as well as by the functional powers of the grey matter. *Can such a minimal underived non-experiential or experiential aboutness in both conscious and non-conscious beings be without an immanent pole of epistemic and cognitive centre?*

I intend to ask the above from an anti-sceptical position. The context for such an anti-sceptic question arises from Searle's formulation that intentional states represent word-to-world fit that relegates Consciousness into the background of cognitive acts. Strawson's minimalism does not allow intentionality quality as the crucial source for gaining experience. The question is further necessitated by the cognitive inputs that go into precise identification of what thoughts are about. Even Searle admits of an identity between "intent" and "intentional acts" that Strawson separates in order to identify what really happens to a subject that has an experience. The idea of "real" in terms of an experience related to an actual happening that positions that Subject to have an experience of what happens brings back the old problem of "external reality" as a substrata of experience. This also nullifies the difference between "intentional objects" and "real objects" in experience, while it gives an a priori determinateness to cognitive intent that precedes all experience. Two distinct factors for a sceptical rendering of these arguments arise here: one, the certitude and uncertainty involving the real world and two, the a priori precedence of intent. Searle would take the first, while Strawson would buckle under the second. For Searle, the intentional content of thought assumes certitude by way of pushing consciousness to the background, while for Strawson, the cognitive intent derives intentionality from consciousness, while its contentful states arise in experience of the externally real. This kind of internalism in Searle, actually relegats his notion of intentionality to a backdrop of unconscious, a reverse form of determinism that is only supplemented by speech, acts and truth claims. Strawson's reliance on cognitively real experiences is a causal account of intent that does not bind itself to an ontologically real commitment. Given these backward and forward causal moves, respectively, by Searle and Strawson, one needs to recover a non-surrogate ground for intentionality from its subsumption under causality.

This line of thinking allows us to posit what Husserl had called the "problem of natural attitude". The problem of natural attitude is that it takes the external world as it is and objects of mental act in all their multiplicity have to somehow "belong" to this world. The relation between mental acts and the "objects" of the external world, to which it necessarily refers to, by way of belonging to the same world. But this relation suffers from an in-built contingency in the criterion of identity between thought and world, especially in cases such as twin earth, swamp creatures, zombies. In contrast, Husserl's attribution of universalizing roles to acts of consciousness that produces intended objects over and above the world of facts, turns out to be the source of cognizing the real world. Through intentionality, that is, the acts of consciousness through which the Subject is directed to the world, performs a constitutive role, it constitutes the sense of the real world, without which the world as a totality loses its being or essence. This kind of a descriptive phenomenology of sense in Husserl, does not foreclose the possibility of a causal explanation of the "worldly" entities, rather intended sense of the world in totality opens up "sense" to a variety of "corresponding" synthesis between "sense" and acts of consciousness. Searle's internalist account hinges on "conditions of satisfaction" of the acts of intentionality by way of treating these "conditions" as "derived" from the worldly state of affairs that always transcends with an external causal role in constituting intentionality. Galen Strawson's externalist account of "underived aboutness" as "states" in the world denies any constitution of sense by intentional acts in the case when it is not causally influenced by the world as such. Such a reductive-minimalist account abolishes the pole of subjectivity in the immanent condition of being a part of the world that can be analysed only in terms of acts of cognition. Therefore, what Husserl characterized as synthesis between "intended object" and "sense" is denied by both Searle and Strawson in their overdetermined causal account of intentionality.

The shortcomings of Searle can be further exposed in the light of Dennett's intentional stance that grants autonomy of/ to consciousness and its being as an ontologically self-sufficient phenomena in living beings. The evolutionary notion of intentionality as presented by Dennett assumes an embodied form of acts of consciousness that sets out an in-built acts of consciousness as a naturally evolved model of "reverse engineering" that pursues the causal connections only in the form of intentionality that evolves into cognitive powers and acts. This idea of reverse engineering saves the analytic destruction of the role of consciousness into bodily experiences and psychological intentionality. I suppose Dennett's intentional stance can take care of causal determinism by way of a reverse engineering that projects intentionality only as a mode of "looking forward" to the all-important "anthropological machine" that imports meanings in the world.

Dennett's later stance on freedom of will[2] as an evolved feature of causal determinism in living creatures distinguishes the "phenomenal" and "phenomenological" character of "experience" from explanatory commitment to facts, events and consequences. The idea of freedom of will is not tied to how will is caused, it is rather an expanded notion of causality in the human world that makes things happen by centring it upon the agent, who can affect the fixed laws of nature. Free

2. Daniel Dennett, *Freedom Evolves*, New York: Viking, 2003.

will is conceived in terms of a basic capability of being human that allows freedom of will as a possibility in the realm of action. The phenomenal feature of free will lies in an intentional stance towards the world, the phenomenological basis of which further lies in an integration between the causal and the agentative.

These argumentative moves overcome causation-centric explanation of the idea of intentionality. Daniel Dennett's powerful moves in rendering the "phenomenal" constitute the realm of the "causal" is an explanatory inversion of the Searlean intentionality that derives its efficacy from the ability to "perform" on an external context. Dennett argues that causal powers of an agent are neither eventual nor are they extensional, in his famous *basic argument*.[3] It is rather the case that "free will" ontologically is separable from "fixed" laws of nature as extendable to the past and this separation yields an instantiation of "acts" that are freely willed by an agent. Such acts by free will do not follow from causal acts and their consequences, they rather turn out to be "acts" without any prior occurrence *in* the context of any possible connection between the acts and the outcomes. This does not entail singularity of acts of free will, but it merely brings out the possibility of an "elbow room" in the natural ontological attitude. Free will as a subject-centric concept often violates the determinism of the "causal" in the realm of the "phenomenal" in order to make itself visible in terms of its enactive role in judging and reflecting on the "experience" of the act. The experiential dimension of the free will makes it intersubjectively available in all possible contexts of human action. *Is free will then constitutive of the "causal"*? Dennett gives

3. Christopher Taylor and Daniel Dennett, "Who's Afraid of Determinism? Rethinking Causes and Possibilities", in R. Kane (ed.) *Oxford Handbook on Free Will*, New York: Oxford University Press, 2001:251-77.

a specific meaning to such questions about the relationship between free will and determinism. The meaning that Dennett gave to the ontological nature of free will in relation to sentient beings is that of "freedom" to choose a course of action and its intended consequences:

> The idea that we have free will is another background condition for our whole way of thinking about our lives. We count on it; we count on people "having free will" the same way we count on them falling when pushed off cliffs and needing food and water to live, but it is neither a metaphysical condition nor a fundamental physical condition.... The atmosphere of free will is . . . the enveloping, enabling, life-shaping, conceptual atmosphere of intentional action, planning and hoping and promising and blaming, resenting, punishing, and honouring. We all grow up in this conceptual atmosphere, and we learn to conduct our lives in the terms it provides.[4]

Dennett provides an all-inclusive characterization of "free will" by turning it into the "background" of activities of conscious, intentional and conceptual thinking and thereby, giving it a phenomenological status, instead of a merely ontological role. The phenomenology of background free will arises in various intentional processes that in themselves carry content in terms of mental, brain and physical states. Such intentional processes work in a manner of "performance systems" that succeed in acting out in reasonably complex, articulatory and competent ways that are decoded in multiple ways. Following evolutionary mechanism, such multiple ways of performance of intentional systems, often by itself have become expressions of free will, the larger causal picture of which can only be retrieved in "external modules". Scaffolding the natural abilities of free will in physical and intentional systems merely produce "responses" from the current state of affairs to

4. *Freedom Evolves*: 10.

imagined and remembered moments. In other words, the directionality of free will operate in merging itself over temporal and spatial markers of experience, which would otherwise not have got encapsulated within the complex action coordianting mechanism of the human mind. Dennett provides an ontological basis for such operations of free will by establishing compatibility between natural laws and levels of description that would lay bare the explanans. Such a compatibility is not the usual synthetic validation of natural laws in a variety of "worlds". Dennett's compatibility assures a non-metaphysical sense of "experience" that selectively chooses to disclose the embedded causal manifold. The "freedom" of the subject acts as a latent factor in determining how various mental phenomena stand in a cognitive relationship with the "worlds" in which causal relations are plausible. Dennett considers both the causal relation between the Subject and the world as well as the free will of the Subject as "latent". Subject can exercise its will to stand in relation to the world without being determined by the embedded causal relations between the subject and the world, which allows the Subject to reflexively feel its freedom in the world.

If Dennett's compatibilism establishes "complementarities" between causality and free will without specifying pathways from one to the other, it only produces various exploratory possibilities for relating them.[5] One such exploratory possibility is embedding of a derivative intentionality in the physical systems that gives it what Strawson called non-experiential underived aboutness, which is a material analogue of "freedom" as it obtains in conscious beings. But free will establishes a wider meaning of "freedom" in human agents by way of relieving it from a necessary connection with anything physical, or rather, by establishing a reflexive

5. Daniel Dennett, *Elbow Room: The Varieties of Freewill Worth Wanting*, Oxford: Clarendon Press, 1984: 77-8.

autonomy of its relationship with the "world" in which it is present in a certain mode. Further, the absence of a conscious being in a world does not theoretically deprive it from the possibility of a biologically conscious agent having free will within itself. This brings about a relational complementarity that does not violate its free will driven cognitive-intentional capability in the absence of a conscious agent, which is only projecting and opening up *of* the possibility of how other conscious agents would relate themselves to the world.

In other words, one can surmise that a compatibilist attempt of reconciling free will and causality needs the capability of projection of free will, which is not exactly equivalent to "causing" things by free will of an indexical agent, but it is rather the case that an agent is temporally prior to make itself into a cause. Dennett puts it in this way:

> . . . consider the tale of Billy and Susie. Both children are throwing rocks at a glass bottle, and as it happens Susie's rock, travelling slightly faster, reaches the bottle first and shatters it. Billy's rock arrives a moment later at exactly the spot where the bottle used to stand, but of course encounters nothing but flying shards. When choosing between $\varphi_1$ ("Susie throws rock S") and $\varphi_2$ ("Billy throws rock B"), we vote for $\varphi_1$ as the cause of $\psi$ ("The bottle shatters"), despite the fact that neither sentence is necessary (had Susie not thrown her rock, the bottle would still have shattered thanks to Billy, and vice versa) and both are sufficient (Billy's throw suffices to produce a broken bottle, whatever his playmate does, and likewise with Susie's). Why? The general notion of temporal priority (introduced above in connection with distinguishing cause from effect) strikes us as one critical consideration. As with priority disputes in science, art, and sports, we seem to put a premium on being the *first* with an innovation, and since rock S arrived in the vicinity of the bottle earlier than rock *B*, we give credit to Susie. Further, it is clear that, although the bottle would still have shattered

> without Susie's throw, the shattering event would have been significantly different, occurring at a later time with a different rock sending fragments off in different directions. We can choose set *X* to reflect this fact (. . .) let it contain worlds in which either (1) the bottle doesn't shatter at all, or (2) it shatters in a way very similar to the way it shatters in reality. Then for every world in *X*,
>
> $\psi \Rightarrow \varphi_1$
>
> obtains; wherever in *X* the bottle shatters, we find Susie throwing her rock first. On the other hand,
>
> $\psi \Rightarrow \varphi_2$
>
> may well fail in *X*; *X* can certainly contain worlds where the bottle shatters but Billy refrains. In short, $\varphi_1$ is "more necessary" than $\varphi_2$, provided that we choose *X* right. The vagueness of *X*, though sometimes irksome, can also break deadlocks.[6]

What breaks the deadlock is both the priority of the agency over the causal sufficiency as it is derived necessarily from agent's acts. Agent's decision to act in a certain way does not necessarily form a causal loop with the consequences, as consequences are not overdetermined by consciousness or any other factor of intentionality. As the consequences assume freedom from the actor, so, by analogy, the conscious intentional act of the agent also remains as the source of exercising "free will" in the context of an action, which is just going to happen. This characteristic of "free will" in being "free" from consequences and yet assuming responsibility are both "parts" of a wholesome causal account that describes the happening only explanatorily. In order to bring in a notion of responsibility as it emerges in the exercise of free will, a strategy of prioritization of the Subject over the world makes it possible to "explain" the "how" of events. The givenenss of

6. Christopher Taylor and Daniel Dennett, "Who's Afraid of Determinism?", p. 272.

the world is altered substantially in the "experienced consequence" from agent's perspective as well as from the projection of such a perspective for analogous agents, which gives a sense to the very functioning of free will.

Analogous agents assume the position of an attributed intersubjective character of agency of free will that merely prioritizes "agency" in an otherwise causally controlled realm of consequences and events. Free will yields a place to the Subject in a causally closed world by redrawing the "world" in the relationship between Subject's cognitive ability and the world as such. Searle, Galen Strawson and Dennett granted an ontological position to the Subject, often ubiquitous by its "intent" that forms "intentionality" on the basis of "free will" and inserts itself in the realm of the "causal". Following Husserl, I would like to put forth the claim that the Subject with free will is ontologically "free" as it merely responds to an emergent phenomenology of free will in the backdrop of its acts. Such "responses" for Dennett is an "unknowable", while for Searle it is non-propositional and for Galen Strawson, it is a "cognitive intent" without "intentionality". Husserl overcame this duality between "states" and "intentionality" in a move that he called "affections", which is a "nexus" between streams of consciousness, lived experience and intentional correlates.[7]

## Husserl's Enactive Subjects beyond the "Elbow Room"

The Subject, for Husserl, willingly suspends its intentionality in favour of what it reflectively acquires about the world, which is the greatest signifier of free will. Free will lies in freeing the Subject from its "inner" and "outer" determinations in a naturalistic sense, which is mostly "causal". Dennett could

7. Edmund Husserl, *Ideas pertaining to a Pure Phenomenology and to a Phenomenological Philosophy*, Second Book, tr. Richard Rojcewicz and Andre Schuwer, Dordrecht/Boston/London: Kluwer Academic Publishers, 1989: 349-70. Henceforth, *Ideas*, II.

only partly do so, as he leaves the scope of manipulation of the Subject by an embedded causality. Husserl's methodical act of tracing the Subject in the causal realm lies in granting it the full room, instead of a mere elbow room. Husserl puts it in this way:

> Consciousness in itself has a being of its own which in its absolute uniqueness of nature remains unaffected by the phenomenological disconnexion. It therefore remains over as a "phenomenological residuum", as a region of Being which is in principle unique, and can in fact the field of a new science — the Science of Phenomenology.[8]

The phenomenological residuum of consciousness occupies the "full room" in the sense of first, being disconnected from the passive doxastic conditions of the "given" in the world as well from ideas that are self-evident and then in the sense of affecting both, the *noema* and *noemata*[9] in an active synthesis. Dennett's so-called elbow room as a room for self-legislation, for Husserl, is much larger than it can be conceived of in a naturalistic manner. Husserl conceived acts of consciousness, as mutually constitutive and constituted of/by the "world" that arises in the noesis of an enactive "self". Husserl's notion of "self" is necessarily the identity pole[10] of intentional life of

8. Edmund Husserl, *Ideas: General Introduction to Pure Phenomenology*, tr. W.R. Boyce Gibson,4$^{th}$ impression, London: Allen and Unwin, 1967: 113. Henceforth, *Ideas*, I.

   Also see, Edmund Husserl, *Experience and Judgment: Investigations in a Genealogy of Logic*, revised and ed. Ludwig Landgrebe. Tr. by J.S. Churchill and Karl Ameriks, Evanston, III: Northwestern University Press, 1973: 42-43. Henceforth, *Experience*.

9. Husserl's notion of noema is the subjective correlate of intentionality, while noemata is the "objective" correlate of consciousness, both of which exist as two poles of noesis, that is, the notion of phenomenological bracketing of the "real".

10. *Ideas*, I: 154-55.

the Subject, which is both actively and passively synthesized and associated in the personal life of the Subject.[11] Such an intentional personal life is constitutive of the "world" of moral associations and it is not merely self-legislation, but it is a formation of the self by phenomenological constitution. A deontological moral self merely "acts" through an already constituted "self", but it fails to integrate the will to legislate for itself, as such, a will is not constitutive of the "agency" of the "self". As a strategy of keeping moral will outside the realm of causality, the very moral experience of the subjects is brought to a mere "propositional attitude" that is only correlative to the availability of norms and experiences. This is where Dennett's free will, without a constitutive Subject and its relationship with others, is denied its intentional basis without the clear priority of the "self" as it arises as a pole of conscious identity in every instance of "experiencing".

Galen Strawson considered such instances of "experiencing" as what he allegorically called as "subjects of experience that are single, mental, *persisting* things",[12] while he attributed "cognitive-experiential intentional intent" to such persistent Subjects in order to enable them to experience. Both, Dennett and Strawson give a naturalistic twist here to the self-world relation, which Husserl turned into a relationship of "disconnection" and "reduction" that allows a phenomenological return to an enactive subjectivity.

An enactive subjectivity is a subjectivity-in-relation that merely is *not* a pre-reflective awareness of self's relation with the world, but it is a structure of transcendental relation that is enacted in intentionality and cognition by leaving

11. *Ideas*, II: 200-01.

12. Galen Strawson, "The Phenomenology and Ontology of the Self", in Dan Zahavi (ed.), *Exploring the Self*, Amsterdam/Philadelphia: John Benjamins Publishing Company, 2000: 47.

consciousness as a residuum over and above what is "constituted" by acts of cognition. Husserl articulates the situation in terms of (1) the way the world is posited by consciousness as sense-data or representation, which is one of the constitutive elements *of* the sense of the world as given by a personal-subjective Self and (2) Consciousness is separated and excluded as a residuum of the cognitive acts of "sense-constitution" in order to bring "reality" back to itself. As far as (1) is concerned, it is an outcome of cognitive-intentional intent of the persistent self that persists temporally through a necessary centre of "self" that accompanies every positing of the world by consciousness. This satisfies Strawson and Dennett's position of a centre of consciousness to which cognition of the world can be predicated.

Specifically for Dennett, this centre of subjectivity works on a multiple possibility of sense bestowal and hence displays an intrinsic free will to an outside observer. The reflexive-indexical propositional attitude of a subject and its sensuous output fall within the work of free will, which Strawson attributed to an "underived intentionality" constitutive of all non-conscious agents as well as cognitively equipped self-persisting agents. Both of them follow a method of reverse engineering of an underived free will or intent in the Subject, but it completely misses how Consciousness cannot be reproduced in a reconstruction of its lived intentionality, which is precisely stated in (2). A compatibilist Dennett misses the point that the work of Consciousness is not merely free from bounds of causal determination, but it can present and absent itself in its acts of volition or willing, right within the very production of the knowledge or representation of the world. Husserl gives a greater priority to the residuum of consciousness as the crucial freewilling agency that excludes itself from what it achieves in a specific contentful state by retaining itself as a residue toward constitution of sense of the world.[13] Strawson separates (1) and (2) by completely subsuming (2) under (1). For Galen Strawson, the self is only a persistent agent that arises and emerges in underived non-experiential aboutness that represents/presents a foundational "cognitive intent". The persistence of the self as an agency of cognition arises "causally" from the possibility of cognitive qualia that is "non-conceptual" and "existential", which again is a qualitative description of the laws of nature for Strawson. Although Dennett is free from this naturalist fixity of Strawson, yet he does not address the question of consciousness in terms of coincidence between (1) and (2), that is, in terms of coincidence of "constituting" and "constituted" poles of intentionality. This is *also* evidenced by Dennett's denial of any constitutive role to free will in agency; rather he structured free will as intentionality and refused to give any role of consciousness in already constituted pole of subjectivity. Dennett's strategy turned out to be freeing "consciousness" from the functions of free will in subjectivity so that intentionality of the Subject can act as the basis of operation of free will and any act of consciousness can't be covered by an operation of free will. One implication of such a strategy is to keep free will in the form of consciousness as the agent of the act caused by it in order to grant consciousness freedom of evolving in a form that fulfils the task of a competent agency, *which does not control how it evolves*. A conjunction between an emergent "freedom" and "intentionality" does not overdetermine the agency role of the subject, it rather suspends the subject in an undecidable structure of goal choice and motor

13. This explains better self-organizing character of symbol using biological-computational systems. For details, Prasenjit Biswas, "Phenomenology of Autonomy in Genes: A Neurobiological Critique of Parallelism", in Partha Ghose (ed.), *Materialism and Immaterialism in India and the West: Varying Vistas,* New Delhi: Centre for Studies in Civilization (CSC), 2010; 709-22.

action. Such suspended subjects can be situated in the space between singularity of first-personal givenness and plurality of its experiences that turn a strict causal embedment of "agency" and "will" into the possibility of a "transcendence". Such a transcendence in lived experiences arises in a state of suspension of subjectivity.

**Humanizing the Naturalists**

Husserl would go further than these limits of a sophisticated theory of emergence and evolution not just in terms of causal realism and moral responsibility, but in terms of projecting ineluctable consequences of conscious acts into a phenomenology of human existence that "humanizes" the transcendental grasp of consciousness over the world.[14] This humanization moves beyond the temporal and spatial limits imposed on free will by a causally closed nature in order to make it possible a returns to a constituting subjectivity. This "constituting subjectivity" remains "transcendent" in lived experiences as well as it remains "immanent" in any experiential content that is a part of subjectivity. What is to be noted in this project of humanization is that every existential instantiation of "constituting subjectivity" sets up a new relation by excluding itself from what it experiences and this is what persists in every diachronic relation between the experiential and the reflexive. This shifting nature of a dialectics between constitution and constituted is clarified by Husserl in this way:

> . . . every experience, however far it extends, leaves open the possibility that what is given, despite the persistent consciousness of its bodily self-presence, does *not* exist. It is

14. Dan Zahavi, "Naturalized Phenomenology", in S. Gallagher and D. Schmicking (eds.), *Handbook of Phenomenology and Cognitive Science*, Springer, forthcoming 2009. Unpublished version as available in Dan's homepage.

> an essentially valid law that existence in the form of a thing is never demanded as necessary by virtue of its givenenss, but in a certain way is always contingent.[15]

This contingency of the givenness of consciousness in every instance of experience arises from the very operation of intentionality as the pole and ideal of an infinite *noematic* determination that paradoxically excludes consciousness from intentional correlates such as "sense" or "meaning". That consciousness is only contingently given in intentional acts does not make Husserl commit to an "underived aboutness" of the natural world or an anthropological free will, as they also are "contingent". Husserl allows a full play of this contingent character of consciousness in the lived intentional life of the subject that constitutes an "agency" for intentional acts. This contingency of givenness of entities is conceived as "real" within natural ontological attitude that posits a fully accessible and reflexive role to the human subject and its consciousness, which can be termed as "metaphysics of presence". Husserl reformulates this contingency of presence as an "absolute immanence" that cannot be determined within a region of being but which can be "transcendently constituted",

> *A quite peculiar* transcendence presents itself a non-constituted transcendence — *a transcendence in immanence.*[16]

This non-constituted transcendence of being allows consciousness to remain "immanent" without being present in the logical conception of the intentional life of the Subject, it is only *noematically* conceived as part of that intentionality. Such a *noematic* conception of consciousness grants the *noema* an originary intelligibility in terms of retention and protention of itself. Such an immanent consciousness becomes

---

15. *Ideas*, I:144.

16. Ibid.: 173.

consciousness of something without ontologically setting up a relation with the world, but by partaking in the lived experience of the Subject. Lived world of the subject is not founded on originary intelligibility of its experiential manifestation, but it "exists" in concrete everyday experiences, whose intelligibility lies in the infinite horizon of events, within which consciousness enables human beings to "transcend" the given "reality". Consciousness starts off with its originary sense bestowing role in the world only to transcend it in its everdayness. Husserl formulates it in this way:

> Every finite substrate has determinability as being-in-something. (. . .) But in the following respect the world is absolute substrate, namely everything is in it, and it itself is not in something; it is no longer a relative unity (. . .) everything mundane, whether a real unity or real plurality is ultimately dependent; only the world is independent, only it is absolute substrate in the strict sense of absolute independence.[17]

The world as an absolute substrate is transcended in its originary sense as bestowed in intentional life of the subject leading the phenomenologist to recover the world in its "absolute independence", which is the task of a rigorous investigation. Husserl makes here a distinction between "originary world" and the "constituted world" in order to recover the "world" as an "absolute substrate" from both the "constituted" and the "originary" worlds. This is a double movement within consciousness, a recovery from the phenomenological to the ontological and then a move from "ontological" to the possibility of a metaphysical substratum. This substratum is metaphysically real as it is supposed to be accessible from "non-constituted transcendence", which is a predicative synthesis as carried out by a knowing subject. This predicative synthesis figures the subject as constituted in the

17. *Experience*: 137-38.

world and hence all its moves within consciousness is an attempt to surpass the given and bring in "phenomenal content" in the interface between subjectivity and the world. Such a phenomenal relationship is "constitutive" of the real in concrete experiences, that is, in the concrete flesh and blood of the lived world. The subjectless, faceless, non-intentional and not-lived world is a "built world" that reinstitutes the Subject in its synthetic originality and constitution. This is the transcendence of the world from the subject of the world. The phenomenological content of transcendence lies in passive synthesis of other minds and subject poles in the constitution of the self/world which gives consciousness an autonomy of self-constitution. Husserl expresses it in this way:

> In the intentional lived experiences, the subject of the stream of lived experiences is conscious of this or that "transcendent" being, visible things, (. . .) things thought of, etc. We speak here hence of three: lived experience, subject of the lived experience and the object of the lived experience in consciousness.[18]

Husserl provides here a schema of constitution of transcendence that involves all the above three that involves a fundamental unity between the subject and the world that gets embodied in the form of belonging in the body. For Husserl, body is not only imbricated in an a priori relation with the surrounding lived reality, but it is the "unity of corporeal apperceptions" and it "has the horizon of causal properties co-constituted in the current actual apperception of experience".[19] Husserl, of course, does not connect causally bodily sensations and mental processes, but they are considered co-constituted in "apperception" of the "self" *because* of the larger transcendental subjectivity that can take a

18. *Ideas*, II: 369.

19. Ibid.: 391, n.1.

"perspective" upon every bodily and mental state.[20] Such a perspective resists reduction of the constitutive sense of every act of intentionality to bodily or psychological properties. At the same time, what is phenomenologically bodily or mental finds its correlate in transcendental subjectivity in the form of *noetic* data, which is owned by a subject who experiences such a phenomenological datum. Such a datum is described by Husserl in the following:

> I consider (. . .) spirits as subjects, just the way they are, as persons, accomplishing acts relating to their surrounding world. I consider the acts and am led back to the nexuses of lived experiences of the persons. And now phenomenology makes known to me the essence of "consciousness", the essence of all types of acts, the essence of the passive modes of lived experience which found them, and in these nexuses phenomenology again discovers quite specific relations between the "I experience" and the sensations, adumbrations, sense-things, etc., and I am led to the implicated "motivations", relations between kinesthetic series and the concomitant visual data, etc.[21]

This is almost like an "I think" that a priori accompany all the representations in Kant. But Husserl attaches greater significance to the *noetic-noematic* constitution of experience in body and mind. Such a *noetic-noematic* constitution brings into picture streams of experience, which all belongs to "one" ensemble of experiences. Such an "ensemble" is necessarily co-conscious of all the sense data that are animated within their passive reception. The reception of experience is passive as their "objects" are transcendent of the sense data and such "objects" are available to awareness through a passive self-

---

20. *Ideas*: 391, Husserl calls for a phenomenological distinction between various kinds of "because" that moves personal subject to various accomplishments.

21. Ibid.: 391.

constitution. This passivity of experiencing as well as constitution of self is part of the relation beween "I experience" and "sensations", which cannot be reduced to bodily and mental phenomenology. Husserl neutralizes the possibility of Galen Strawson kind of phantasmic experience of one's own pre-reflective self available to thought and action by taking two steps here: (1) phenomenal qualities of experience is separated from sense-data as belonging to reflective and transcendental subjectivity and (2) transcendental subjectivity is merged passively with an active and vigilant "I" constituted as an existent "I". This can be contrasted with what Galen Strawson declared:

> What I want to put in place is a distinction between one's experience of oneself when one is considering oneself principally as a human being taken as a whole, and one's experience of oneself when one is considering oneself principally as an inner mental entity or "self" of some sort — I'll call this one's self-experience.[22]

One's experience of oneself, for Husserl remains immanent in transcendental subjectivity's merger with an active self and vice versa that receives sense data and experiences their phenomenal properties as "transcendent" of all that is present and *de re* presented in a moment of knowing one's own mind. For Husserl, phenomenological self is atemporal and it is pre-constituted before any act of experiencing and hence its inner mental qualities are "phenomenal" and "transcendent" to any objective sense data. Does this phenomenological self make the existent self appear? For Galen Strawson, the existent self and the phenomenological self are diachronic as the former is categorical and the latter is experiential. For Husserl, such a diachrony arises out of a fundamental misconception about the nature of temporal constitution of subjectivity, which, in

22. Galen Strawson, "Against Narrativity", in *Ratio* (new series) vol. XVII, no. 4, December 2004, p. 429.

his phenomenological reflections, is a "temporal genesis" that throws up various instantiations of a moving, shifting and phenomenally predicative subjectivity. The genesis happens in "passivity" as temporalization of self does not face a diachrony between phenomenological and existential, it rather mitigates the difference between the two in a genetic sense of owning various instances of subjective life. Such instances of subjective life are themselves a "series of changes in real properties", a part of the causal nexus in constituting the reality for the Subject.[23] This causal nexus exists in temporal flow of consciousness that often creates a constitutive manifold of the Subject. The Subject places itself within the temporal mode of experiencing in the manifold of subjectivity, which does not any longer belong to the place of origin, and instead, assumes another origin in the sense bestowing activity of the Subject, which is a transcendental move within the horizon of consciousness. The supposed diachrony between phenomenological experiencing and the existential location of the subject and object is overcome by this move of temporalization, which is indeed "passive". The passivity of transcendental move is a process of "becoming" in which the subject finds itself:

> . . . this Ego itself belongs to its own surrounding world in virtue of self-consciousness and in virtue of the possibility of all sorts of self-directed comportment; the subject is *"subject-object"*.[24]

This becoming of the subject into a relation called subject-object is a passive constitution that works through the acts of consciousness. The "passivity" becomes a genetic relationality between one subject and another and also between the subject and the object with "one surrounding world with an open

---

23. *Ideas*, II: 49-53.

24. Ibid.: 205.

horizon".[25] The experience of the surrounding world undergoes change every moment and this change is experienced in the temporal character of sense formation and their continuous transformations.[26] If the surrounding world marks the existential character of the acts of consciousness, the relationship between one subject and another marks the "origin" of "sense formation" that simultaneously transcends and places itself within the existential world. The "origin" is passive and it goes all along transformation of sense in the subject through various acts of consciousness in unifying a variety of realities in its constitutive partaking in the horizon of the world. Interestingly, Daniel Dennett confounded this multiple ways of phenomenologically fitting the subject in the world as "deflationary" as it merely expresses its experiences reflexively in the states of the Subject. Dennett's term for this is heterophenomenology, but unfortunately, it does not address how reflection is possible on a variety of experiences without just being "subjective" or "objective". Husserl's notion of intersubjectivity gives intentionality an orientation to the other in mutuality that allows an understanding of how consciousness is effective in "originally" bringing the world through originary acts of consciousness. This world brought to the subject by conscious acts of intentionality leaves the residuum of consciousness to reflect, reconstruct and transform the "world" into "constitutive acts of subjectivity". Dennett's moves to deflate and naturalize achievements of consciousness as disconnected from its "originary" engagement with the "world" constructs a hierarchy between "outputs" of constitutive acts of consciousness and intentional acts of

25. *Ideas* II: 205.

26. Ibid.

consciousness.[27] For Dennett acts of consciousness are constituted by acts of intentionality, which curtails the place of conscious subjectivity in nature to a mere appropriating, computing and other such intentionally driven mechanisms. This is an inversion of the role of consciousness into products of consciousness in order to invert the full phenomenological participation of implicit causal-intentional structure of consciousness into a subjectless and objectual material phenomenology of nature that lies completely outside the lived world. This is a deviant-insurgent *coup d'état* through an "eliminative" natural scientific causality that lacks its primary substrate of availability of the nature or the world to the Subject.

**Dennett and Husserl: Agency versus Consciousness**

In sharp contrast to Dennetian "heterophenomenological" elimination of the subject as well as of the world, Husserl propounded a radical view of an experienced objectivity as opposed to mere conditions of its existence. The reason being, the objective conditions of existence cannot be without the possibility of their access and reflection by the Subject. Such an accessibility discloses for reflection on the "world" to which intentionality is directed. Such a "world" is constituted by awareness of temporally differentiated sense-content that the world brings to the experience of the Subject.[28] The possibility of reflection arises from both, intended as well as intentional objects, in such a manner that experience mediates between intentional object and the "object" intended in an act of intentionality. The existence-independence and concept-independence of such intentional and intended objects are ontologically "sensed" within the reach of reflection, but such

27. Daniel Dennett, "Who's On First? Heterophenomenology Explained", in *Journal of Consciousness Studies*, vol. 10, pp. 19–30.
28. Edmund Husserl, *Analyses Concerning Passive and Active Synthesis: Lectures on Transcendental Logic*, tr. Anthony J. Steinbock, Dordrecht: Kluwer, 2001: 42-43.

acts of reflection establish the free will and autonomy of the Subject in the realm of the intersubjective. The crucial autonomy of the subject lies in living a pre-reflective state of consciousness on which consciousness reflects upon and in the process passively synthesizes the sensuous and the intended and through introspection it is further able to identify and understand the phenomenal content that arises in this exercise of reflection in an individuated and fine-grained manner. This is the intentional-experiential perspective that not only guides the autonomous subject, but it can also guide any attempt to understand the subject in the realm of the intersubjective. But most often, the role of the subject in reflecting and individuating intentional content is confused as an act of representation in the absence of the actual. This act of reflection is supposed to be an act performed by an individual subject under all conditions of a third and first-person perspective. Dennett retains the agency of the Subject in its passive acts of synthesis that it actually can perform in the absence of an intended object, and project this capacity of the Subject in the realm of third-person perspective as semantically evaluable, recursive and fit to be interpreted as "data". Dennett preserves the agentative role of subjective consciousness in both, intentional and non-intentional contexts, in order to evolve a compatibilist account of a unified structure of consciousness within which representation of the absent object/content as well as an act of presentation of what is present can be performed with a disjunction as well as conjunction between presence and absence. The unifying role of consciousness in subjectivity not only restrains an apparent chasm in mind between presence and absence, but it also bridges up free will and causation with a temporal priority of the subject herself. The priority of "representation" of the subject in any representational act by the subject seems to be a phenomenological ploy of Dennett in order to identify the cause of free will in the realm of the intentional stance. Husserl would be issuing here two very important correctives: (1) the presence and priority of the subject is only intersubjectively available, as the consciousness of an individual subject excludes itself from any of its conscious achievements by "passive synthesis", the subject-object; (2) the free will and intentionality of the subject arises from "transcendental subjectivity" that brings a constitutive-constituted relationship between the experience and the object. Apparently, Dennett goes with (1), but rejects (2) as a mere methodological step. The absence of consciousness from the "data" that it generates about the world as well of its own procedure of reflection does not find a mention in Dennett's unifying procedure of first-person with third-person intentional stance. As far as (2) is concerned, Dennett sees here free will without an agent causation, that is, a portrayal of a phenomenology without an ontology. Dennett's subjectless objectual phenomenology treats free will as the cause, while it treats the subject causing the free will as located in the world without a necessary transcendence. It is the demonstrable free will of the subject in the acts of consciousness that, for Dennett, frees the consciousness from evolving into an agency in all its causal interrelationship with itself as well as with the world. Galen Strawson frees consciousness further, by freeing it from free will as well as its causal bounds only to minimally deploy it in the "underived" form as it may obtain in all non-experiential beings and relegate it to the sphere of God.[29] Husserl, in sharp contrast to Dennett, identifies the "transcendental structure of consciousness" as the ground of reflection on any representational or phenomenal content, but the representational/phenomenal content only provides a "clue" to the lived reality of which the agency of the subject is one of the constitutive elements. This transcendental structure of

29. Galen Strawson, *Real Intentionality*: 308.

consciousness, as the very ground of acts of consciousness transcends those acts, that is, it can directly relate the "transcendental subjectivity" with those poles of subject and object as disclosed in the lived reality of the Subject even without the presence of the centre of consciousness, which traditionally is self or subject. Transcendental subjectivity can passively reconstitute the absent subject of the world by its internal time consciousness within the stream of lived experience. This is a temporal return to subjectivity as a return to the empirical self-world relationship as it happens within the demonstrable acts of consciousness, which for Husserl, is not a mere relationship between free will and the agency that it constitutes, but is much more than that. Demonstrable acts of consciousness establish connections between the same things and same connections between same things, over a period of time. Transcendental subjectivity can retrieve the lived connections between a plurality of subjects who are differentiated, individuated and distinguished on the basis of "experience of single, mental and persisting things", pace Strawson. If Strawson's characterization of such singular individuated subjecthood is correct, then it should be identifiable in naturalizable, underivedly intentional agents, on which he leaves room for speculation. Husserl would have taken such speculative needs not just to the "cognitive intent" of the Subject, as it is available within the intersubjective grasp of the transcendental subjectivity, but to an altogether new way of phenomenological inquiry to the very nature of subject and self, which is not confined to the self-made selves or the minimal intentionality of the non-experiential creatures. Suffice it to say that an ontological confusion between temporal structure of consciousness and its static "acts" perpetually haunts a metaphysical inquiry into "cognitive intent" or subject of experience, as displayed in Searle, Strawson and Dennett. All of them attempted to turn the hard problem on its head, by either bringing "intentional" under "physical" or "mental" and then leaving the room for speculating about a naïve/ sophisticated anthropology of physicalism-naturalism as a third-person science. Husserl introduces the crucial element of transcendental subjectivity in its temporal dimension that can recover its structure of experience from the individual subjectivity, that lives in it and reflects on it. Without such a content of reflection and without such a subjectivity, that is aware of itself in acts of reflection, any intersubjective determination and differentiation between "events", "causes" and "processes" would only be speculative as it would lack a structure of genesis. Searle commits a greater mistake that libertarians do: reducing intentionality to a constitutive element of the causal order but without making it the determinant of the "effect" that is going to come. This is an epistemic fragmentation of not just the temporal structure of causation, but it is also a fragmentation of the agent within a narrow realm of the intentional that ascribes "content" in a context, without allowing it the crucial capacity of intentional genesis of external natural order with its internal time consciousness. Husserl's pointer to Searle and Dennett's "intentional fallacy"[30] of "intension with an *s*" and "third person perspective" would lie in two aspects: (1) temporal structure of consciousness and its intentional genesis and (2) temporality of transcendental consciousness that goes deeper than specific conscious events in a given, publicly

30. I use this phrase to connote how acts of intentionality are exhausted in the identity of objects, causes and events by Dennett, as he treats these "objective correlates" of subjectivity as "intended". Galen Strawson attempts to widen the net of objective correlates by including how "intentionality" drops out in the face of the "non-experiential" within the structure of "causal relations". Searle reduces intentionality to causal power of the mind and consciousness in their connections with nature as such. All the three commit a naturalistic fallacy of assigning intentionality an "objective" meaning.

available, intersubjective and third-person field of scientific objectivity. For example, if we follow Searle and Dennett, it is possible to conceive mental states such as shame, fear, empathy, etc. as causal occurrences and as states of the subject directed upon an intentional act or object locatable in the world, it wouldn't be possible to get a full perspective on how such states establish an interface with other subjects from either first-person or third-person points of view. One needs to adopt a second-person point of view, which is new phenomenology based on how states relate between one subject and another, which is different from how those subjects are *in* those states. In other words, for a Husserlian subjectivity, existence is not a given, but it belongs to a "region of being", especially in the region of "being-meant-as-real", which translated in phenomenological terms, signifies availability of the sensible and phenomenal "content" as an "orginary synthesis". This "originary synthesis" is always constituting-constituted through free will of the subject and "conscious experience" immanent in it. Further, this "originary synthesis" is the source of decision that synthesizes "perception" and "memory", what is perceived "now" and the memory of this act of intentionality, which is simultaneously a co-reduction between "existence" and "experience". Husserl describes the moment of synthesis in this way:

> Pure consciousness in its absolute Being (. . .) remains over as the "phenomenological residuum" we were in quest of: although we have suspended the whole world with all things, living creatures, men, ourselves included. We have literally lost nothing, but have won the whole of Absolute Being, which, properly understood, conceals itself in all transcendences, "constituting" them within itself.[31]

This phenomenological residuum is the residuum of the "real" that is contained within the constituting-constituted

31. *Ideas*, I: 154-55.

relationship of transcendental constitution and transcendental becoming, which takes the form of "being meant to be transcendent". This is how the world is constituted in transcendental subjectivity without being deprived of its transcendence. The truly intended object of the world, which for natural consciousness is a transcended object remains transcendentally immanent within transcendental subjectivity in order to be given as "real" without any presupposition. Intentionality only provides "sense" to transcended object between consciousness and reality by directing consciousness to the specific object of the world, which is backed up by the entire work of transcendental subjectivity. Every act of transcendental subjectivity is potentially and actually a way of intending an "object" constituted within transcendental subjectivity, which is a "surplus", as it is an addition to what has been already achieved by transcendental subjectivity. Each fresh addition to the pre-constituted knowledge of the world needs to be investigated through their passive pre-constitutions in subjective origins. This can also be an investigation, the "origin" of constitution in general, which is constituted by "givenness" of consciousness in its relation with how it appears to itself in its "absolute facticity". The project of Phenomenology here becomes a reflection on the facticity of consciousness in its transcendental constitution, which is a relationship with an original ontology.

Husserl's projection of such an "originary" consciousness as the source of all the embodied and intentional acts of the subject necessarily binds each "experience" with another, which is a unity of the concrete multiplicity. This unity is experienced as a "stream of consciousness" that is a flow of "pure time" leaving us with only a residuum of a passive form of "lived experience" as "now". Husserl puts it in this manner:

> The actual *now* is necessarily something punctual and remains so, *a form that persists through continuous change of content.*[32]

This brings us to a closer approximation of how an intended object persists, it persists through "puctuation", which is a temporal self-structuring of transcendental consciousness by way of appearing as "then", which further is a continuous change of content in order to arrive at an intentional genesis. Transcendental self-constitution of consciousness, therefore, turns out to be genetic through its internal residuum, the objects that are already constituted in a time "past", which undergoes a different transformation in the punctuating disruption by the "now". The pointlike form of many "nows" implies a topos of interminable retention of the already constituted pasts, which is directed to many possible "nows" that are going to come. Husserl attributes this whole process to a "unity" in the Kantian sense of time as a form of possibility that acts as the condition for experience. In Husserl's inimitable words:

> An objective time being constituted in all their subjective times and (. . .) an objective world itself being constituted in objective time.[33]

This is retention of the changing content of temporal flow, which is constituted in senses and every moment it is modified in order to give the idea that existence is no longer originary constituted by a transcendental gaze. That it is a process of becoming in subjective times, which is a pointlike constitution of object in "objective time". This process of becoming is made "transcendentally intelligible" by a mish-mesh of subjectivity in the objective and objective in the subjectivity, which is an entry into the experiencer as well as the experience of intentional phenomena. This entry into the process of

32. *Ideas* I: 237.

33. *Experience*:166.

experiencing through temporalisation of the subjective is a mapping of how the intentional processes work and how this map is accessible to the very subject himself or herself in person. What is needed to be distinguished here is that an understanding of the structure of subjectivity or, how the subject constitutes the "object" is *not same as* how the subject self-reflexively understands and wills the same. Husserls' notion of posits of the world as residuum, both in the real of the subjective as well as in the objective, helps us to understand how the subject constitutes the world without presuppositions through pure phenomenological moves that meets an ontology in temporal flows in experience. His notion of "sense" tells us how this process that goes within the subject is decoded by the very subjects in relation to each other for an intersubjective and social world. This giving "sense" to "posits" is an active synthesis between acts of consciousness and its achievements in the world, which in itself, is a move within transcendental subjectivity. Husserl constantly dissolves the notion of an agency that exercises its intentionality in the domain of transcendence, which may regionally offer an "intentionality with an "s" or "t". This regional structure of intentionality does not give us the causal relation between these two modes of intentionality as ascription of self to both or any of these modes is only a passé in the process of constitution of "world" by thought. The gap between *de re* thought and *de dicto* thoughts leads to a chasm between intentional ascription of self and the phenomenal quality of thought as "felt" without its causal locus in the subject. The contextual ascription of *de re* thought to the singular subject or the so-called semantic opacity of *de dicto* thought ignores this aspect of self-reflexivity and its upward transcendental moves.

### The Possibilities of Transcendental Subjectivity

Husserl's notion of transcendental subjectivity does not posit "self" as an agent of intentional acts of consciousness. Rather a phenomenological understanding of knowledge and sense is a "passive synthesis of the existent with the existent" that is an activity of the subject to the extent that its "mineness" characteristics gives an access to its own constituting role in what is mine. This access to constituting and constituted roles of subjectivity is not a by-product of the subject-object relationship, it is rather a temporalized form of subjectivity. This temporalized form is disembodied, as the relation between the subject and the world disappears in subject's awareness of itself, only to re-appear in the form of a "stream of consciousness" that erases the originary self as an agent.[34] Stream of consciousness is "non-intentional" and "pure", a wholly other to one's intentional consciousness that gives the subject its "transcendental subjectivity". This Husserlian transcendental subjectivity brings into picture a layered and plural "ontology" of subjectivity, the existent "I" appears before the phenomenological "I" only to constitute and then the phenomenological "I" disappears before the disembodied transcendental subjectivity which makes it possible to return to an enactive phenomenological subjectivity. This phenomenologically constitutive subjectivity worlds itself in phenomenal and conceptual achievements of consciousness qua mind and self. This is where consciousness becomes intersubjective and publicly available. The example of "empathy" shall make it clear. The phenomenal and conceptual structure of empathy as a state of subjectivity is an opening up to the other, who may be engaged or not, and in a theoretical sense who is a pre-constituted other available for an empathetic understanding. Empathy leads to a transcendence of the difference in the "intentional horizon" within which the other is intimated in the sense that the difference with the other brings in a new relationality, not so far constituted within the being of transcendental subjectivity.

---

34. *Ideas*, I:173.

In both these modes of transcendental subjectivity in discerning how it relates to itself and in difference to an other in order to retain its originary intentionality within its horizontal space of relations.

This Husserlian description of disembodied transcendental subjectivity as "pure being" never progresses without an opposing discourse intersubjectivity within which it makes itself functional. The opposing discourse of intersubjectivity frames itself in relationality between operative intentionalities within the horizon and beyond this relationality. The disembodied and yet intersubjective nature of transcendental subjectivity in its temporal constitution assumes the role of the observer who "observes" itself by assuming the position of the "other" who can be touched, seen and known in the immediate and distant neighbourhood. An ontological dissociation between the absent subject with an absent body of transcendental subjectivity and really existing subjectivites is only "phenomenological" which is bridged up in the relationship with the other. This lies in sharp contrast to self-enclosure that merely "refers" to the other as, say, the different, or say, the "hand of the other" as opposed to intersubjective notion of "self-reference" or "ego-reference" of transcendental subjectivity, which is a "diaphanous" non-being. The diaphaneity lies in a set of transparent and introspectively available properties such as "being identical with *X*", where *X* is any property of consciousness. Identity with any such property bridges up the distance between "constitution" and "essence" as created in transcendental subjectivity. The transcendental non-being can also turn self-referential by following an intransitive subject such as "I". Such a subject is intransitive and diaphanous as its relations are merely a supplement to the lack of the other. Closure of the self as an agent in its body and consciousness "limits" the possibilities of phenomenological constitution, hence it requires an openness without closure. Husserl celebrates this phenomenological openness of the transcendental subjectivity and characterizes it as an open horizon that is present to consciousness as a horizon of presumptively actual and really possible objects, and as soon as it becomes intuitive as an open infinity, it gives itself as an infinitude of particularizations of the transcendental subjectivity. These particularizations of transcendental subjectivity are arranged in temporal self-structuring, which is "comprehensive experience of the existence of the other" as well as an,

> If we examine the structure of consciousness that constitutes a thing, then we see that all of nature, with space, time, causality, etc. is completely dissolved into a web of immanent motivations. . . .[35]

This web of immanent motivations is included in the lived experiences, of which the subject is aware of and which conditions the temporal dimension of every judgemental act of intentionality. Such judgements bind us to a "comprehensive" and "apprehensional" relationship with the other, which are nothing but "apperception of spirit" that can be transferred to one's own ego.[36] This apperception of spirit functions as a "non-objectivated pure ego" that is one of the elements of the "web of immanent motivations". Husserl explains it in a "fundamental analysis" when he describes it as:

> All this is accomplished in the spiritual attitude, without any "naturalizing". But we know already that we can turn *every man as a comprehensive unity* into a unity of nature, a biological and psychophysical Objectivity, in which pure spirit no longer functions as member of a comprehensive unity, but instead a new phenomenal unity, an Objective thinghood, is constituted. This is transferred to me myself

35. *Ideas*, II: 238.

36. Ibid.: 254.

> as an Object of nature, in a very mediate way of representation, as one can say.[37]

This non-objectifiable pure ego is a transformative step in changing the reflexive self-apperception *to* what he called as the "ultimate foundation" of philosophizing, which is, "self-responsibility" in the sense of responsibility to make truth appear for no other purpose than truth itself.[38] This responsibility is presented by Husserl in terms of the absolute Being of transcendental consciousness as under:

> It is thus clear that in spite of all talk-well-grounded no doubt in the meaning intended-of a real (*realen*) *Being of the human ego*, and its conscious experience *in* the world and of all that belongs thereto in any way in respect of "psychophysical connexions" — that in spite of all this, Consciousness, considered in its "purity", must be reckoned as a system of Absolute Being, into which nothing can penetrate, and from which nothing can escape, which has no spatio-temporal exterior, and can be inside no spatio-temporal system; which cannot experience causality from anything nor exert causality upon anything, it being presupposed that causality bears the normal sense of natural causality as a relation of dependence between entities.
>
> On the other side, *the whole spatio-temporal world*, to which man and the human Ego claim to belong as subordinate singular realities, is *according to its own meaning mere Intentional Being*, a Being, therefore, which has the merely secondary, relative sense of a Being for a consciousness. It is a Being which consciousness in its own experiences posits, and is, in principle, intuitable and determinable only as the element common to the motivated appearance-manifolds, but *over and beyond* this, is just nothing at all.[39]

---

37. *Ideas*, II: 238.

38. *Husserl Archive* VIII: 197; V: 139.

39. *Ideas*, I: 152-53.

The ontological Being of the human ego, which is non-objectifiable is a state of disembodied transcendental subjectivity that arises from the real in a non-causal sense in order to disconnect the constitutive power of subjectivity from consciousness, which is both a transformation of human individual ego as well as a transcendence from the nexus of lived experience. This transcendental subjectivity differs from empirical ego-subjectivity in the sense that the difference is non-supplemental and a kind of radical difference that does not presuppose even a common semantic notion of difference. Husserl articulates this non-supplemental sense of difference as two different ways of being: actual consciousness is immanent and it is absolute and transcendental, while intentionality is noematic-constitutive. Transcendental subjectivity includes this noematic-constitutive intentionality without a fixed centre of a conscious agency, as agency is already dispersed in what is anterior to noetic and noematic sense. This inclusion of noetic-noematic intentionality within transcendental subjectivity is the non-self originary consciousness that has never been at the exterior of the lived subjectivity. Such a consciousness does not require the unstable, incompletely formed and metaphysically suppressed position of Subjects as "agency", as such an agency arises only in a new constitution of "objectivity" that "abjects" the unstable subjectivity. This prevents simulation of the "self" and its representation at the level of conscious acts, rather, it becomes an experience of reflexivity on a situation that drives the subject "over and beyond" the "state" of abjection where it reconstitutes itself as neither a subject nor an object in the "world" but as a de-centred entity engaged with the situation. It is at this stage that neither the "body" nor the "self" of the "subject" can be present to an enclosed intentionality of performing an act in the world, but they are transcended in the very act of which they are traces of an agent.

Transcendental subjectivity achieves an almost magical disconnect from the reflexivity of ego-constitution and in principle becomes a non-intentional egoless bodyless "form", which can only be iterated in situations. Such iterations allow a complete sovereignty of transcendence in order to self-govern and be autonomous of its "phenomenal states" in such a manner that states and situations of the erstwhile subjectivity appear only as a means for acquiring its own subjectivity. These forms of disembodied transcendental subjectivity, for Husserl, can be represented as "transferred to me myself as an Object of nature", which is "a very mediate way of representation".[40] This is a "new phenomenal entity" that consciously represent itself by disconnecting from the situations in which it arises, it is rather transferred to its appropriate "object", which is a rediscovery of the subject-object connection lost and purged out in ego's constitutive self-representation. What is reflectively achieved by this transcendental phenomenal unity between the subject and the object in the state of being disembodied and decontextualized are not the truths of the pre-phenomenological life-world, but the transcendental sense of birth and death of subjectivity. This is what Husserl means by self-responsibility as the "ultimate foundation" of reality and knowledge, which is a "form of intentional genesis" through which truth finds its "Absolute Being". This seems to be a "finished constitution" in such a manner that what is at first noetic-noematic constitution ascribed to nature and history is now decontextualized in its phenomenal form only to re-situate it in the sovereign and autonomous region of Being that does not depend on nature and history. This is abjection of all those markers of belonging that suppress its own exterior in order to recover and leave them as they are. One phenomenologically recovers the givenenss of the being from its constitutive determinations, which is "transcendental" in

40. Supra note 36.

terms of the lived experiences that synthesizes both objectivity and subjectivity with world given beforehand in intuition. This recovery institutes and embeds agency in the acts of consciousness which truly recovers its grounds of being.

# 8

# Collective Agency and Social Action*

*Bijoy Boruah* and *Bhaskarjit Neog*

## Introduction

OUR being in the world as active individual persons is defined by two contrary agential features, namely independence and interdependence. There are ways in which we individually, hence independently, do things to bring about desired changes in the world. And there are ways in which our doing things in the world requires us to depend on other individuals. We understand our independent actions in terms of certain states or attitudes formed by individual minds. The explanatory mental state is internal to the concerned individual subject of the action. We might call this the "internality constraint" of the explanation of action by reference to intention. While the intentional explanation of independent action evidently conforms to the internality constraint, it is far from obvious whether an intentional explanation of interdependent action can be shown to conform to this constraint. Since doing an interdependent action involves the participation of more than one individual person, there is no way of attributing the explanatory intentional state to any single member engaged in accomplishing the interdependent act.

* An earlier version of this paper appeared in *Journal of Indian Council of Philosophical Research*, vol. XXVIII no. 3, pp. 1-32, July-September, 2011 with the title "Collective Agency".

If we attach importance to the internality constraint in explaining an action, performed independently or interdependently, then it would appear that the idea of the later kind is unintelligible from the explanatory standpoint. However, there is no question of de-recognizing the reality of interdependently performed actions, which are the action-types that define our existence as social beings. It therefore means that there has to be some complex account of the possibility of human beings acting interdependently, which makes the concept of cooperative or collective action intelligible without conflicting seriously with the intuitive plausibility of the internality constraint.

The concept of cooperative or collective action has already been an issue of fervent philosophical discussion in recent philosophy of mind and action. The crux of the discussion has been to analyse it in terms of the possibility of collective intention. Prominent among the philosophers who have dealt seriously with this issue are John Searle, Raimo Tuomela, Michael Bratman, Margaret Gilbert and David Velleman.[1] They have addressed themselves to the question of what makes our social life possible, or, more specifically, what it is for us to intend to do something together. They are centrally concerned with spelling out the complex notion of collective intention conceived as the underlying mental state that explains the possibility of collective action. However, their final aim seems to come to terms with a particular conception of collective agency on the basis of their analysis of the idea of collective intention.

Irrespective of their individual differences on the notion of collective intention, they are unanimous on the point that the

1. John Searle (1990; 1995), Raimo Tuomela (1994; 1995), Michael Bratman (1999), Margaret Gilbert (1989; 1996; 2003; 2005; 2006), J. David Velleman (1997).

existence of collective intention is a necessary condition for the possibility of collective agency. But what remains still a moot question is whether collective intention is a sufficient condition for collective agency. And this latter question deserves to be critically examined. Indeed, the question of sufficiency raises the issue of whether collective intentional goal-directedness has to be supplemented by an evaluative conception of the goal as being worthy of pursuit on the part of the agent.

In this paper, we critically examine the intention-based account of collective agency and argue for its radical insufficiency. The proposal we intend to proffer here is that efficacious collective agency is a far more robust notion than what comes forth in the intention-based approach. Collective agency must be predicated upon the collective's ability to form an internal evaluative perspective for the execution of its intention to accomplish the goal that it sets for itself. In point of fact, it is the presence of this perspective that is responsible for endowing cohesiveness and robustness to the collective as a proper agent.

**Action, Intention and Agency**

We, human beings, are capable of doing many things. We do things by exercising our agential power. We are what we are because of our actions. Our actions or doing things are essential to much of what we cherish as human persons. One of the basic features of human action is that our doing something brings about a certain change in the world. The change that is brought about is owed to the doer. Changes in the world that merely happen are not owed to anyone because these are not doings of anything by anyone. Such changes occur as part of the natural course of events ultimately subject to the laws of nature and available for causal explanation. It is, of course, not that human actions are not causally connected with human agents, but there is much more to the relation between action and agent than mere causation. Actions involve practical deliberation on the part of the agents, and such deliberations are in turn sustained by beliefs, desires, and goal-directed attitudes or predispositions of the agent. Given these deliberative elements constitutively involved in the mental make-up of agency, the agent intends to do what he or she eventually does.

Wittgenstein made a brilliant point by asking: "What remains if I subtract the fact that my arm went up from the fact that I raised my arm?"[2] Here a conceptually crucial distinction is being drawn between "arm rising" and "arm raising". It is obvious that when I raise my arm, my arm rises; but there is more to the fact that I raise my arm than the fact that my arm rises up in the air. My arm can rise up in the air due to air pressure forcefully applied to my arm, in which case I do not raise my arm but my arm rises because of causal forces of nature. On the other hand, when I do raise my arm, the arm rises up in the air because of my willing, or intending, to do so.[3] There is, thus, a state of intention that crucially determines the agential role, and thereby shapes the agential status, of me in my raising the arm.

But one's agential role or status can be comprehended only when there is a reasonable balance between one's state of intending to do something and his or her ability to execute the intended goal. I can intend to do something only when I am minimally confident of fulfilling the intended goal. Indeed, the content of my intention must be in line with what I believe about the possibility of executing the intention successfully. I can, for example, intend to climb up to the Himalaya, but I cannot intend to fly from the top of that mountain and land in my favourite Buddhist monastery in Nepal. There must be a

2. Wittgenstein, 1958: §. 621.

3. The subtle difference between intending and willing, if there is any, is of negligible importance in this context, and hence ignored here.

reasonable match between the content of the intention and the capacity to execute it. One cannot intend something which one is perfectly sure that one is unable to perform it. This, of course, does not mean that one must be certain of being able to do what one intends to do. For instance, one can intend to publish a paper in a most highly acclaimed academic journal in the hope of winning a most prestigious award, even though the probability of succeeding in achieving that goal is pretty low. Intention and possibility may go side by side, but intention and impossibility do not at all go together.

The conceptual link between intention and possibility needs to be interpreted in a rather careful way. It would seem to be an abuse of the term "intention" if I say that I currently intend to climb up to the Mount Everest given my actual expertise in mountaineering, which is much too inadequate to fulfilling the intended goal. There is a serious mismatch between actual agential ability and the ability actually required in accomplishing the intended action in the stipulated period of time. It would be more appropriate, in such a case, to use the term "desire" instead, even though it would then be viewed as an "irrational" desire given the mismatch between my present agential ability and the possibility of success in accomplishing the desired goal. The point is that a desire can be rational or irrational depending on whether there is a significant discrepancy between the agent's ability to attain the desired goal and what level of agential capacity is demanded by the goal that is desired to be attained. By contrast, an intention cannot be either rational or irrational; it can only be rational, where its rationality is a function of the matching relation between agential ability and the demand the intended action makes upon the agent.

The flip side of the intention-action relation is the relation between intention and agency. Actions at the individual level

— i.e. individual actions — are clearly interpreted or explained by reference to the intention formed by the agent. Depending upon agential self-knowledge, or self-knowledge of agential ability, the agent is rationally self-confident about the possibility of accomplishing the intended action.[4] In the case of a normal individual action, I as an individual agent am rationally confident about my possible agential success, because my intention to do the act is rationally measured against my agential ability under normal circumstance. But if I say, for example, that I, as a single agent, intend to construct a multi-storeyed building, overlooking the fact that such a task requires the agential role of various other people of technical and non-technical expertise, my intentional self-confidence would be questionable. Would it also be irrational?

It would be irrational only if I am so stupid as not even to realize the magnitude of the task in relation to my standard agential limits. What I am supposed to realize is that the task intended by me is a collective action, and hence my singular agential power or role is most inadequate to executing the intention for successful completion of the action. The question relevant to this realization is whether the required intentional interpretation of such a collective or social action must advert to an agency of a non-singular kind, i.e. plural or collective agency. Must collective or plural actions be intended by collectives or plural agents?

This question is most pertinent to the theory of social explanation in social sciences, especially with regard to the role of collectivity concepts in social explanation. According to the central precept of what is known as methodological

4. The notion of "rational self-confidence" on the agent's part is elaborated in terms of the "Principle of Intentional Self-confidence" by Hans Bernhard Schmid in Schmid (2008). The Principle of Intentional Self-confidence was first introduced by Annette Baier in her paper "Act and Intent" (1970).

individualism,[5] of which Max Weber is one of the founding fathers in sociological theory, the only agents that social sciences know of are individuals. The so-called collective agents are social fictions that have no place in social explanation. Weber's rejection of collective agency is believed to be predicated on his conviction that only individuals can be treated as agents in providing an intentional interpretation of actions. For Weber, group or collective agency does not make any sense. It is because collective actions cannot be separated, as distinct from identical actions of many persons, and because groups, unlike the individuals who belong to them, cannot think as groups or formulate intentions of the kind normally thought to be required to actions.[6] Collectives are simply not suitable candidates that can be meaningfully invoked in intentional interpretation of social action.

Weberian methodological individualism is clearly a challenge to any theory of social explanation that considers group agency to be a necessary as well as viable explanatory notion for our understanding of social action. It may be wondered whether, in addition to his belief about intentional interpretation of action in individual agential terms, Weber harbours any worry about endorsing collectives as *bona fide* candidates for explaining collective action. In his most recent and fascinating paper, Hans Bernhard Schmid conjectures that Weber's main worry underlying his strong allegiance to methodological individualism is his principled commitment to what Schmid calls individual intentional autonomy, which means: "Under normal circumstances, each individual's

---

5. The first use of the English translation of the German phrase *methodische Individualismus*, coined by Weber's disciple, and the famous economic theorist, Joseph Alois Schumpeter, is to be found in his *Quarterly Journal of Economics* paper "On the Concept of Social Value".

6. Weber 1968.

behaviour has to be interpreted as his or her own actions."[7] Given this commitment, individual behaviour is the proper object of intentional interpretation, and thus individuals alone are the agents of the behaviour that instantiates their actions.

The alleged worry is therefore that conceding any other type of agency than the agency of the participating individuals in a group would "impair" or "compromise" their individual agency and autonomy. Collective agency, considered as a distinct form of agency, would render the agential role of the participating individuals into mere instrumental roles in the execution of some collective will. The individuals would then not be proper agents any more behind what they do as contributing participants in the collective enterprise.

What is really important about this worry, if the said conjecture is justified, is the question of alleged incompatibility between individual intentional autonomy and the impossibility of collective agency on methodological individualist ground. For the truth of the principle of individual intentional autonomy that lies at the heart of methodological individualism is sacrosanct. And yet, it is not obvious that any concession to collective agency necessarily involves betrayal of this principle. We shall take up this problem towards the end of the paper. Meanwhile, we need to enter into a detailed discussion of the distinction between individual and collective action, with the intention of concentrating on the complex nature of the latter.

## Collective Action and Intention

Actions can be classified into two broad categories from the point of view of agency, namely individual and collective. Collective actions require the participation of at least two people. Examples of collective actions may include: jointly writing a paper, singing a duet, playing a symphony, dancing

7. Schmid 2008: 34.

on a tango, pushing a car together and the like. One of the striking features of these actions is that all the members of the collective in question engage in their actions in order to arrive at a single goal. The goal is not pursued severally by the individual members of the collective, as it happens in the case of the passengers of a single bus getting off the bus in an airport in order to embark an aeroplane. The reason why a collection of passengers engaged in the act of embarking the same aeroplane is not a case of collective action is that there is no collective intention on the part of the passengers. No doubt the goal here is a common one, a common end that they all are pursuing. But the pursuit of the common goal is not sustained by a common intention.

If an action is conceptually tied up with an intention, then the question of the relation between a collective action and intention is as pertinent as it is in the relation between an individual action and intention. Two perplexing problems surface here. It is clear, in the latter case, that the intention to do *X* by an individual *S* is a mental state or attitude attributed to the individual mind of *S*. But a collective action, not being a matter of individual agency, cannot possibly be tied up with a mental (intentional) state of any particular individual subject. Must there be a collective intention as distinct from individual intention or a collection of individual intentions? This, the issue of the possibility of collective intention, is one problem. The other problem relates to the fact that what we individually intend to do is always within our individual control. The execution of the intention to do something is entirely up to the person who intends it. But since, in a collective action, the performer is the entire collective, how can the individual members of the collective individually intend to do something, the doing of which depends on all the members of the collective?

By way of addressing ourselves to these two aspects of this problem, we may further analyse the structure of collective intention. It is evident that I cannot intend to *X* if *X-ing* is a matter of collective performance, in which you also have a part to play. But it is possible that I intend that we *X* together. There is a difference between intending-*that* and intending-*to*.[8] Intending-*to* is something where the agent is the sole author of what he or she intends to do. But intending-*that* refers to a situation where the agent does not have the complete authorship over the intended action, and yet he or she is somehow connected with it.

Further, intending-*that* itself admits of two different senses. In the first sense, I intend that someone else *X-es*, in which I myself have no agential role to play in *X-ing*. For instance, I can intend that my wife join academics instead of joining management service. Intention in this sense is more like my wanting or desiring — that my wife *X-es* rather than *Y-es*. In the second sense, I intend that we *X*, where the authorship of the intended action is shared with others. For instance, in my intending that we renovate the club, I exercise my agential power in co-operation with the exercise of agential power by other members of the club.

What is the relevance of this distinction between two types of intention with regard to the issue of collective action? The relevance is that intention in the sense of intending-*to* is not a constituent in the structure of collective action in the paradigmatic sense of the phrase — the sense in which we address ourselves to the problem of collective agency. However, there is a loose sense of collective action in the structure of which this sense of intention does fit. To cite an example, an autocratic king fights against and defeats his enemy. He of course performs this task by employing his soldiers to bring about the desired end, which makes his task one of collective action. In this case, despite the fact that it is a collective action, the

8. M.E. Bratman, 1999: 142-61.

action is the result of executing the intention of one particular individual, namely the king. Therefore, the intention involved in this action can be described as the king's — rather than the collective's — intending to defeat his enemy.

It is obvious in the above example that there is no collective intention that plays the explanatory role in relation to the so-called collective action. It is therefore clear that such an action — where the collectively brought about consequence is due to individual intention — cannot properly be described as a collective action. There is, in point of fact, no operation of collective agency in this action; for the king has coercively thrust his autocratic intention upon the collection of soldiers fighting for him. It is therefore no wonder that this so-called collective action is amenable to explanation by reference to "intending *to*" rather than "intending *that*".

We can now reinforce the point about collective action proper in terms of the involvement of genuine collective agency. The examples cited in the beginning of this section — playing a symphony, jointly writing a paper, singing a duet, unanimously approving a bill in the parliament, etc. — all fulfil this condition of exercising collective agential power, where the following five conditions are satisfied:[9]

> Members of the collective each intend that they engage in the intended action.
>
> They each intend to do their part in this engagement.

9. These conditions are formulated, by Pettit, Philip and Schweikard, David in "Joint Action and Group Agents", in *Philosophy of the Social Sciences*, vol. 36, no. 1, March 2006, pp. 18-39. Pettit and Schweikard have acknowledged that the requirement of these conditions is closest to Bratman's analysis of shared co-operative action presented in Bratman (1999). The description of the conditions formulated by Pettit and Schweikard is rendered here in our own terms.

They each believe that the other members intend to do their part as well.

Because of believing this, they each intend to do their part of the collective action.[10]

We may explain the requirement of these conditions in terms of a concrete example. Consider the case of writing this paper by the two of us — you and me. We the authors individually intend that we involve ourselves in writing the paper, and thereby intend to play our individual intellectual roles in the joint engagement. We each believe that the other member intends to play his role as well by exercising his intellectual ability towards completing the paper. And it is because of this belief that each of us intends to play our individual roles in collectively writing the paper.

If each of the two of us intends that the other plays his role in jointly accomplishing the intended goal, then it should be clear that the primary intention in such a joint action is that we together complete writing the paper. Of course, each of us individually intends that we do this act, and only come to make one's individual contribution towards jointly completing the paper as a result of that *we*-intention. Thus, primacy is given to the we-intention over the *I*-intention in the case of joint action.[11]

---

10. Pettit and Schweikard mentions a further condition, namely "they each believe in common that the other clauses hold". We, however, think that this further condition is in fact a meta-condition, i.e. a condition that the other conditions hold. For our purpose, the inclusion or exclusion of this condition is irrelevant.

    The account of collective agency discussed in the paper mentioned above is further developed in relation to collective responsibility in Pettit (2007). The specific notion of "group mind" invoked in the explication of collective agency is introduced by Pettit in Pettit (2003).

11. The distinction between *we*-intention and *I*-intention is derived from a more fundamental distinction that Raimo Tuomela (1994) makes between the *we*-mode and *I*-mode of performing an act.

Michael Bratman throws more light on the explication of the concept of collective action by stressing its shared character.[12] Three basic features of the shared character of collective action cited by Bratman are: (1) mutual responsiveness to each other's intention and action; (2) commitment to the joint activity; and (3) commitment to mutual support in performing the joint activity. The thrust of these features is the idea of commitment with which the members of the collective are jointly engaged in performing the collective action. This emphasis on joint commitment is not quite apparent in the set of conditions cited by Pettit and Schweikard. In particular, the commitment that the individual members have in being supportive to one another in attaining the common goal is what lends cohesiveness to the joint activity.

An adequate account of joint commitment is made available by Gilbert.[13] The essence of collective intention, according to her, is best reflected in the notion of joint commitment. Commitment is a matter of will, and such a commitment may be personal or joint. If a person is subject to a commitment in virtue of making a decision to do something, then he or she has a sufficient reason to act in accordance with it. The decision to which the person is committed carries its normative force until the person rescinds or fulfils it. In a personal commitment, the subject commits himself to doing something, such that he creates the commitment on his own and is in a position unilaterally to rescind it.

By contrast, a joint commitment is made by more than one person, but it is not a conjunction of one's personal commitment and separate personal commitments of the others

---

12. This dimension of shared character is emphatically put forward by Michael Bratman (1993).

13. M. Gilbert 1989: 39-64. The idea of joint commitment is further elaborated in several of her later papers. The idea of joint commitment is further elaborated in several of her later papers.

who join together in the act of making that commitment. Rather, it is a single commitment made by all of them. All the members of a group are equally subject to the same commitment and, therefore, it can only be rescinded by their concerted action. Each one of them is supposedly obliged to do his or her part of the action to make it the case that they all act as a body.

We now need to address ourselves to a new question regarding the idea of joint commitment. The question is whether the members of a collective jointly act together because of their being jointly committed to one another, or it is in virtue of their acting together that they are jointly committed to one another. Supporting the latter view, Pettit and Schweikard writes: "it is in virtue of their jointly acting together that people [i.e. members of the collective] are jointly committed to one another, not that it is in virtue of their being jointly committed that they jointly act together".[14] Contrary to this view, Margaret Gilbert, attaching primacy to the former, says:

> Persons *A* and *B* are collectively doing *A* if and only if they collectively intend to do *A* . . . and each is effectively acting, in light of the associated joint commitment, so as to bring about fulfilment of this intention.[15]

What is at stake behind this controversy regarding the question of prioritizing joint commitment over joint intention or action, or the other way round, is the issue of the normativity of collective action, i.e. whether normativity is intrinsic to the structure of collective action. In case joint commitment is said to have primacy over joint intention and/or action, there would be an implication of normativity in virtue of the fact that joint commitment would oblige the members of the collective jointly to intend to pursue their common goal. Mutual reliance and expectation would ensue from the commitment,

---

14. J. Searle 1990: 32.

15. M. Gilbert 2005: 12.

which in turn would necessarily invite obligatory or normative considerations. It would also imply their mutual commitment to support one another in the collective performance aimed at the common goal. There would then be mutual responsibility on the part of the individual members of collective intention to accomplish the intended collective action.

On the other hand, attaching priority to joint intention or/and action over joint commitment would mean that no such normative implication is intrinsic to collective intention or/and action. Since joint commitment is a result of joint intention or action, any normative import that the intention or action might bear would, in that case, be consequential rather than intrinsic.

Our position on this controversy is not identical with either of these two parties, but closer to Gilbert's stance. However, we believe that intending to do something collectively is surely a matter of being mutually committed to taking the *we*-intention minimally seriously. Unless the constituent members minimally seriously commit themselves to the performance of the jointly intended collective action, what they jointly engage in doing would not really be a joint action proper. Besides, it is primarily the joint commitment that constitutes the condition for the possibility of collective agency. Of course, there could be a collection of people who happen to get together in a common place and coincidentally engage in an act directed at the same goal. For instance, several people coming from different directions happen to assemble in place P1. They then see someone at place P2 throwing a basketful of gold coins for some peculiar reason, and then they all run towards P2 to grab as many gold coins as possible. This act can, in a loose sense, be attributed to a collective. But there is not collective agency here because no collective intention is formed by mutual consent and commitment with respect to the goal of grabbing the gold coins.

Our argument that joint commitment is intrinsic to

collective intention or/and action has been directed at strengthening the claim that collective intention or/and action is intrinsically normative. But it may be alleged, as Bratman does,[16] that no such normative implication is entailed by joint commitment made towards engaging in a shared co-operative activity. For, the allegation continues, it would be "too strong" a claim to say that collectively intending to do something, and thereby being jointly committed to doing that act, necessarily implicates the constituent agents in being mutually obliged to engaged in the co-operative activity, and entitled to press upon others so to engage if the obligation is not fulfilled by them. What instead can rightly be claimed, according to Bratman, is that even if such mutual obligation and entitlement somehow attach to collective intention, that attachment is not intrinsic to it, but a consequence of it.[17]

Even though we have argued that our position is closer to that of Gilbert's, we do not consider that the answer to the question of normative implication depends on the primacy of joint commitment over collective intention or/and action. In

16. Talking about joint commitment in terms of "mutual obligation and entitlement", Bratman says the connection between shared intention and mutual obligation is "too strong" to be true. He adds: "Even though the normal etiology of a collective intention does bring with it relevant obligation and entitlements when the collective activity is itself permissible, this etiology is not essential to collective intention itself." On his view, therefore, this obligation and entitlements are a consequence of the collective intention. — Bratman 1999: 132.

17. Bratman is trying to disclaim the intrinsic normativity of collective intention by regarding any likely normative attachment to it as a matter of consequence. Suppose we grant that it is a matter of consequence. We are then entitled to question whether this is a contingent or non-contingent consequence of collective intention. Bratman of course thinks that such a consequence is contingent. — 1999: 130-41.

point of fact, there is no question of prioritization here, because these two concepts are not related to one another in terms of dependency of the one upon the other. Rather, the relation is an internal one in the sense that being involved in joint intention/action is expressive of being jointly committed to executing the intended act.

**Collective Agency and Plural Subject**

Given that collective action is performed by more than one individual, it should be obvious that collective agency is constituted of a plurality of individual agents. The notion of agency, whether collective or individual, is of course the notion of a single unit. However, the notion of collective agency is the notion of a single unit that does not consist merely of a single individual. In other words, the notion of collective agency connotes a single unit without it being the case that the agential unit is singular.[18] The "singleness" of collective agency is a direct consequence of the fact that all the members of the collective share the same intention to pursue a common goal. It is because of this singleness that there is unity in the collective action.

There is, however, a conceptual complexity in the notion of collective agency if it is interpreted as a single unit of a plurality of individual agents. Apparently, there is a kind of "agential interweaving" of distinct individual members in the constitution of collective agency. Is there a "fusion" of distinct agential attitudes that yields, rather mysteriously, a collective mind or group consciousness, as the locus of collective agency? One can readily suspect that this sort of a construal of collective agency will invite fierce criticism on the ground of mystification. Indeed, several philosophers of empiricist orientation have dismissed any construal of collective agency

18. This is comparable to Velleman's remark, made in connection with Gilbert's notion of "plural subject", that a plural subject is a single subject without being singular. See J.D. Velleman 1997: 30.

that resorts to the metaphor of fusion. The driving force behind this dismissal is basically a set of two reasons: (1) ontological parsimony on Ockhamian ground, and (2) avoidance of any metaphysically loaded concept. John Searle, for one, says that since society consists entirely of individuals and, hence, only of individual minds/brains or consciousness, any talk about group mind or group consciousness is "at best mysterious and at worst incoherent".[19] In the same vein, but by resorting to the concept of shared intention, Bratman is dismissive of any move to explain the notion of collective agency by invoking the idea of a collective mind. He contends:

> [S]hared intention is not an attitude in the mind of some super-agent consisting literally of some fusion of the two (or more) agents. There is no single mind which is the fusion of your mind and mine.[20]

If there is no super-agential subject of shared or collective intention, no group mind or consciousness, what kind of image of the subject of collective agency is reflected in the views of Searle and Bratman? Given their individualist ontological persuasions regarding mind and agency, it can be inferred that both of them would explain the possibility of collective action in terms of shared or collective intention, without thereby resorting to any explanatory connection between such an intention and a corresponding non-individual agent-subject. In the case of Searle, there is just the individual subject or agent who forms, in appropriate social context, *we*-intentions that are directed at attaining a collective goal. The capacity to form *we*-intentions is biologically innate, and it presupposes certain other background capacities which help us to sense others as candidates of co-operative action.[21]

19. J. Searle 1990: 404.
20. M.E. Bratman 1999: 98.
21. J. Searle 1995: 37.

In the case of Bratman as well, the agent-subject of shared intention is individual. But, unlike Searle's (essentially singular) *we*-intentions, which get their collective character from a social context, Bratman's shared intentions are "complexes of appropriately constrained individual intentions interrelated in appropriate ways".[22] Different individual intentions together form an interlocking web, yielding thereby a collective intention. The content of each individual intention is essentially collective in the sense that all the participants are committed to the same intended goal.

A question naturally arises here as to why the presence of a collective or shared intention does not necessitate the corresponding collective agent-subject which is not an individual subject. Bratman avoids having to commit himself to the existence of a literally collective agent-subject by treating a shared intention (between two persons) as not being a mental state, or an attitude in the mind or minds of either or both participants. It rather is "a state of affairs that consists primarily in attitudes (none of which are themselves the shared intentions) of the participants and interrelations between those attitudes".[23]

Treating the notion of shared intention as referring to a state of affairs rather than a "shared" mental state of some kind may be a clever way of diffusing the problem of having to deal with collective agency at the "collective-subject" (as opposed to individual-subject) level. But the price one has to pay for persisting in such an arch-individualist construal of the problem of collective intention or/and action is not negligible. What suffers under such a construal of the agent-subject of collective intention/action is the collective character of the agency. If the intention to attain a common goal is shared by you and me, and there is no more unity and integrity

22. M.E. Bratman 1993: 34.

23. M.E. Bratman 1993: 108.

between you and me than the fact that we each share the same intention to reach the common end, it then looks as though the individual agential roles of each of us have just been co-ordinated in the sense of dovetailing two distinct sources of agential power geared to a common action. The palpably "plural" character of collective agency seems to be betrayed by efforts to project the agent-subject of collective intention in terms of singular subjects.

An interesting exception to the empiricist orientation on this complex issue is the stance taken by Margaret Gilbert,[24] who proposes the idea of "plural subject" in order to explain what it really means for something to be a collective agent. It is not obvious whether Gilbert intends the term "plural subject" to refer to collective or group mind. None the less, this new concept seems to have explanatory advantage over the empiricist-cum-individualist attempts to explain collective action/agency inasmuch as the centre of attention shifts to a new and complex concept. The complexity is that a plural subject is not just a plurality of subjects, but subjects who combine or integrate in such a way as to constitute one subject, "a special kind of thing — a 'synthesis *sui generis*'".[25] Each of these individual subjects or persons offers his or her will to be part of a "pool of wills" dedicated, as a whole, to a single goal. "Thus," adds Gilbert, "what is achieved is a binding together of a set of individual wills so as to constitute a single, 'plural will' dedicated to a particular goal."[26]

Consider two people, *A* and *B*, are walking together, where *A* and *B* perform the joint action of walking together by being entangled in the same intentional state, namely the state of intending to walk towards the nearby park. According to

---

24. Gilbert (1989).

25. M. Gilbert 1996: 268.

26. M. Gilbert, op. cit., p. 185.

Gilbert, during the process of jointly intending to go for the walk, the two individuals form a new entity called the "plural subject". They form a plural subject by mutually expressing their willingness, with their common knowledge about the goal, to be jointly committed to the performance of a particular action. A collective agent, in this sense, is none other than such a plural subject.

But is this a viable notion of what it really means to be a collective agent? The reason why this question is paused is that it is far from clear how one can locate what we call a collective agent understood as a plural subject. To refer to the given example, whereas we can locate agent *A* and agent *B*, there allegedly is the third complex agent other than *A* and *B* that qualifies the status of a "new entity". But since this new entity cannot be located at all, what justifies the postulation of such an entity? Is this notion of a plural subject then a reification of the fact that a plurality of individual wills intermingle to form a single will? Indeed, suspicion of such unwarranted reification is already manifest in a remark, made by J. David Velleman, who conjectures that Gilbert is "using talk of a plural subject as a mere *façon de parler*, a convenient way of summarizing facts about a collection of subjects who never actually meld".[27] How important and cogent is this suspicion of reification and the surmise that nothing really hangs on the creatively coined phrase with which Gilbert wants to score a substantive point over Searle and Bratman?

We have already argued that any account of collective action that undermines, whether reductively or otherwise, the collective character of agency is to that extent counterintuitive. Our dissatisfaction with Searle-Bratman type individualist accounts of collective intention/action is grounded in our realization that their individualist, "singularist" construal of the agent-subject of such intention/

27. D.J. Velleman 1997: 31.

action misrepresents the agential image lurking in collective action. It therefore seems to us that Gilbert's "non-singularist" characterization of collective agency in terms of "plural subject" is at least a move in the right direction of formulating a tenable theory of social action.

Whether Gilbert's plural-subject view of collective agency and/or intention is in fact a reification of something vulnerable to Ockham's razor depends on how the *sui generis* status accorded to it is to be countenanced. To allege that it is a new kind of entity over and above the individual subjects who form a "pool of wills" is an unwarranted exaggeration, and a failure to recognize the spirit (rather than the letter) of the assertion under the pressure of a patently literal reading of it. We are therefore inclined to think that a judicious interpretation of the non-singularist projection of collective agency will attend to the collective salience of agency forcefully indicated by the notion of plural subject.

## Internal Evaluative Perspective of Collective Agency

Talking about the collective salience of the plural subject gives us the opportunity to explore the further, and foremost, issue of what constitutes a collective or social agent in the robust sense of the term. While we take Gilbert's lead in this direction as important, and consider this lead as facilitating us towards our own position on this issue, we believe that the prospect of her theory being adequate is weakened by a limitation inherent in her own position. The limitation is that her attempt to depict the picture of collective agency through the sketch of the plural subject is constrained within the structure of collective intention. What we do get in that depiction is the ontological outlines of what it is to be an agent of collective action. But the plural agent-subject inherent in that structure does not represent the perspective or standpoint that crucially determines the collective identity of the agent.

This limitation is endemic to any account of collective agency that is restricted to analysis in terms of intention. It therefore applies as much to Bratman and Searle as it does to Gilbert. The general character of this limitation can be brought to light by linking the notion of agency to the idea of an "intentional system" famously introduced, and expounded in terms of "intentional stance," by Daniel Dennett.[28] An agent is so structured as to exhibit an appropriate pattern of rationality in its behaviour, given that agency is an intentional notion and rationality is constitutive of the idea of the intentional or mental, à la Donald Davidson.[29] The Davidsonian idea of rationality in intentional behaviour is interpreted by Dennett in epistemic and instrumental sense. In this interpretation, even a chess-playing computer, in virtue of its displaying a pattern of instrumental rationality in the moves it makes, is a *bona fide* agent, having beliefs and desires concerning the chess game that rationally motivate its behaviour.

The attribution of agency to a dynamic intentional system is of course predicated on the way the system functions towards an appropriate goal. Goal-directed behaviour is thus a constitutive feature of agency. But the important question is whether we get a full-blown notion of agency when goal-directed behaviour is in conformity with instrumental rationality. Although we might concede that a chess-playing computer's goal-directed, game-winning behaviour is structured by patterns of instrumental rationality, the computer is not motivated to pursue its goal because of any sense of significance or worth of that goal. It is not an agent that evaluates the goal before embarking rationally on the task of accomplishing that goal. The chess-computer therefore exhibits rationally mediated goal-directed behaviour that has no

28. Daniel Dennett (1987).

29. Donald Davidson 1980: 207-25.

evaluative perspective from with which the agent forms its reason for pursuing its end.

What emerges from this discussion is the difference between agency in the sense of instrumentally goal-directed behaviour, and agency motivated by the agent's desire to pursue its goal because of the value it finds in that goal. We believe that the robust or full-blown agency is instantiated only by agency of the latter kind. The crux of the difference is that robust agency is characterized by a rationality that is adequately sensitive to the evaluative significance of the end intended by the agent. The evaluative perspective is intrinsic to the structure of robust agency.

This distinction between instrumentally goal-directed and evaluatively goal-directed senses of agency applies to the case of collective agency as well. Thus, the behaviour of a collective intentional system, such as that of a selection committee meant to appoint someone belonging to a specific category of caste or economic status, is rationally instrumentally driven to make the selection in terms of the fulfilment of these two criteria. The collective behaviour of the members that make up the system exhibit a pattern of goal-directedness is mediated rationally through its two informational states, namely the candidates belonging to the specific caste and their having the specified economic status. There is no concern, on the part of the members of the committee, for the worthiness or otherwise of the end that it intends to accomplish.

By contrast, a robust or full-blown collective agency, such as a football team playing against a rival team, is motivated to score the winning goal by its rational evaluation of the worth of attaining this end. Its collective goal-directed behaviour is governed, not merely by means-ends strategies of instrumental rationality, but by the realization of the significance, to them, of winning the game. This implies that there is an internal evaluative perspective that shapes the structure of such agency, even though the evaluative weight of the perspective may be minimal. The perspective also substantively determines the identity of the collective agency precisely because it is integral to the collective's agential constitution.

The crux of what has been discussed above with regard to the distinction between full-blooded collective agency and quasi-agential collective systems is quite similar with the insightful comments made by Helm (2008) in his paper on plural agents. But, this does not mean that there is no essential difference between his view on the issue and our way of dealing with it. The attraction of Helm's explanation is the presence of the mutual emotional care between individual persons in the group. For Helm, the cementing force needed for collective agency is held to be emotive, even though the collective psyche of the plural agent is drawn towards the collective goal by its perception of the worthiness of the goal. Surely the perception of the worthiness of the goal is a normative condition. But what is not clear is whether it is because of emotional connectedness and mutual care that the plural agent considers the collective goal to be worth pursuing, or the members become united by mutual emotional care because of the fact that they all believe the collective goal to be worth pursuing.The important issue is whether or not the priority is to be attached to mutual emotional care among members over the group's normative perception of the goal. If mutual emotional care among the members of a group is more of an instinctive nature, as it often is in a family, then the group intention to act towards a particular goal may or may not be guided by an evaluative conception of the goal.

The more important issue is whether, in such a case, we can talk about collective agency and collective intention/action in the proper senses of these terms. The connection between collective agency and intention is a rational one in that the agent recognizes the reason why it intends to achieve its goal. Both the rationality and intentionality of the action cannot be accounted for independently of the way the goal is conceived. This means that the agent has a belief about why it ought to pursue the goal, and what sense of value regarding the goal yields the group-desire to fulfil the intention of attaining the goal. Without bringing the conception of the goal under this normative light, neither the agency nor the intention and action of the collective can properly be described to be a case of collective agency and collective intention/action. Thus, what is crucial to collective agency as well as collective intention or action is not group-internal emotional care, but group-internal evaluative perspective.

Robust collective agency is group agency in a fairly substantive sense, because the group as a whole rather than the members that make up the group is the (plural) subject of the evaluative attitude towards the collectively intended goal. The group as a whole — the group subject — experiences a sense of concern and makes evaluative judgements about the end it is set to attain. However, the group subject of collective agency is not, contra Searle and other individualists, metaphorically ascribed evaluative concern and judgement in regard to the visualized end. For the appropriate pattern of rationality exhibited by the behaviour of the group is a projection of the group itself. The overall pattern of rationality projected by the group behaviour is, as it were, woven by the rational interconnectedness of attitudes and allegiances of the individual members forming the group, or the group subject. It is not that distinct evaluative behavioural responses to the goal exhibited by the different members merely happen to coincide in such a way that there emerges an overall pattern of rational responsiveness to the world for the entire group.

We have thus talked about a joint evaluative perspective, an evaluative perspective shared by each member of the group.

The projectible pattern of rationality in the group's responsive behaviour constitutes that perspective, which is jointly held by the members such that each — each of us — can be held rationally accountable for his or her responses in the light of that joint evaluative perspective. Indeed, it is from the joint or shared evaluative perspective that the goal of our collective intention assumes significance for us, or matters to us. We together constitute the evaluative perspective of us (the plural agent-subject), and each one of us is answerable to the demand of the perspective. We each become rationally beholden to the same evaluative perspective and so answerable to ourselves jointly. It is the jointly owned evaluative perspective that constitutes the desired end as having collective significance for joint pursuit.

Sharing an evaluative perspective in the constitution of collective agency has a phenomenological shift of stance that must not be neglected in the articulation of robust group agency. As members of the group, our individual evaluative attitudes towards the desired end must be transformed into attitudes we each have as one of us: i.e. I thus become an "organic" element of we in being an agent-subject of that attitude and the appropriate responsive behaviour in regard to the envisaged end. I am responsive to the "call" of the end not merely because it is of value to me, but because it is valuable to me inasmuch as it is valuable to us. My sense of concern and care for the desired end is for our sake, and is for my sake as well only because I feel myself inalienably bound up with the collective *we*-identity. Because of this sense of group-identity or cohesiveness, my individual agential identity becomes an "organic" element of an agent-subject that has plural identity.

## Conclusion

Reconciling the unity of action with the plurality of agents is manifestly the crux of the problem of collective agency and social action. What precisely is the sense in which there is one composite but unitary action which is performed by two or more people jointly intending, qua a group to accomplish the task? In the current debate on this issue the dominant trend is to invoke the concept of shared intentionality in providing an answer to this question. Since it is unclear what exactly it means to share an intention, most authors in this debate tend to understand this phrase as a metaphor. Their understanding at bottom is that in sharing an intention, each participant individual has his or her own intention, all of which interlock to form a web of (token) intentions. No single (token) intentional state is there that is shared by the participants in the straightforward sense of the term. Intentional states referred to in the interpretation of individual behaviour are all and only individual states: in short, the thesis of intentional individualism, as formulated by Schmid.[30]

There is the almost universal endorsement of intentional individualism on the part of those who discuss the problem of collective intentionality in the individualist framework. Being wedded to intentional individualism, these thinkers are necessitated to adopt a distributive conception of shared or collective intentionality. But the distributive conception is plagued by a vicious circle: whatever it is that two or more individuals intend when they participate in a joint intentional activity already presupposes the shared intention. There is, thus, a commonality in the (token) intentional state that pre-exists the act of forming a joint intention by the participant individuals. This irreducible property of "intentional commonality" renders the notion of a shared intentional state into a distinct kind of state with an independent status characterized by unique psychological efficacy.

Once the irreducibility of collective intentional state is established, and thereby its psychological efficacy in explaining

30. Schmid 2008: 48.

the participatory individual behaviour is legitimized, the falsity of intentional individualism becomes evident. The participant individual's own behavioural contribution towards the goal of a joint intentional activity is ultimately interpreted or explained by reference to a shared intentional state rather than any individual intentional state of the participating agent. Nevertheless, the participating individuals intend their contributive actions individually, because they individually own these actions within the collective enterprise. Thus, there is no reason for the Weberian worry mentioned earlier, that joint intentional activity explained in terms of group agency will impair or compromise individual intentional autonomy.

If each individual agent in a group action intends to do his or her own part individually, then it of course implies that the participatory individual intentionality of each agent is derived from an intention that is not individual, i.e. a shared intention to bring about a common end. This is precisely what characterizes the sociality of social action: a shared or common intentional state ultimately responsible for motivating collective engagement aimed at the common goal. We have already discussed much earlier in the paper that this shared intention need not be construed as a psychological state of any particular mind, let alone of a collective mind of some mysterious sort. It rather is a shared intentional "state of affairs" that creates a particular sort of social or group environment, and the group environment is none the less psychologically efficacious in motivating the participant members individually to intend to make the goal-directed contributions.

We thus believe that the idea of shared intentionality, or intentional commonality, must be articulated in terms of the projection of a psychologically efficacious collective social environment that sets the scene for robust collective agency. And we now wish to claim, rather emphatically, that it is the stronghold of the internal evaluative perspective, by which the group intention to achieve the common goal is shaped and motivated, that lends, quite significantly though partially, the peculiar motivational efficacy to the group-psychological environment. In the absence of such an environment, there would be no true unity of actions that are necessarily performed by a plurality of agents.

## References

Bratman, M.E. (1999), *Faces of Intention*. Cambridge, MA: Cambridge University Press.

Baier, C. (1970), "Act and Intent", *The Journal of Philosophy*, vol. 67, pp. 648-58.

Davidson, D. (1980), "Mental Events", in his *Essays on Actions and Events*, Oxford: Clarendon Press.

Dennett, D. (1987), *The Intentional Stance*, Cambridge, MA: MIT Press.

Gilbert, M. (1989), *On Social Facts*, New Jersey: Princeton University Press.

———, (1996), *Living Together: Rationality, Sociality and Obligation*, Lanhan, MD: Rowman & Littlefield.

———, (2003), "The Structure of the Social Atom: Joint Commitment as the Foundation of Human Social Behavior", in F. Schmitt, *Socializing Metaphysics*, Lanham, MD: Rowman and Littlefield, pp. 39-64.

———, (2005), "Rationality in Collective Action", *Philosophy of the Social Sciences*, vol. 36, no. 1, March, pp. 3-17.

———, (2006), "Who's to Blame? Collective Moral responsibility and Its Implication for Group Members", *Midwest Studies in Philosophy*, XXX, 94-114.

Helm, B.W. (2008), "Plural Agents", *Nous*, 42, (1), pp. 17-49.

Petersson, B. (2007), "Collectivity and Circularity", *The Journal of Philosophy*, vol. CIV, no. 3, March.

Pettit, P. (1993), *The Common Mind: An Essay on Psychology, Society and Politics*, New York: Oxford University Press.

Pettit, P. and Schweikard, D. (2006), "Joint Action and Group Agents", *Philosophy of the Social Sciences*, vol. 36, no. 1, pp. 18-39.

Petit, P. (2003), "Groups with Minds of Their Own", in F.F. Schmitt (ed.) *Socializing Metaphysics: The nature of Social Reality*, Lanham, ML:

Rowman and Littelfield, pp. 167-94.

Pettit, P. (2007), "Responsibility Incorporated", *Ethics*, 117, January, pp. 171-201.

Schmid, H.B. (2008), "Plural Action", *Philosophy of the Social Sciences*, vol. 38, no. 1, March, pp. 25-54.

Searle, J. (1990), "Collective Intentions and Actions," In P. Cohen, J. Morgan, and M.E. Pollack, eds., *Intentions in Communication*, Cambridge, MA: Bradford Books, MIT Press.

Searle, J. (1995), *The Construction of Social Reality*, New York, N.Y.: Free Press.

Tuomela, (1984), *A Theory of Social Action*, Dordrecht, Boston and Lancaster: D. Reidel Publishing Company.

Tuomela, R. (1995), *The Importance of Us: A Philosophical Study of Basic Social Notions*, Stanford: Stanford University Press.

Velleman, J.D. (1997), "How to Share an Intention", *Philosophy and Phenomenological Research* LVII: 29-50.

Wittgenstein, L. (1958), *Philosophical Investigations*, tr. G.E.M. Anscombe, Englewood Cliffs/N.J: Prentice Hall.

Weber, M. (1968), *Economy and Society: An Outline of Interpretative Sociology*, ed. Guenther Roth and Claus Wittich, N.Y: Bedminster Press.

# 9

# Updating Practical Wisdom[1]

*Rachana Kamtekar*

## Empirical Challenges to Practical Rationality

RECENTLY, students of virtue ethics have responded to the empirical-psychology-inspired assault on character[2] by calling to attention the crucial role of practical rationality, and its excellence practical wisdom, in virtue.[3] In our view, failure to

1. For comments on ancestors of this paper, I'm grateful to audiences at the University of Denver conference on Situationism and Virtue Ethics, the Jawaharlal Nehru University conference on Self-Knowledge, and the Northwestern University Virtue Workshop, and to Joshua Knobe.

2. John Doris (2002), *Lack of Character: Personality and Moral Behavior* Cambridge: Cambridge University Press; Gilbert Harman (2000), "Moral Philosophy Meets Social Psychology: Virtue Ethics and the Fundamental Attribution Error", in *Explaining Value and Other Essays in Moral Philosophy* Oxford: Oxford University Press, pp. 165-78.

3. Julia Annas, (2011), *Intelligent Virtue*, Oxford: Oxford University Press; Rachana Kamtekar (2004), "Situationism and Virtue Ethics on the Content of Our Character", *Ethics*, vol. 114, no. 3. I cannot here take account of two notable books published since my paper was written, Nancy Snow's (2008) *Virtue and Social Intelligence*, New York Routledge, and Daniel Russell's (2009) *Practical Intelligence and the Virtues*, Oxford: Oxford University Press. Both books find empirical support for an Aristotelian conception of virtue in the cognitive-affective personality system in social psychology described in Mischel and Shoda (1995) "A cognitive-affective system →

understand that character is animated by and expressed in practical reasoning leads to a false expectation that character-traits will yield behaviour in a mechanical fashion. The empirical evidence that such mechanical entities do not generate cross-situationally consistent behaviour, we have argued, does not bear on virtuous character as conceived of in virtue ethics. But quite apart from whether empirical psychology undermines virtue ethics and the possibility of developing a virtuous character in particular, there is a far more relevant and pressing question: what is the bearing of empirical psychology on the very possibility that practical rationality — whether on the classical virtue ethicist's, Kant's, Bentham's, or ordinary people's interpretation — has a role in determining our behaviour?

Surprisingly, at least some empirically inclined students of ethics have embraced the view that practical rationality is not important in determining what we do. For example, according to John Doris:

> Given the quantities of empirical work with apparently "bleak implications" (Nisbett and Borgida 1975) for human rationality, . . . practical rationality is not a promising entrée to an empirically sustainable psychology of character.
>
> — Doris, *Scepticism about Persons*, 10/5/05

In this paper, I examine some of the empirical evidence that allegedly has these "bleak implications for human rationality". First, I look at two examples of weaknesses in inferential reasoning much discussed in the "heuristics and biases" literature in cognitive psychology: the overconfidence bias and the neglect of the base rate or prior probabilities. Then, I look at experiments that study the effects of "priming" on our behaviour and that have been used to characterize our

---

→ theory of personality: Reconceptualizing invariance in personality and the role of situations" in *Psychological Review* 102.2, pp. 246-68.

behaviour as produced "automatically" by environmental stimuli without any rational mediation.

Although I will be arguing that this research does not warrant the pessimistic conclusion that practical wisdom, or at least significant improvement in practical rationality, is incompatible with an empirically sustainable psychology of character, my interest in this empirical work is not purely negative, for the empirical research also suggests concrete ways in which we can improve as practical reasoners. And those of us who have argued that practical wisdom is at the heart of the ideal of virtue have acquired the burden of putting some flesh on the mostly negative (anti-Platonic) skeleton of an account of practical wisdom we have inherited from Aristotle. Much of Aristotle's discussion is an attempt to distinguish practical wisdom from scientific knowledge and knowledge of first principles, which, according to Aristotle, Plato mistakenly supposed could guide our attempts to live well. Aristotle's own positive characterization of practical wisdom — a true and reasoned state of the capacity to act with regard to human goods (EN 1140b20, cf. 1140b4-6), acquired by experience (1142a15) — is disappointingly thin. Recent work in cognitive and social psychology makes this thinness harder to ignore, because by detailing the cognitive errors to which we are prone in reasoning, this work demands that we say more than that practical wisdom is a sensitivity to all the ethically salient features of a situation and that this is what our upbringing, experience and reflection should be aiming to inculcate. We need to be able to say what specific abilities such a sensitivity would consist of, and how we can develop these abilities so that the weaknesses that seem to pervade our practically oriented faculties do not determine what we do.

**Heuristics, Biases, and their Corrections**

According to the "heuristics and biases" programme in cognitive psychology, we use certain heuristics to make quick inferential judgements, and while these often serve us quite well, they also lead us into error. One pervasive heuristic is "representativeness", the expectation that causes will be like their effects and whole classes like the instances we have sampled (or stereotypes); we use this heuristic, it is argued, to the exclusion of statistically more significant factors like the base rate or incidence of a characteristic in a given population. For example, given a character sketch of "Steve" as shy, helpful, and with a passion for detail, people say that Steve is more likely to be a librarian rather than a farmer — ignoring the fact that there are many more farmers in the population than librarians. Another pervasive heuristic is "availability", the use of information that is vivid, perhaps because it is familiar or fits into a script we already know, to assess probability. Because factors other than frequency affect availability, relying on availability can lead us astray. For example, when people are asked to estimate whether there are more men than women on a list, they judge that there are more women if the women on the list are more famous than the men, and vice versa.

Nevertheless, our heuristics are valuable: as Tversky and Kahneman say about the availability heuristic in an early article:

> Lifelong experience has taught us that, in general, instances of large classes are recalled better and faster than instances of less frequent classes; that likely occurrences are easier to imagine than unlikely ones; and that the associative connections between events are strengthened when the events frequently co-occur. As a result, man has at his disposal a procedure (the availability heuristic) for estimating the numerosity of a class, the likelihood of an event, or the frequency of co-occurrences, by the ease with

> which the relevant mental operations of retrieval, construction, or association can be performed.[4]

Still, it is a problem that in experiment after experiment we have been shown to use these heuristics to the exclusion of information highly relevant to making predictions.[5]

The bearing of these heuristics and biases on practical wisdom should be clear: practical reasoning is reasoning about what to do, so judgement under uncertainty — about what other people are like, or how it is likely to be with them, or what they are likely to do — is central to our deliberation and decision-making. Making inferences about the likelihood of an event, or the distribution of some property in a population, etc., is central to practical rationality. And to the extent that our inferences are biased, we fall short of excellent practical reasoning or practical wisdom. Can we improve, that is, can we approach practical wisdom?

In their classic work, *Human Inference*, Nisbett and Ross recommend that everyone studies statistics in high school, and among their preferred inferential practices they highlight the following:

(i) when establishing covariation between two variables, pay attention to all four possibilities (variable 1 present/variable 2 present; variable 1 absent/variable 2 present, variable 1 absent/variable 2 absent, variable 1 present/variable 2 absent);

(ii) avoid data known to be vivid but not relevant (like job interviews);

---

4. Amos Tversky and Daniel Kahneman, "Judgment under Uncertainty: Heuristics and Biases", *Science* (n.s.), vol. 185, no. 4157, 27 September 1974, pp. 1124-31, at p. 1128.

5. See, e.g., Richard Nisbett and Lee Ross (1980), *Human Inference: Strategies and Shortcomings*, Prentice-Hall.

(iii) if your own judgement or action is surprising to you, ask yourself why you made it or did it;

(iv) prefer collective over individual reasoning.

However, they and other cognitive psychologists caution that such remedies are not always available or appropriate in the heat of action, and that when they are reasoning intuitively, trained statisticians themselves routinely make the errors they have studied.

The persistence of errors in inferential reasoning despite statistical training may be explained by the hypothesis that we have two independent systems for inferential reasoning, an associative intuitive system that uses heuristics to give us the quick and dirty results we need to get by, and a rule-based one that uses formal logical or statistical methods.[6] Some suggest that the associative system, which we use in everyday reasoning, is automatic, is not capable of being brought under rational control or being taught the superior inferential methods of the rule-based system; among the reasons they give is that our heuristics operate below the level of consciousness.

Although the heuristics and biases programme identifies many errors — the effect of arbitrary anchors on estimates, availability biases, non-regressive predictions, and others[7] — this paper focuses on errors involving subjective probabilities, because some research on this topic shows a way ahead for improving practical reasoning.[8]

---

6. Steve A. Sloman, "Two Systems of Reasoning" in Griffin, Gilovich and Kahneman (eds.), *Heuristics and Biases: The Psychology of Intuitive Judgment*, Cambridge, 2002.

7. See Tversky and Kahneman 1974, remarked by Kahneman and Tversky (1996), "On the Reality of Cognitive Illusions", *Psychological Review*, vol. 103, pp. 582-91, at p. 583.

8. And so I ignore a number of cases where the alleged error is in fact the psychologist's error. For example, take the "inclusion" bias. Subjects are supposed to be guilty of this bias when they say that →

## OVERCONFIDENCE

In one kind of study of overconfidence, participants are asked many questions of the form,

*Which city has more inhabitants?*

(a) Hyderabad (b) Islamabad

---

→ (1) "Robins have ulnar arteries, therefore birds have ulnar arteries" is a "stronger" argument than (2) "Robins have ulnar arteries, therefore ostriches have ulnar arteries". The psychologists fault the judgement that (1) is a stronger argument than (2) on the grounds that ostriches are included among birds, so (2) is at least as strong as (1); they explain the faulty judgement by the representativeness heuristic: robins but not ostriches being paradigmatic birds. (Osherson, Smith, Wilkie, Lopez and Shafir, 1990; reported in Sloman, p. 387). But is the judgement faulty, in the first place? The conclusion of (2) may be no less likely than the conclusion of (1), but in (1) the conclusion is obviously related to the premise, whereas in (2) the relationship between premise and conclusion has to be made via some argument like (1), the conclusion of which would be the missing major premise in (2). Since in (2) there is no direct relationship between premise and conclusion without introduction of the conclusion of (1), it is reasonable for people to say that (1) is the stronger argument. Similarly, in the so-called conjunction fallacy, viz. the judgement that Linda, who is "single, outspoken, bright, concerned with discrimination and social justice and anti-nuclear" is more likely to be a feminist bank teller than a bank-teller, the conversational implicature of the "bank-teller" alternative would seem to be "and not a feminist". And is that really more likely than that she is a feminist bank-teller? (This possibility is recognized in Gilovich and Griffin's introduction to *Heuristics and Biases*, p. 12; Tversky and Kahneman recognize that rules of co-operativeness in conversation demand that information be given that has high value, even if the trade-off is reduction in probability, but they think that their experimental subjects distinguished clearly between the instruction to rank statements by probability and ranking of statements by their expected information value. "Extensional versus Intuitive Reasoning", in *Heuristics and Biases*, pp. 46-47.

*How confident are you that your answer is correct?*

50 %   60 %   70 %   80 %   90 %   100 %

The experimenter then counts how many answers in each of the confidence categories were actually correct. Typically, in cases where the participants say "100 per cent", the relative frequency of correct answers is 80 per cent; and where they say "90 per cent", it is 75 per cent, and so on.

Overconfidence is defined as mean confidence minus relative frequency of correct answers. Two experts, Von Winterfeldt and Edwards, say about the overconfidence bias,

> Overconfidence is a reliable, reproducible finding. Can anything be done? Not much.[9]

But are we overconfident? In two studies (Gigerenzer, Hoffrage, and Kleinbolting 1991), participants were asked either

(i) how confident are you that you got this question right? about each question, OR

(ii) how many of these 50 questions do you think you got right?

In (i), the mean confidence minus relative frequency of correct answers was +13.8 per cent and +15.4 per cent; i.e., the subjects were significantly overconfident.

But in (ii), the mean confidence minus relative frequency of correct answers was -2.4 per cent and -4.2 per cent. That is, subjects were slightly underconfident.

What could explain these findings? The overconfidence

9. Quoted in Gerd Gigerenzer, *Adaptive Thinking: Rationality in the Real World*, Oxford, 2000, p. 247. The reference: W. Edwards and D. von Winterfeldt, "On Cognitive Illusions and their Implications" in H.R. Arkes and K.R. Hammond (eds.) *Judgement and Decision-making: An Interdisciplinary Reader*, Cambridge, 1986, pp. 642-79. My discussion above is indebted to Gigerenzer, pp. 245-48.

hypothesis has no explanation of the underconfidence in response to question (ii). Gigerenzer points out that there is no contradiction between believing that the probability that a certain event *E* will come about is 100 per cent and believing that the frequency of events of type *E* is 80 per cent. The two beliefs, one about single-event probability, and the other about frequency, are logically independent. Lay people hear a difference between the question, "how confident are you that you got this question right?" and the question, "how many of these questions do you think you answered right?" Statisticians do not, because they have been trained to convert both single-event and frequency judgements into degree-of-confidence judgements.

It may seem that even if single-event probability and frequency are logically independent, there is still a contradiction between saying of every question on the test that you are 100 per cent sure you got it right and at the same time saying that you think you got 80 per cent of the questions right. But this is the attitude of a conscientious author in the preface of a book: she takes responsibility for any persisting errors, feeling sure that there are some — but of any particular statement in the book, she is as sure as she can possibly be that it is correct. (If she weren't, she'd correct or at least qualify it.)[10]

If overconfidence is an artefact of the framing of information in an unfamiliar, theoretically-dictated format, as Gigerenzer claims, then improving our practical reasoning in such cases will not involve somehow compensating for overconfidence, but rather, translating information from a subjective probability format into a frequency format. Identifying just what our errors are is crucial for improving our reasoning. I will return to the topic of what kind of improvement is needed and is possible after discussing a second heuristic-and-bias, neglect of the base rate.

---

10. I owe the analogy with "the paradox of the preface" to Tad Brennan.

## NEGLECT OF THE BASE RATE

According to the heuristics and biases programme, we neglect base rate information in favour of information that is "available" to cognition or information that we (wrongly) take to be "representative".

> Over the past few years much experimental evidence has accumulated which indicates that people underutilize an important source of information in making predictions. That source is base-rate data, that is, prior probabilities, population proportions, or information about central tendencies in the outcome domain. The same evidence shows that intuitive predictions usually overutilize information about the target case, that is, the particular object or person about which predictions are made.
>
> — Nisbett and Ross 1980, pp. 142-43

In an experiment designed to demonstrate neglect of the base rate, 60 students and staff at Harvard Medical School were asked,

> If a test to detect a disease whose prevalence is 1/1000 has a false positive rate of 5 per cent, what is the chance that a person found to have a positive result actually has the disease, assuming you know nothing about the person's symptoms or signs?

Over half of the experimental subjects answered that the probability was 95 per cent, and only one-third of them gave the correct answer of 2 per cent.[11]

Again, alternative framing of the question produces very different results. In another study, Stanford undergraduates were told:

---

11. Gigerenzer p. 251, reporting A. Tversky and D. Kahneman, "Evidential Impact of Base Rates", in D. Kahneman, P. Slovic, and A. Tversky, *Judgment Under Uncertainty: Heuristics and Biases*, Cambridge, 1982, pp. 153-60.

> One out of 1000 Americans has disease X. A test has been developed to detect when a person has disease X. Every time the test is given to a person who has the disease, the test comes out positive. But sometimes the test also comes out positive when it is given to a person who is completely healthy. Specifically, out of every 1000 people who are perfectly healthy, 50 of them test positive for the disease.

They were then asked:

> Imagine we have assembled a random sample of 1000 Americans. They were selected by a lottery. Those who conducted the lottery had no information about the health status of any of these people. How many people who test positive for the disease will actually have the disease? . . . out of. . . .

The correct answer, "one out of 50 (or 51)" (2 per cent) was given by 76 per cent of participants.[12]

What explains the difference between these two results? The Harvard Medical School subjects who gave 95 per cent as the chance that a person who tested HIV positive was in fact HIV positive seem not to have been underestimating the importance of the base rate — at least not in the way that someone who assumes that the dark-skinned man walking down the street is a criminal is ignoring the base rate. This person knows that not every dark-skinned man is a criminal but ignores that information; the Harvard Medical School subjects, however, seem not to have understood that the 5 per cent false positive figure had anything to do with the population at all and to have thought that 5 per cent was the chance that this individual might test HIV-positive when he

12. Gigerenzer, pp. 251-54, reporting L. Cosmides and J. Tooby, "Are Humans Good Intuitive Statisticians After All? Rethinking Some Conclusions from the Literature on Judgment Under Uncertainty", in *Cognition* 58 (1996), pp. 1-73.

was not. Perhaps they didn't connect this single-event probability with the frequency or prevalence of HIV in the population, or perhaps they thought that the 5 per cent figure meant that of 100 people who test positive, 95 will in fact be HIV positive (that would be to confuse the rate of false positives with the sensitivity or "hit rate" of the test).[13]

So in at least the cases of overconfidence and neglect of the base rate, it looks as if our inferential errors are due to an unfamiliar information format, rather than to an inability to reason statistically. Our ability to reason using information in the natural frequency format in which we usually experience probabilities may be quite adequate for our purposes — except to the extent that we are increasingly given information, about our health, safety, educational success, and so on, in the unfamiliar formats in question.

One may wonder whether this sensitivity to information formats is evidence for or against our ability to predict accurately and use base rate information appropriately. One wouldn't say, of someone who couldn't solve multiplication problems using Roman numerals, but had to be given them using decimal numbers, that he didn't know how to multiply. On the other hand, one would say of a person who couldn't process English sentences in the passive voice, but had to be

13. Gigerenzer's explanations are different, but not incompatible: (i) that medical personnel might ignore base rate information because in their experience, a person who shows up for an HIV test is not randomly selected; (ii) that presenting the false positive rate as a percentage or relative frequency (5 per cent) conceals information about the base rate in the population, whereas ordinarily, people acquire frequency and base rate information as a package; (iii) that (as in the overconfidence case) people do not calculate single-event probability (in this case, the likelihood of the individual's being HIV-positive) on the basis of frequency (the prevalence of HIV in the population).

given them in the active voice, that he didn't know English. It is worth asking exactly what the competence with probabilistic reasoning is supposed to consist of. Does it, for example, involve a competence across information formats, or the ability to translate information from one format to another?

In any case, converting statistical information from difficult-to-manipulate probability or percentage formats into more user-friendly natural frequency formats (e.g. to translate information from the format given to the Harvard Medical School subjects into the format given to the Stanford undergraduate subjects) would seem to be a highly desirable reasoning skill. According to Gigerenzer, who has been designing tutorials to teach people how to effect these conversions, people can apply and retain their ability to reason using natural frequencies much better than they can formal statistical training.[14] To illustrate: if you are told that for a given cancer screening, the false positive rate is 10 per cent, the prevalence of the cancer 1 per cent, and the test's sensitivity 80 per cent, and then asked, what are the chances that someone who has tested positive actually has the cancer, Gigerenzer's tutorial teaches you to reason as follows: the prevalence figure tells you that 10 out of every 1,000 people have the cancer. The sensitivity figure tells you that 8 of these 10 will test positive for the cancer. The false positive test tells you that of the remaining 990 [who don't have the cancer], 99 will test positive. So how likely is it that the person who has tested positive will have the cancer? 8/(8 + 99), or less than 8 per cent.[15]

14. "Ecological intelligence" is discussed in Gigerenzer pp. 55-76. So we can use Bayesian reasoning in natural frequency formats by keeping track of: cases of evidence-borne-out and cases of evidence-not-borne out and dividing the former by the sum of the former and the latter.

15. However, Gigerenzer exaggerates in his *How to Make Cognitive Illusions Disappear*, pp. 241-66 — his own numbers show that the illusions do not completely disappear with reframing information in frequency formats.

So far, I have gone along with the assumption of the heuristics and biases programme that formal statistical reasoning is normative reasoning. But whereas the goal of statistical reasoning is accuracy in prediction, everyday reasoning is constrained by other goals as well as accuracy; for example, a simple result that is simple to use again,[16] or a speedy result, or even a result that others in the group will accept. Is it right to expect that in reasoning what to do we should first attain the accuracy required of statistical reasoning and then plug that information into deliberation? If an increase in accuracy on one inferential task can only be had at the price of a too-slow reaction time, or a neglect of the other practical tasks required for living one's life, then perhaps taking statistical reasoning as normative is repeating the mistake Aristotle convicted Plato of.

Compare two departments at Princeton University. Because of the "interview illusion" — the fact that job interviews give highly available information that trumps the more accurately predictive information provided by letters of recommendation, written work, etc. — the Princeton Philosophy Department do not interview job candidates. But the Princeton Psychology Department, although they accept that there is such a thing as the interview illusion, having done much of the work to establish it, continue to interview job candidates, on the grounds that doing so promotes departmental harmony. Which department's policy is the more practically rational? Perhaps the end of academic success is specified somewhat differently for each department: perhaps academic success in psychology requires greater collaboration and so greater departmental harmony than does academic

16. Gilbert Harman suggests this as one explanation for our preference for simplicity in theoretical explanations. "Practical Aspects of Theoretical Reasoning" in Alfred R. Mele and Piers Rawling (eds.), *The Oxford Handbook of Rationality*, Oxford, 2004, pp. 45-56.

success in philosophy. But in any case, the example shows that pursuing accuracy wherever possible may not be the most practically rational thing to do.

### Automaticity: A More Radical Challenge

So far, my discussion has tried to show that we may hope to improve our practical reasoning if we can better understand why we make the sorts of inferential errors we do. However, according to proponents of the "automaticity hypothesis" Bargh and Chartrand, the more fundamental mistake is to think of us as engaging in practical reasoning — well or badly — at all. For although

> much of contemporary psychological research is based on the assumption that people are consciously and systematically processing incoming information in order to construe and interpret their world and to plan and engage in courses of action

in fact

> . . . most of a person's everyday life is determined not by their conscious intentions and deliberate choices but by mental processes that are put into motion by features of the environment and that operate outside of conscious awareness and guidance. . . — Bargh and Chartrand 1999[17]

If this is right, then deliberation and decision, for long the focus of moral philosophers since Aristotle, do not properly characterize most of our practical behaviour: we are on automatic pilot in most respects and for most of the time that we act.

---

17. John Bargh and Tanya Chartrand, "The Unbearable Automaticity of Being", *American Psychologist* July 1999, pp. 462-79. For a thoughtful discussion of how we should think of the way normativity operates in lives mostly lived automatically, see Railton, Peter, "Normative Guidance" (2006), *Oxford Studies in Metaethics*, vol. 1, ed. Russ Shafer-Landau.

But what are the implications of this fact for the role practical rationality can play in our lives? One position, that of John Doris (*Skepticism about Persons*), is that if unconscious processes determine our behaviour, then rational processes, like reflection, deliberation, etc., are epiphenomenal — we may be able to come up with reasons for our actions, but they are post-hoc rationalizations.

Let us first consider some evidence cited in favour of the irrelevance of practical reasoning to our behaviour. Psychological studies on the behavioural effects of priming indicate that our behaviour is affected by environmental factors that subliminally produce in our minds the idea of some action or the other, which we then are likely to do. So, for example, 67 per cent of experimental subjects exposed to words related to rudeness in what they were told was a "language experiment" went on to interrupt in a later conversation, by contrast with only 16 per cent of subjects primed with "polite" and 38 per cent of subjects in a "control" condition.[18]

But even if most of our behaviour is prompted by causes to which we have no conscious access, it does not follow that we do not have control over that behaviour, or that the reasons we may produce for that behaviour are just post-hoc rationalizations. (I also doubt that the fact that we do not have infallible introspective awareness of these causes means that we have no conscious access.) To see this, we should think about the ways in which we may have control over our behaviour.

One way in which I can control my behaviour is by monitoring it as I go.[19] But — and this is the truth in the

18. John Bargh, Mark Chen and Lara Burrows, "Automaticity of Social Behavior: Direct Effects of Trait Construct and Stereotype Activation on Action", *Journal of Personality and Social Psychology* 71 (2), pp. 230-44 (1996), reported in Bargh and Chartrand 1999, p. 466.

19. Note that John Bargh defines control as experienced occurrent conscious control: he is talking about controlled processing, and →

automaticity hypothesis — it would take too many mental resources for us to monitor all of our behaviour all of the time and so most of our behaviour must be automatic. But I also control my behaviour by formulating explicit goals which rule out goal-undermining behaviour. (The ruling out would seem to happen consciously as well as unconsciously.) For example, we might ask whether someone interviewing for a position as a waiter or receptionist would be so vulnerable to the rudeness primes described above.

It seems that we also exert control over our automatic behaviour by instituting mental overrides to interrupt automatic behaviour upon receipt of certain kinds of information.[20] So, for example, knowing about the bystander effect, one can put in place overrides to interrupt one's ordinary reliance on others for having a correct grasp of the situation and for doing the right thing, in cases in which (for example) someone seems to be in great distress.

Now consider the case of behaviour in which no override is activated, my explicit goals don't affect what I do, and I am not consciously monitoring my behaviour. Is such behaviour

---

→ says that in controlled processing you are able to reflect on yourself processing; you experience yourself as the agent of your own behaviour; you experience yourself making the effort to process, and you are aware that automatic processes may be occurring and are motivated to be able to counteract them. See John Bargh, "The Four Horsemen of Automaticity: Awareness, Efficiency, Intention, and Control in Social Cognition", in R.S. Wyer Jr. and T.K. Surll (eds.), *Handbook of Social Cognition,* (2nd edn., pp. 1-40, Erlbaum, 1994.

20. H. Pashler, J. Johnston and E. Ruthruff, "Attention and Performance", *Annual Review of Psychology* 52 (2001), pp. 629-51 discuss the related idea of "off-line control"; the recent studies they review indicate that top-down goals influence the intake of external stimuli without conscious monitoring, just as a thermostat's setting turns the furnace on only when the temperature falls below a certain level.

in my control or not? Bargh and Chartrand themselves acknowledge that there are two routes to the development of automatic processes: behaviours may be first-time automatic responses to current environmental stimuli or they may have become automatic through consistent and frequent repetition of mental-process/situation pairings (e.g. through habituation and practice). These differences in history seem relevant to whether the automatic behaviour we are considering is in our control, and indeed the result of intention and deliberation, or not. Behaviour that originates in an agent's decision and becomes unconscious and automatic as a result of the adoption of a policy is surely a central case of intentional behaviour, behaviour that is in our control. From the agent's point of view, the disappearance of conscious choice is not a loss of control but its victory. For example, an agent whose table manners now unreflectively and automatically conform to bourgeois European etiquette due to a past decision to develop such manners surely has not lost control over his table manners. Automaticity may entail loss of control if we are engaging in behaviour that has no historical connection to any decision or intention on our part, or in behaviour that we could not consciously endorse. But this is not the case with consciously chosen behaviours that become second nature as a result of practice.

Interestingly, agents engage in situationally driven automatic behaviour of a sort they do not or would not endorse much less if they have previously articulated reasons for behaving in the ways they do endorse. So, in one experiment, participants in one group were asked to list reasons for and against treating people equally (in a "test of abstract writing skills"), while participants in another group were merely primed with words related to equality (in an anagram-solving task) and participants in a third group underwent no manipulation. Subsequently (in a "test of decision-making"), each of these groups was divided into a "red" and a "blue" team and asked to play a round of 20 questions at the beginning of which they were to assign future "red" and "blue" teams a number of initial points. If they gave more points to future players on their own colour-team, they received more points themselves. The participants who had listed reasons for treating people equally showed much less in-group favouritism [M=4.08] than did a control group [M=6.75] and a group primed with equality-related words [M=7.02], even though the groups did not differ in how important a value they took equality to be.[21]

If articulating reasons enables people to withstand situational effects, then one might expect that people who have articulated reasons for behaving in one way (e.g. politely) would continue to act politely when primed with words suggesting the opposite behaviour (the rudeness-related words), and the size of such an effect might be of considerable impact for understanding the behavioural relevance of automaticity *vs.* rational control.

One might raise another worry about habituated automatic responses, though, and this is that automatic responses, whatever their history, are not as sensitive to situational

---

21. Maio, Olson, Allen and Bernard (2001), "Addressing Discrepancies between Values and Behavior: The Motivating Effect of Reasons", *Journal of Experimental Social Psychology*, 37, pp. 104-17. We might raise some worries about this study: what counts as a reason? (It looks as if everything countenanced as a reason is instrumental.) Further, is it a failing of the subjects that they lack cognitive support for some of their values? Musn't justification come to an end at some point? Finally, is the phenomenon of greater belief-behaviour consistency among those who have articulated reasons for their beliefs about value due to the increased cognitive support they now have for their values? Or does reason-giving just have a polarizing effect?

specificities, and especially specific differences from past situations, as morality requires. Perhaps the criterion of right action is the principle of utility, and the habit of helping your neighbour becomes less and less a contributor to overall utility as your neighbour becomes better and better off. But being automatic, your helping-your-neighbour behaviour may well continue when the morally right thing to do is clearly (and it would be clear to you if you were reasoning about it) to help the distant poor. This may be an inadequacy we just have to live with, and make the best of by engaging in periodic personal policy reviews. It may be a reason to believe that even the best life will contain regrets about particular actions.

**Conclusion**

The improvements in practical reasoning that I have been collecting here — training in converting information into natural sampling formats, monitoring and preparing overrides for behavioural-determinants anticipated to be problematic, periodic policy reviews — do not (and wouldn't even if I'd collected more of them) add up to the kind of perception-like sensitivity to whatever is ethically salient that is often associated with Aristotle. Aristotle does, of course, think that the virtuous person takes pleasure in things of genuine value, and that the virtuous person's motivations are characterized by harmony. But it doesn't follow that deliberation — reasoning about what to do, what means to adopt to one's ends — of which practical wisdom is the excellence is effortless or indeed unnecessary. What does follow is that a virtuous person won't chafe at the means identified by practical wisdom as the means to her end. So, for example, it may take quite a bit of thought for your virtuous and practically wise friend to determine the best way to support you when you have just lost a loved one. What it seems has to be spontaneous, or "automatic", on her part is wanting to do the best thing she can to support you, and picking up on your various needs through careful observation and empathetic identification. Her thinking about what to do might have the character of perception not in that she immediately and effortlessly determines which actions are called for in the situation, but instead in that it involves the activation of an already well-developed disposition to attend to a bereaved friend's concerns — whatever that involves. Rather than being undermined by empirical findings about perennial weaknesses in human reasoning, an Aristotelian ideal of virtuous character can be informed by empirical findings about the ways in which we can improve as reasoners.

# 10

# Negotiating Practical Identities

*Meena Dhanda*

PRACTICAL identities are unstable. They change. There is no halo of permanence and immutability around them. Even so, my practical identities constrain what is morally possible for me. Further, people are known to take up arms, kill others, or die for the sake of their identity! Struggles for identity fuel resistance and rebellion; sacrifice and martyrdom too are offered for the sake of identity. When seen from the point of view of the one who puts her life on stake, we encounter different layers of meaning of the elusive term "identity". An identifiable person, with *a* name, sometimes stigmatized, undergoes changes — in personality and in bodily comportment — through ageing, through accidents of circumstance, through multifold requirements of practical life, through aesthetic self-fashioning and through transformative protest. This is one meaning of identity: negotiating the continuous process of becoming different.

A different meaning of the term identity comes into play in differentiating a person from non-persons. A person's identity makes her a member of a special class of beings, whose specialness is marked in one or another way by consciousness, the ability to feel pain, to communicate, to reflect, to formulate projects and to form relationships amongst other features. In what follows I first develop the notion of *moral identity* to mark this specialness of persons along the lines that what makes someone a person, thereby a member of a special class of beings, is the exercise of their ability to respond to others *as* persons.

I then introduce the idea of *practical identity* as a constellation of negotiated roles, some of which people *identify with* alongside others they are constrained to inhabit. Finally, I explain the relationship between moral identity and practical identities, and argue for a conceptualization of identities as negotiated (Dhanda 2008a).

## What I Mean by Moral Identity

Moral identity is the identity of the person *as a person*. It is expressed in the values one holds dear. These are values that, all other things remaining the same, a person would not set up for bargaining. One's moral identity in my sense:

(i) sets the limits of what one may do,

(ii) guides one's choices within those limits and thus,

(iii) defines what it is for one to act in character.

Moral identity is a necessary identity of persons. It is clear then that I take moral identity to be the sense of one's own identity as a person as such. It is the sense of oneself as a person, as a being who exercises her/his ability to respond to others as persons.

A comparison with the use of the term "moral identity" by some other thinkers might be of help to specify the meaning I propose.

## Is Moral Identity about the Kind of Character One Has?

Someone's "moral identity", in my usage, is not to be understood in terms of whether that person is, say, generally speaking modest or indecent, courageous or cowardly, charitable or selfish. Amelie Rorty (1993) has pointed at the importance of this way of talking about persons' identities, which shows the way in which social morality is tied up with the identification of persons as having such and such a moral character. This is not what I mean by "moral identity". I do not mean by it the "type" of person someone is. In my analysis, concerns about being cowardly or courageous are tied to one's location and hence are an aspect of one's practical identity. One's moral identity defines what it is to act in character (as when one asks: am I being myself?) it does not specify any particular kind of character, e.g. moral as opposed to an immoral character. It does not tell whether one is a "courageous type" or "cowardly type" of person. Because of the way in which moral identity and practical identity are linked together, there is no context-free way of talking about the type of person someone is.

### Is One's Moral Identity One's Singularity or Uniqueness as a Person?

My view also differs from the diametrically opposite position to the above, namely that by moral identity is meant that which resists typecasting persons. Respecting someone's moral identity on such a view would be recognizing their uniqueness. It would highlight the difference, as Bernard Williams says, between loving Mary and loving someone exactly like her.[1] It may equally be brought out in the difference that underlies the first-person concern that one be loved for oneself rather than for the qualities that one has. Someone else may have many of the qualities that one has, perhaps in an even more refined and pronounced a measure than oneself. If qualities were loved and not the person herself then someone else might be deserving of more love. But it can hardly be accepted as love of oneself, if it may be conferred on another with greater justification. And, so it may be argued that moral identity is

---

1. This uniqueness for Williams is provided by one's unique bodily identity.

not qualitative. It is the foundation of acknowledging each person as a unique person. Typecasting denies the individuality of persons, and moral identity provides the basis for resistance to it. While close to my own view, this foundational view of moral identity too is unsuitable as an articulation of the sense in which I use the term "moral identity". The main reason for differing with what I am calling the "foundational view" is that, according to my analysis, one's moral identity is subject to the constraints of negotiation in which there may be times when it is justified to identify with a practical identity that may appear to involve a denial of one's moral identity. On the foundational view, such a denial could never be justified.

### Does Moral Identity Rest in Fundamental Commitments or "Ground Projects"?

There is the view espoused by Bernard Williams that moral identity consists in an "internal" necessity to act and live and follow certain projects.[2] Should chance or necessity radically change these projects, one could be robbed of the very core of one's being. One's moral identity, on this view, is sustained by living a life one considers to be worthy of oneself. What in fact makes a life worthy of oneself may be a range of factors not all of which are mutually supportive. But the variety of worth-conferring projects is not of itself held to be of any consequence, unless it leads to a situation where the (dis)joint(ed) pursuit of conflicting projects, each worthy in themselves, poses a threat to the very integrity of the subject.

The most extreme form of the threat to moral identity of the subject on this view is manifest in the reduction of the subject to a mere object in the hands of other subjects. Chance, social necessity or irrational ambition may place one in such a calamitous state of affairs. Since it could happen that a

2. I take this to be Bernard Williams' view in Williams 1993, which he labels as "Necessary Identities".

particular life becomes unworthy of living from the point of view of one who is constrained to live it, it is clear that there is a question of identity involved here. Such a "metamorphosis" is well exemplified in the most feared prospect of life in ancient times, the prospect of a free person becoming a slave (Williams 1993: 108). The opposite change, from being in someone's power to becoming a subject of rights, is no less drastic, though it cannot for obvious reasons be described as a loss of worth, or as being "robbed of the very core of one's being". A comparison of the two movements in opposite directions shows that on Williams' view the loss of the subject status is not simply the linear opposite of the loss of the "object" status. In the one case, the change in the social identity (from being free to being a slave) involves a diminution of moral identity. In the other case, the change in social identity (from being a slave to being free) is the acquiring of a new moral identity. This new moral identity brings with it a new sense of "ownness".

On Williams' view of identity, a slave does not have a moral identity to begin with, and only acquires one through the process of becoming a free person, while the free person, on being taken into captivity as a slave, is increasingly brought under pressure and threatened with erosion of his moral identity by the changed circumstances of his life. Clearly, in this circumstance having a moral identity is having the status of a subject, and not simply figuring as an object in the lives of other subjects. It is only as a subject that one has the "internal" necessity to act and live in a way that one can be a subject in the eyes of other subjects.

My use of the term "moral identity" does not emphasize the importance of "freedom" in having a moral identity, rather it takes "responsiveness" to be central. In my view, even in captivity, slaves have moral identities, to the extent that they are capable of responding to others' acknowledgement or lack of acknowledgement of them.

To summarize the differences between my view of moral identity and those of others, I should say the following. First, I do not mean by moral identity a full-bodied characterization of a person's identity, in terms of her manner of conducting herself in moral matters. Likewise, while the uniqueness of a person is important to personal identity, that too is not what gives one a moral identity in my sense of the term. Finally, being an autonomous subject, while providing a basis for self-worth, and hence to some degree, for moral identity, is not the core of moral identity for me.

**How Does One Acquire a Moral Identity?**

One way of coming to understand what it means to have a moral identity is to note the passage from being a child to becoming an adult. As adult human beings we seek the recognition and love of others. But when does our wish to be loved become a concern? Our wish to be loved can be traced back to our very early childhood, but our concern grows out of more complex understandings. It is only when we have a self-understanding and judge ourselves to be fit objects of love that we can begin to expect others to love us. It is only when we are in a position to judge that our expectation is not being met, that the lack of love becomes a concern. Being afraid of loss of love, which is a primordial sentiment, and being concerned that one is not loved are two different matters. Somewhere in the interim period we move from fear to self-concern, from feelings to self-understanding. This passage could be called the acquiring of a moral identity.

Moral identity is the identity of a person as such. It is not a matter of degree. There may be some temptation for introducing degrees of moral identity at the early stages of a human life, in line with the attribution of degrees of personhood[3] in this learning phase. Leaving aside the question

3. See Parfit 1985.

of uncertain boundaries, at least beyond the very early stages of a child's upbringing into becoming a member of society, a person necessarily has a moral identity.

In the early stages, as the child gradually acquires linguistic skills she learns to make comparisons, to show discrimination, to make judgements and to be corrected. Language acquisition is the prime mode of being moralized (in the sense of moral identity that I am using here). In the very practice of orderly speech, using words to mean something, a child learns several things. In repeating after an adult, the child learns discipline. In noticing similarities and differences, the child learns discrimination. The child also learns freedom and the use of imagination in asking questions, and in venturing to anticipate answers. When the child succeeds in communicating, she learns trust. When she fails, she learns struggle.[4] Thus, the complex activity of language-acquisition, and creative imagination together constitute the basic materials from which a moral being is fashioned[5] (Tugendhat 1993; Noam and Wren 1993).

The next step in my argument is to introduce the concept of practical identity. An explanation of what I mean by

---

4. Some theorists, mostly psychoanalysts, such as for example Lacan, would say that in entering the linguistic world a child also suffers repression. But this is not contrary to my claim that the child acquires moral identity, because for these theorists, acquiring moral identity is precisely the process of being repressed. A contrary view is Ernest Tugendhat's, who writes that "children are socialized into all sorts of special skills, they are also being socialized into one fundamental skill, which is the skill of behaving as a member of the community, or more generally, as a member of society" (Tugendhat, 1993: 5).
5. I should like to add here that I agree with Williams that the explanation of our human disposition to see ethical similarities in different cases, necessary to make ethical judgement, "does not lie in postulating a stateable rule, which the respondent has internalized and unconsciously consults" (Williams 1985: 98).

practical identity is followed by a critical appraisal of Christine Korsgaard's arguments with a view to highlighting the difference in our positions on "practical identity".

## What I Mean by Practical Identity

My practical identity is a disjunction of roles, which normally form an ordered constellation. Each of these roles may be radically questioned, redefined or even opted out of, at different times but all of these cannot be side-stepped or given up altogether. There is a complex reason for this. Practical identities cannot be given up altogether because in becoming a person one's life is embedded in norm-governed interpersonal relations, both institutional as well as non-institutional. One must be seen as following these norms, in order to sustain those relationships. These norms define, for example, what it is to be a mother, an employee, or a citizen, within respective institutional frameworks and practices. When the institutions are in flux and practices themselves are in tension, practical identities may generate conflicts. For instance, lack of childcare support, institutional or familial, may generate the conflict for a woman between being a mother and being an employee.

By "practical identity" I also mean what one provisionally identifies with. Using the language of roles it could be said that at any point of time one may be identified with and be identified as having different roles to play. Not all of my practical identities are necessarily endorsed by me. Even so, I may act from these identities tied to my location, reluctantly, resentfully or simply nonchalantly.

One may have several actual or potential practical identities at any one point of time. One may be a mother, a philosopher, a national of a particular country, a person with a particular sexual orientation, a speaker of a particular mother tongue, a member of a particular social class and so on. These are practical identities in that they locate one's actions within limitations and boundaries set by habit, conventions and rules of established practices. One's actions and one's projects spring from one's orientation within the practical world of limited choice-making. Likewise, one's judgement of others' actions is guided by one's understanding of this practical world.

Seeing practical identities in this way shows why loss of a job, breakdown of a relationship, or loss of one's citizenship are seen as threats to one's identity. An appropriate response when someone says "I am no longer the same person" would be to ask, as indeed we normally do ask in these circumstances, "Why? What has happened? What has made you feel this way?" It is a change in their orientation in the practical sphere that we expect. If we take identity to be matter of identification with a higher-order self, as Charles Taylor and Harry Frankfurt do, then changes brought on by practical upheavals need not be experienced as a threat to one's identity.

### Christine Korsgaard on "Practical Identity": A Critical Appraisal

Christine M. Korsgaard has effectively used a comparable notion of "practical identity" to the one I am employing. She writes:

> for most human beings on most occasions, the only thing that could be as bad or worse than death is something that for us amounts to death — not being ourselves anymore.
>
> — Korsgaard 1996: 17-18

According to Korsgaard, our human or moral identity induces our obligation to other people. However, she argues that in order to understand how and why ethical concepts have a grip on me I must appreciate the mediating role of my practical identity.[6] This is how she defines practical identity:

---

6. Her earlier work was a pertinent attack on the move to undermine the notion of identity by the use of metaphysical arguments; there →

> The conception of one's identity in question here is not a theoretical one, a view about what as a matter of inescapable scientific fact you are. It is better understood as a description under which you value yourself, a description under which you find your life to be worth living and your actions to be worth undertaking. So I will call this a conception of your practical identity. — Korsgaard 1996: 101

The key contrast for Korsgaard is between the theoretical conception and the practical conception one has of who one is. The conception of practical identity that I am putting forward is not one with a unifying force for the person because there are plural practical identities and not all of them are value-conferring. I think that we may value ourselves under some practical identities because we are identified with them, but many are just given. These practical identities may serve to prohibit certain actions for me, but not necessarily with the force of an obligation that I "must" obey. They may issue nothing more than commands, which I may even have moral reason to disobey. For example, mutual trust within relationships is one such command, which I may have reason to disobey in an exploitative relationship.[7]

If it comes to a clash, Korsgaard says,

> it is better for us to think of ourselves, and more essentially

---

→ she reminded us of the "practical" basis of identity (Korsgaard 1989).

7. Annette Baier is exceptional in arguing that betrayal of trust may even be a moral response in some situations, for example, she writes:

> When the trust relationship itself is corrupt and perpetuates brutality, tyranny, or injustice, trusting may be silly self-exposure, and disappointing and betraying trust, including encouraged trust, may not be merely morally permissible but morally praiseworthy. Women, proletarians, and ex-slaves cannot ignore the virtues of watchful distrust and of judicious untrustworthiness. — Baier 1995: 120

> to value ourselves, just as human beings than, say, as men or women, or as members of certain religious or ethnic groups, or as the possessors of certain talents.
>
> — Korsgaard 1996: 117

I do not agree with this general approach of making our moral identity as human beings trump our particular practical identities because what it is to be a human being may itself come under question in situations of conflict. Here I am in agreement with Richard Rorty (1989): it is a mistake to presuppose a fixed idea of what it is to be a human being. Sometimes, if one holds on to a practical identity in the face of conflict with whatever is the accepted notion of being human in one's community, one may bring to the fore a valuable, though hitherto unacknowledged, aspect of humanity. If we are evolving creatures, then new circumstances and new conflicts may generate new capabilities of expressing humanity. That, in my view, is a sufficient reason to be suspicious that it is "better" for us to think of ourselves "just as human beings".

For Korsgaard, conflicts between practical identities may in some cases lead one to discard a particular practical identity. All conceptions of practical identity are contingent in this sense, but "What is not contingent is that you must be governed by some conception of practical identity" (1996: 120).

Korsgaard draws the questionable conclusion that our identity as moral beings "stands behind" (1996: 121, 129) our more particular practical identities. She also makes a guarded comment about the respective places of moral and practical identity in our lives, in that "Moral identity does not swamp other forms of identity: no one is simply a moral agent and nothing more" (1996: 125). She grants that consideration of myself as a legislative member of the Kingdom of Ends is one among many descriptions under which I can value myself. Nevertheless, according to her, it is our moral identity that gives worth to any practical identity. She is quite emphatic in stating that "Practical conceptions of your identity which are fundamentally inconsistent with the value of humanity must be given up" (1996: 130). The example she briefly mentions in this context is that of an "assassin". Being an assassin would be ruled out, she argues, because in so far as this identity derives its importance from the value of humanity, it "does not make sense to identify oneself in ways that are inconsistent with the value of humanity" (1996: 126). But such an example is precisely what should lead us to question whether a "practical identity" derives its importance from the value of humanity in the first place. It is more likely the case that the importance of a "practical identity" for a person derives from upbringing, habit, or simply from some practical necessity.[8]

### The Importance of Practical Identity

The conception of practical identity I have developed has a mediating potential between rival theoretical accounts of moral identity. Ironists, like Rorty (1989) and Appiah (1996), while arguing against any essential identification, have reason to welcome the element of practicality in identification. Communitarians, while rejecting the implication that value-conferring identifications possess a merely "practical" validity, have reason to welcome the element of self-identification. Feminists, standing on both sides of the divide, have reason to welcome the idea of practical identity because it makes the force of moral demands depend upon lives that are actually lived and not merely upon those imagined or idealized by people (Benhabib 1992; Nicholson 1996; Young 1990, 1994).

An early feminist insistence on the practical is evident in the following response from Simone de Beauvoir, when asked in an interview about how to determine "real" change in a man's sexist ways:

---

8. We are partly led to chase or reject certain practical identities because of the imprints we carry from our childhood, as Freud suggests.

**Gerassi**. But is it real? I mean. I've learned, for example, never to use the word "chick", to pay attention to women in any group discussion, to wash dishes, clean the house, do the shopping. But am I any less sexist in my thoughts? Have I rejected the male values?

**Beauvoir**. You mean inside you? To be blunt, who cares? Think for a minute. You know a racist Southerner. You know he's racist because you've known him all his life. But now he never says "nigger". He listens to all black men's complaints and tries to do his best to deal with them. He goes out of his way to put down other racists. He insists that black children be given a better-than-average education to offset the years of no education. He gives references for black men's loan applications. He backs the black candidates in his district both with money and his vote. Do you think the blacks give a damn that he's just as much a racist now as before "in his soul"? A lot of the objective exploitation is habit. If you can check your habits, make it so that it's "natural" to have counterhabits, that's a big step. If you wash dishes, clean house, and take the attitude that you don't feel any less "a man" for doing it, you're helping to set up new habits. A couple of generations feeling that they have to appear non-racist at all times, and the third generation will grow up non-racist in fact. So play at being non-sexist, and keep playing. Think of it as a game. In your private thoughts, go ahead and think of yourself as superior to women. But as long as you play convincingly — that you keep washing dishes, shopping, cleaning the house, taking care of children — you're setting precedents, especially men like you who have a certain macho "pose". The trouble is, I don't believe it. I don't think you really keep doing what you say. It's one thing to wash dishes; it's another to change diapers day in, day out. — Gerassi 1976

The key moment to pause for thought is when Beauvoir says:

"The trouble is, I don't believe it". On the one hand, it is difficult to believe that a well-intentioned man could give up a sexist practical identity simply by choosing to do so, when everything around him conspires to remind him of the benefits of sexism. On the other hand, should he actually succeed in playing at being non-sexist, in my terminology, if he succeeds in sustaining the practical identity of "a non-sexist man", according to Beauvoir, it matters little what he thinks "in his soul". What he does is more important than what he thinks. My slight disagreement with her, deriving from my work on dalits' experience of pervasive discrimination is that in a clash of practical identities, attempts to sustain counter-habits through the process of complex negotiations of practical identities risk being jeopardized without the support of deep commitments. Merely playing at being non-casteist without foundational beliefs of human equality is vulnerable to being unsettled when the going gets tough. A non-sexist, non-racist and non-casteist manner of being is practically very demanding.

## Identity as an Outcome of Negotiation

I shall attempt in the remainder of this chapter to offer a new description of the notion of personal identity. My aim is to do some justice to the concern with identity of individuals, belonging to groups whose members have been compelled for various reasons of historical "chance", "necessity", or design, as the case may be, to re-evaluate their standing as individuals. In some cases these individuals have been systematically divested of their standing. In other cases they have been threatened by the loss of any standing that they may have achieved. They live under the constraint of continually confronting the pessimistic prospect of never gaining an equal standing in the larger society in which they have managed to survive. I have in mind members of different oppressed collectivities, particularly dalits in the Indian context.

### Why Talk of Negotiation?

Charles Taylor (1989) helpfully reminds us that our deepest moral intuitions are interlinked with our notions about "what it is to be a human being, a person or a self". An important task of a moral philosopher must be to explore the "background picture" lying behind our moral and spiritual intuitions. It is clear that Taylor commits himself to just such a task when he writes that:

> my target is the moral ontology which articulates these intuitions. What is the picture of our spiritual nature and predicament which makes sense of our responses? "Making sense" here means articulating what makes these responses appropriate: identifying what makes something a fit object for them and correlatively formulating more fully the nature of the response as well as spelling out what all this presupposes about ourselves and our situation in the world.
>
> — Taylor 1989: 8

Fuelling this enterprise is the belief that it is possible to share an understanding of, and to rationally argue about, ontological claims. Richard Rorty, in contrast, has a way of doing philosophy whereby:

> The method is to redescribe lots and lots of things in new ways, until you have created a pattern of linguistic behaviour which will tempt the rising generation to adopt it, thereby causing them to look for appropriate new forms of non-linguistic behaviour. . . . This sort of philosophy . . . works holistically and pragmatically. It says things like "try thinking of it this way" — or more specifically, "try to ignore the apparently futile traditional questions by substituting the following new and possibly interesting questions."
>
> — Rorty 1989: 9

The picture of intellectual and moral progress on this view is one of "a history of increasingly useful metaphors rather than of increasing understanding of how things really are".

Both the pictures in their extremity and exclusiveness, if I may put it that way, are not very helpful, either for the purpose of understanding "better" or for the purpose of "attracting" followers. Taylor's picture of seeking to unravel underlying structures of our moral intuitions and our view of what it is to be human promises a false finality, a promise of arriving home. Such a promise cannot be truthful (and "truth" is what he must surely want) to the actual process of negotiating an identity, which is shot through with uncertainties and attendant tentativeness.

In contrast, Rorty's picture is so imbued with the spirit of playfulness, that it robs the identity-making enterprise of its seriousness. Therefore, it cannot be very attractive to the persons who struggle to search and keep/preserve their identity, sometimes to the point of sacrificing their lives in the endeavour.

A corrective is thus needed: a middle way. One needs a fusing of the concerns of both, searching for identity and making it. At the outset there may seem to be no way of doing this at the same time. What I am attempting, therefore, is to offer a description of negotiations of personal identity in the Rortian way, which in the course of its elaboration, I hope, will make an appeal to the "truth" of structures seen as underlying concerns for identity, somewhat in Charles Taylor's way.

The idea that I have tried to make use of is that of negotiation. Identity, as I understand it, is something that one negotiates. It is at once a process and the (tentative) end of a process, a path of struggle punctuated by resting points in it. Negotiation in its literal meanings is both cutting out a path for oneself and bargaining with others, from a standpoint with which one identifies, for a better, more acceptable agreement than one currently has.

Where does "truth" come in this? And where is the "play"? There are several points of entry of the ideal of truth into negotiation, but one, which has already been indicated by the literal meanings of negotiation above, is in the sense of direction that must accompany any cutting out of a path. The overall direction must be regulated by the ideal of "truth", if any negotiation is to lead to a (tentative) conclusion. An analogy might help to understand this following of directions.

Imagine going to a new area in your town/city, or to a new village near your own. You have to meet a friend whose new address you do not have. You cannot use a map to reach the new address because the names of streets have changed since your friend lived there. You need to have an overall idea of the direction in which the area where your friend once lived, lies. You can use a map or a compass (think of rules, institutions) to head in that direction, but you cannot risk going too far on the basis of the direction alone, for you may shoot out of the relevant area. What is the way to get around the problem? Quite simply, once you are in the broadly specified relevant area, you ask around.

Being guided by "truth" as a regulative idea is analogous to heading for a loosely specified area that once might have been more specifically identified, and hence provided a definite goal, but which is now only a possible focal point. The other analogy is between the way we arrive at the "truth" and the possible ways that could be employed in our imaginary search for the new address. One can either narrow down the search area, heading for it with the use of efficient means such as maps and compasses, or one can expand the search area, and once in it, use more primitive means of finding out. The first way has a higher probability of hitting or alternatively missing altogether, but it is admittedly a quicker and easier way. The second way is more tentative, tedious, frustrating and might seem interminable, but it has, in the long run, if the long run is possible, less likelihood of being an outright failure.

I think that the second way reflects better the regulative idea of "truth" in struggles for identity than the first way. It also fits better the meaning of negotiation, as a cutting through of a path. The slack in certainty may be taken up by perseverance and a willingness to follow, if need be, a zig-zag rather than a straight path.

The second strand of the meaning of negotiation, of bargaining for a better, more acceptable agreement, reflects the "play" in settling for an identity. It is important to give an account of how negotiation in this way is possible. I suggest that the key to an account lies in the constitutive role that language plays in the acquisition of an identity/identities.

The idea that language plays a constitutive role in the acquisition of identity is common to both Taylor (1989) and Rorty (1989). Only the manner in which language constitutes us is conceived of differently by both. Here's my own version of the role, a version that, I think, explains better, makes more sense, and — as Rorty might describe it — is more attractive to me.

We have at least a double relation to language. We learn to describe things, in terms of the language of truth and falsity, reality and appearance, goodness and badness. But we also learn to establish our relation to the world by the evocative use of language. Here playing on ambiguity, make-belief, deceit and fantasy all have a role to play. Together, both aspects of our relation to language offer us a mixed bag of resources, which contribute to the negotiation and re-negotiation of a person's identity. In using the idea of negotiation, it becomes necessary to re-describe the concept of the "given" on the one hand and that of the "alterable" on the other. There are limits to what may or may not become the subject of negotiation at any given point of time. Altered relations of power shift those limits too.

## An Example: Women Negotiating

What women are negotiating for in a particular instance may be more complex than is apparent in the policies that are issued on their behalf. The crisis following upon the French government's decision to impose the unveiling of Muslim girls in schools in France, is an interesting example of a complex negotiation of identities though not for the first time in recent French history. Franz Fanon[9] writes about an earlier, murkier period:

> After the 13th of May, the veil was resumed, but stripped once and for all of its exclusively traditional dimension.

Fanon underscores the "historic dynamism of the veil", which has been "a mechanism of resistance":

> The veil was worn not only because tradition demanded a rigid separation of the sexes, but also because the occupier *was bent on unveiling Algeria*. . . . The veil was abandoned in the course of revolutionary action. What had been used to block the psychological or political offensives of the occupier became a means, an instrument. The veil helped the Algerian woman to meet the new problems created by the struggle.
>
> The colonialists are incapable of grasping the motivations of the colonized. It is the necessities of combat that gave rise to new attitudes, to new modes of action, to new ways.
>
> — Fanon 1989

The adoption, the abandonment and the re-emergence of the veil is a striking example of the negotiation of practical identities of women that I have explored more fully elsewhere (Dhanda 2008b).

---

9. See "Chapter I: Algeria Unveiled", in *Studies in a Dying Colonialism*, rev. edn., London: Earthscan Publications, 1989, pp. 35-67.

### General Presuppositions of Negotiation of Identity

The first presupposition to note is that anyone undertaking a negotiation must grant that prior to the negotiation, there is no settled view about what the final outcome of the negotiation will be. Without this presupposition there cannot be a genuine negotiation. In the context of negotiating for an identity, this implies a degree of "openness" about what one might end up identifying with.

Connected with the first, the second presupposition is that there is no finality about the outcome of negotiation. Unlike a quest, the point of negotiation is not to establish an essential meaning but to arrive as acceptable agreements. All accepted agreements in one location may turn out to be unacceptable at another location. Thus, the need for negotiation and further re-negotiation may arise endlessly.

The third presupposition is that there are some givens, from which the negotiation begins. In the context of identity, I suggest that we think of the "given" as that which defines one's "practical identity". Our practical identities locate us in a particular time and place. All our negotiations for identity must proceed from this location.

The fourth presupposition is that negotiation takes place between real people. When we negotiate for our identities it is not "ideas", "moralities" or "powers" that confront each other, but embodied people. Of course, embodied people may and do negotiate for the sake of ideas, moralities and powers. One important aspect of this presupposition is that not only the objective of a negotiation, but also characteristics of the particular embodiment of negotiators enter into the negotiation. Their strength of purpose, their willingness to meet halfway, their anger and their satisfactions are expressed in the bodily comportment of the negotiators (Young 1990a). Paying attention to these expressions is as important for the outcome of negotiations as paying attention to what is said. If one were to take negotiations as merely confrontations of "ideas" or "moralities" or "powers", then one would fail to engage with this bodily aspect of negotiation, especially relevant in the case of stigmatized identities, as is the case of dalits (Guru 2009).

Thinking about negotiation as taking place between embodied agents brings the differences between the relations each person has to their practical world into the picture. Being a man or a woman, being young or being old, being black or being white, are aspects of one's embodiment that crucially alter one's relation to the world. Any negotiation of identity that ignores this fact and takes persons as merely repositories of "ideas", "moralities" or "powers" either remains ineffective or may even be counter-productive.[10]

The fifth presupposition is that there are always some limits within which negotiations take place. Not everything is negotiable at the same level. In order for a negotiation to take place at one level, an agreement about what would be non-negotiable at that level must be negotiated at a higher level. Of interest to us for negotiation of identity is the limit on negotiation placed by one's moral identity. Since, one's moral identity is expressed through one's practical identities, if only one practical identity remains the operative one, then that becomes the non-negotiable identity.

Finally, in the sense that negotiation for an identity is "a cutting through of a path", there is a presupposition that our

---

10. Philip Roth's Coleman Silk, in *The Human Stain* does not ignore the fact of his being black; he actively hides it. The success of his negotiation of a different practical identity (he re-creates himself as a Jew), based no doubt on his lies, depends upon how things outside his control turnout. Luckily for Coleman, his children turn out not to be black, and his secret remains safe as long as he lives. See Roth 2000.

identities are reiterated only in the face of obstacles. If it was possible to live a life of identification with whatever it was that one identified with, in other words, if there was no obstacle to one being whatever one cared to be, there would be no need for a negotiation. That there is negotiation for identity presupposes that there are obstacles to one's living according to one's identifications. But that is not to suggest that all conflicts between one's practical identities could one day finally be eliminated through some utopian reorganization of society. This ineliminability of conflict is not an expression of pessimism. Identities are negotiated in situations of conflict. In a world with fewer conflicts, there would be fewer concerns with identity. Struggles for identity are so many signs of the wrongs of this world. However, struggles for identity may be aimed at setting the wrongs right and therefore, must not themselves, be seen as wrong. To the extent that a world with fewer conflicts would be a better world than a conflict-ridden one, we should expect that if we were moving in the direction of that better world, some identities would no longer need to be negotiated. For example, in a world where feminine gender was no longer a handicap, women would not need to negotiate for their identity as women.

In Charles Taylor's account of the making of identity, "identity" is an honorific term. According to him, what is good about the modern concern with identity is that it expresses our aim to be authentic (Taylor 1992a). But I think that the concern with authenticity becomes a concern only when one's authenticity is challenged. Had we lived in a world where mutual respect and care could be taken for granted, and where self-expression in its many forms could be fearless, because it creates no risks, there would be no concern with authenticity. Only the fear of deception, the doubts about being misunderstood and the hurt of being unaccepted lead to the need to negotiate and to assert one's identity.[11]

Thus, until the conflicts themselves, over the sharing of resources and over unequal distributions of burdens are resolved, conflicts of identity will persist. As Bernard Williams helpfully puts it:

> Conflict, in particular ethical conflict, may be the appropriate response to some kinds of situations. If these situations are to be eliminated, it will be a matter not only (perhaps not mainly) of reforming the psyche, but of changing society. — Williams 1985: 47

The way to direct attention to problems of fair distribution that sometimes underpin struggles of identity is not to undermine negotiations of identity, as some thinkers, like Richard Rorty, suggest. Even if negotiations of identity are seen as a sign of other struggles, it may not be available to those involved in the negotiation for identity to wage those other struggles by any other means. In such a situation, to suggest that they must abandon the negotiation for identity amounts to asking them to abandon those other struggles as well.

It follows from the connection between moral and practical identity and the need for a non-negotiable practical identity that if one wants to negotiate for the displacement of a practical identity that is "too narrow", or not conducive to human flourishing, then the only way to do so will be to make available other practical identities through which one may express one's moral being.

---

11. Boxill 1995 describes how doubts about herself/himself lead a powerless but self-respecting person to "protest" and thus to assert and to affirm that she/he has rights. "When he has to endure wrongs he cannot repel and feels his self-respect threatened, he will publicly claim it in order to reassure himself that he has it." (Boxill 1995: 102)

Negotiations would not take place, if there was no struggle for power and recognition involved. But the play for power does not have to be unidirectional. Indeed it is a presupposition of entering into any negotiation that power differences affect all negotiators, although not in the same way or to the same degree. Pervasive power differences may leave less "play" for those who are the subordinates in a particular negotiation for identity. Acknowledgement of their practical identity might be one way of empowering those subordinates engaged in a negotiation. This, I think, is true of the practical identity of being a dalit, a case illustrative in many ways of the conceptualization of embodied identities through the framework of negotiation.

## References

Appiah, K.A. (1996), "Race, Culture and Identity: Misunderstood Connections", in *Tanner Lectures on Human Values* (Delivered on 27 & 28 October 1994) vol. 17 (Salt Lake City: University of Utah Press), 51-136.

Baier, A.C. (1990), "Why Honesty Is a Hard Virtue", in *Identity, Character, and Morality: Essays in Moral Psychology*, Cambridge: MIT Press.

——— (1995), *Moral Prejudices: Essays on Ethics*, Cambridge, Massachusetts: Harvard University Press.

Benhabib, S. (1992), *Situating the Self: Gender, Community and Postmodernism in Contemporary Ethics*, Cambridge: Polity Press.

Boxill, B.R. (1995), "Self-respect and Protest", in Robin S. Dillon (ed.), *Dignity, Character and Self-Respect*, London, New York: Routledge.

Gerassi, J. (1976), "The Second Sex 25 Years Later: An Interview with Simone de Beauvoir", *Society*, January-February (available at: http://www.marxists.org/reference/subject/ethics/de-beauvoir/1976/interview.htm).

Guru, G. (ed.) (2009), *Humiliation: Claims and Context*, New Delhi: Oxford University Press.

Dhanda, M. (2008a), *The Negotiation of Personal Identity*, Saarbrücken: VDM Verlag Dr Müller.

——— (2008b), "What does the hatred/fear of the veil hide?", *Ethnicity and Inequalities in Health and Social Care*, 1 (2) December: 53-57.

Fanon, F. (1989), *Studies in a Dying Colonialism*, rev. edn., London: Earthscan Publications.

Korsgaard, C.M. (1989), "Personal Identity and the Unity of Agency: A Kantian Response to Parfit", *Philosophy and Public Affairs*, 18 (2) Spring: 101-32.

——— (1996a), *The Sources of Normativity*, ed. Onora O'Neill, Cambridge: Cambridge University Press.

Nicholson, L.J. (1996), "To Be or Not to Be: Charles Taylor and the Politics of Recognition", *Constellations*, 3 (1), April: 1-16.

Noam, G.G. and T. Wren (eds.) (1993), *The Moral Self*, Cambridge: MIT Press.

Parfit, D. (1985), *Reasons and Persons*, Oxford: Oxford University Press.

Roth, P. (2000), *The Human Stain*, London: Jonathan Cape.

Rorty, A.O. and Owen Flanagan (eds.) (1993), *Identity, Character and Morality: Essays in Moral Psychology*, Cambridge, Massachussets: MIT Press.

Rorty, A.O. (1993), "What it takes to be good", in G.G. Noam and T.E. Wren (eds.), *The Moral Self*.

Rorty, R. (1989), *Contingency, Irony and Solidarity*, Cambridge: Cambridge University Press.

Taylor, Charles (1989), *Sources of the Self: The Making of the Modern Identity*, Cambridge: Cambridge University Press.

——— (1992a), *The Ethics of Authenticity*, Cambridge, Massachusetts: Harvard University Press.

——— (1992b), *Multiculturalism and 'The Politics of Recognition': An Essay by Charles Taylor* with commentary by Amy Gutmann (ed.) et al., New Jersey: Princeton University Press.

Tugendhat, E., (1993), "The Role of Identity in the Constitution of Morality", in G.G. Noam and T.E. Wren (eds.), *The Moral Self*, Cambridge: M.I.T Press.

Williams, B. (1981), *Moral Luck*, Cambridge: Cambridge University Press.

——— (1985), *Ethics and the Limits of Philosophy*, London: Fontana Press.

——— (1993), *Shame and Necessity*, Berkeley: University of California Press.

——— (2002), *Truth and Truthfulness: An Essay in Genealogy*, New Jersey: Princeton University Press.

Young, I. M. (1990), "The Ideal of Community and the Politics of Difference", in L. Nicholson (ed.), *Feminism/Postmodernism*, New York: Routledge.

——— (1990a), *Throwing Like a Girl and Other Essays in Feminist Philosophy and Social Theory*, Bloomington and Indianapolis: Indiana University Press.

——— (1994), "Gender as Seriality: Thinking about Women as a Social Collective" in *Signs: Journal of Women in Culture and Society*, 19 (3), Spring: pp. 713-38.

# 11

# Self and Morality
## Cross-cultural Perspectives[1]

*Richard Sorabji*

My expertise is limited to the history of Western philosophy, but in taking up a few topics concerned with self and morality from that tradition, I shall cross-refer to what I believe to be some analogues in Indian thought; analogues which, however, are sometimes worked out in India in interestingly different ways. I shall take up five topics.

### Reincarnation

Nationality and ethnic origin can form a large component of someone's idea of their own self. I was always very proud of being half-Indian as well as half-English. But although I could not, in ordinary contexts, imagine not being at least half-Indian, reincarnation is not an ordinary context and it raises the prospect of becoming very different. It is a view with strong implications about the nature of the self, although in the Buddhist versions, selfhood is denied. Like the alternative Christian belief in resurrection, it raises many interesting questions.

On many views one might be reincarnated as an animal, and some say as a tree, which can create a pleasing concern

1. Versions of this paper were delivered at JNU and as the D.M. Singhvi Memorial Lecture at the India International Centre in January 2007. A short version appears in the *India International Centre Quarterly* 2007.

for garden plants.[2] Some (not all) of the ancient Greeks believed in reincarnation and of these Empedocles remembered what it felt like to be incarnated as a bush.[3] Gandhi's autobiography reports his wife as saying that it is rare to be incarnated as a human. If the possibility of return as an animal can be accepted so easily, is it easier to imagine being reincarnated as a human, but of a totally alien culture and religion? Or is that, strangely, harder to imagine? At any rate, it seems to be less discussed by Greeks and Indians alike.

Another Greek, Plotinus, had an interest in India, and tried but failed, to get there. He saw a difficulty about reincarnation in the Greek version. One person, Socrates, might be the reincarnation of another, Pythagoras, but it is hard to think that two such distinctive philosophers were the same person.[4] Reincarnation meant that it was the same soul, not the same person. For what could link them? Empedocles could by a great effort of concentration "remember" twenty incarnations.[5] But how strong a link is the apparent memory of incidents? If on my deathbed somebody says to me, "Cheer up. When you are dead, someone will vividly picture your experiences as his own", why should I think that person would be me? Here I think Indian philosophy makes a difference. According to some versions of Buddhism, aspirant *bodhisattva*s can remember a forward-looking aspiration in earlier lives to progress towards Buddhahood, and to postpone escape from reincarnation until all suffering is removed. Memory of anticipation is found in Jainism too, if the most recent divine

2. Cornelia Sorabji, "Pundit-je", in her *Love and Life Behind the Purdah*, Freemantle, London 1901, pp. 231-39, repr. Delhi: Oxford University Press, 2003, pp. 106-10.

3. Empedocles (fifth century BCE Pythagorean), fragments 103, 110, 117, Diels-Kranz.

4. Plotinus (third century CE Neoplatonist), *Enneads* 5.7. 1 (1-11).

5. Empedocles in Porphyry, *Life of Pythagoras* 30.

incarnation, Mahāvīra, recalled its being declared seven incarnations earlier that he was to be so incarnated.[6] Although it was not the Buddhists' intention to endorse the idea of an individual self, the idea that we have got the same individual person is much more strongly supported, I believe, by forward-looking links than by apparent memory. At any rate the great Russian neuro-psychologist A.R. Luria found that forward-looking projects are much more important to preserving personal individuality than mere memory.[7] The "remembered" prospect, absent from Greek accounts, and "remembered" fulfilment, of progress through successive lives, towards an aspiration that is central to you should both give a sense of its being you in other lives and be potentially cheering. Not everyone has this experience, but some examples could suffice.

There is yet another difference beween Greek and Indian ideas of reincarnation. Although Empedocles believed that his reincarnations below the former semi-divine form were a punishment for eating his relatives through eating meat in an earlier incarnation,[8] the most influential theory of reincarnation was Plato's quite different one, which interposed choice and lottery in the chain of events, thus precluding any idea of mechanical effects in reincarnation.[9] Before the next incarnation, each soul can choose its next life, and the military hero Odysseus chose an insignificant life next time, so as to avoid the trials of his previous life. Admittedly, some choices (like being King of Troy) might have been pre-empted by a previous chooser, but the order of choices was decided by random lottery, not mechanically. This rules out any mechanical

6. I owe this information to Stephen Phillips.

7. A.R. Luria, *The Man with a Shattered World*, New York, 1972, London, 1973.

8. Empedocles, fragments 136, 137.

9. Plato (fifth century BCE), *Phaedrus* 249B, *Republic* 617D-E.

application of *karma*, or of reward or punishment in the next rebirth.

Previous lives by contrast had a strong role for the clients of one of India's legal pioneers who worked for the rights of women in north-east India secluded by purdah from public associations in the early twentieth century. One client, for example, grateful for the sympathy this pioneer showed for the sufferings of women over their children, said, "You have had so many children". The pioneer, in fact, was childless, but her client thought that irrelevant. She meant that such understanding must come from having had many children in past incarnations.[10]

But if previous incarnations have too strong a role to play, a problem arises about the role left over for parents in parenthood. In my travels in India this year, I was told about someone's friend, Ajit, who felt that his children were not really his own, because they were born with their lives shaped by their previous history. That made me understand something I had noticed, but not understood, about Plotinus. He gives two inconsistent accounts of the role of parents. On one account, the child's character is due to the forms that dominate in the parents, and the proportion of hot, cold, wet and dry in the embryo.[11] But on the other account, the soul to be reincarnated helps create its own body by a process which is compared both with drawing and with dancing a part.[12] Evidently, this is not just a slip; rather it is difficult to decide how to share responsibility between parents and past incarnations. At a further point, Plotinus seeks to withdraw the idea of the soul helping to create its body, when he says

10. Cornelia Sorabji, *Letters to Elena*, 22 October, 1915, Richard Sorabji collection.

11. Plotinus 5.7. 2 ( 6 and 11, form = *logos*), 4.3. 23-26, 4.4. 31 (42 proportion = *krasis*).

12. Plotinus 6.7.7 (8-16), 1.1.11 (8-15).

that there is a body similar to the soul itself waiting for it,[13] but this does not tell us how the soul gets to the right body.

One possible solution is mentioned in Tibetan Buddhism in the Tibetan *Book of the Dead*.[14] Although the parents create the new body, one can by concentration choose a womb, instead of being drawn to one. In that case we can see how the parents and the reincarnated one *share* influence on one's future characteristics. Another possibility appears in Jainism.[15] Mahāvīra's embryo was transferred by the God Indra from the womb of a brāhmaṇa woman to that of a warrior caste woman, who was deemed more appropriate. Once again, a selection is made, this time by a God, not by the reincarnated one. But since the god is responding to a series of incarnations that have been leading up to this one, the role gained for the parents is still a limited one.

Giving the parents too much role to play is only one of the ways in which the influence of past incarnations might be weakened. Another way would be to allow a great deal of power to prayers, or ceremonies conducted by others to counteract the effect of past lives. This reduces the influence of past lives in a different way from Plato's introduction of choice of next life, since the effect of ceremonies is not in the hands of the deceased person. The clients of the Indian pioneer whom I have mentioned above tended to assign great influence both to past lives and to counteractive ceremonies, without deciding whether that diminished the influence of one or the other.[16] If, however, the influence of past lives had

13. Plotinus 4.3.12 (37-39).
14. James Ponnaiah, "The Buddhist view of death: a critical study of the Tibetan Book of the Dead", *Jñānadīpa, Pune Journal of Religious Studies* 9, 2006, 63-81 at 66 and 73.
15. Paul Dundas, *The Jains*, London, 1992, p. 23. I owe the information to Marcus Banks.
16. Cornelia Sorabji, *India Calling*, Nisbet, London, 1934, pp. 132, 134, Delhi, rpt. 2001, pp. 99-100, 101, Nottingham, 2004, pp. 87-88.

been diminished too much, the same clients would have felt that this affected ethics. One said that hopes and fears about the next life were what kept her good.[17] And the pioneer lawyer felt, in the context where past lives were allowed such a dominant influence, that her clients could not question why some people were more disadvantaged than others.

There is, in fact, no need for past lives to be given overwhelming importance, and the easiest view to maintain might be that past lives are only one influence among many others. At the same time, however, if there are to be some examples of remembered aspiration fulfilled, frustration from parentage (or curses) must be limited. And here the Indian choice of next *womb, rather than the Greek choice of next life,* may be the best compromise.

We find diverse views on how reincarnation works, both within Indian thought and as against ancient Greek thought, and the differences may at first sight seem somewhat small. But when we look at the ethical implications, these can be very large.

## Higher and Lower Selves

I want in the second topic to say a little bit more about Plotinus, the founder of Neoplatonism in the third century CE.[18] He grew up speaking Greek, but in Egypt, in Alexandria, which was then chiefly Greek-speaking, and he was very very interested in India and tried hard to go there. The only way to go, in those days, was to join an army which was seeking to invade India. But as the army was defeated, he never got there and had to content himself with setting up a school in Rome. His view, which was surely influenced by what he had heard in

17. Cornelia Sorabji, *Letters to Elena*, British Library, Asia, Pacific and Africa Collections, European manuscripts, F165/47, 1 February 1933.

18. For references, see Richard Sorabji, *Self: Ancient and Modern Insights about Individuality, Life and Death*, Chicago and Oxford 2006, Ch. 6.

Egypt about Indian views, was that each one of us has several selves. The lowest self is the soul that is totally interested in our bodies, and a higher self is a soul that is interested in step by step reasoning, which is a characteristically human sort of soul. But above that we have within us the divine intellect which does not need to engage in working things out by reasoning any more, because it totally understands, and what it understands is the world of Plato's Forms. These Forms are unchanging universals such as Justice, Truth, Beauty. Moreover, the divine intellect's awareness of these Forms is uninterrupted and unchanging, yet most of the time we are not conscious that it is thinking of them. Plotinus is a philosopher of the unconscious. He further believes that the intellect's thinking about these universals is outside of time.

I do not fully understand what it means for thinking to be outside of time, but that certainly is his view, and he sometimes had the mystical experience of identifying himself with the divine intellect within him by becoming conscious of its thoughts. His experience was then as if he had escaped from time. Of course, people who were watching him would say, "You seem to have been in a trance and it lasted five minutes". But to him it seemed that no time was passing and he did not conclude that that was an illusion. What he concluded was that at last he had broken through to reality, through to the timeless world. The ideal thing would be to identify yourself with this timeless intellect within you which is uninterruptedly thinking of changeless things. That intellect is your true self, very different from the self that we are familiar with in everyday life. But you have to become your true self by identifying yourself with it.

But then Plotinus feels a worry. If he achieves the ideal of identifying himself with the divine timeless intellect, would it still be him? He has two opposite reactions to that question. One reaction is to think that he would be better off if he completely shed his lower selves which are interested either in the body or merely in working things out by reason and thus became just this intellect. He would be better off because he would be identified with God. The intellect within him is God. And yet he feels a certain anxiety whether he would lose himself. And so he says that in a sense individuality would be preserved. In what sense?

All he can do once again is to tell us a metaphor. He offers the metaphor of a theorem in a mathematical system. Such a theorem is not totally individual because you cannot fully understand any particular theorem in a mathematical system without understanding the entire system. It does not stand independently on its own. On the other hand, each theorem in a mathematical system has a unique point of view within that system. It emphasizes some propositions in the system and de-emphasizes others. So it has a certain individuality. That is only a metaphor. If after death, when we have shed our bodies, some of us manage to become a timeless intellect thinking of changeless universals, in one way there would be no individuality because each of these thinkers would contain exactly the same thoughts and nothing else. So they would not be distinguished from each other, neither by their thoughts, nor by their bodies, because they would no longer have any bodies. And yet, a certain individuality they would have, because one thinker, by analogy with a theorem, would in his thoughts be giving prominence to some of these universals in Plato's system, another to others. So, there would be for each one a distinctive focus of attention, even though every one of these disembodied minds would have the same thoughts. That is how Plotinus tries to preserve a certain limited degree of individuality within the timeless intellect.

The great Islamic philosopher Ibn Sina, around CE 1100, agreed that the true heaven involved union with the Divine Intellect. Why, then, did the Koran give such a physical account of heaven? Because most people are not capable of deciphering the true heaven, and so God, in his benvolence, gives them a dream-heaven which they merely comprehend and dream, corresponding to their own aspirations.[19]

I believe that students of Sāṁkhya Yoga and the subsequent tradition of Advaita Vedānta will see some analogy with its views about what the true self is. There is even a further analogy in so far as that philosophy believes that the self with which we are familiar is surrounded by physical sheaths and we have to get through five illusions, and strip away these five physical sheaths, before we find the true self, which is *Brahman* and which has a form of consciousness quite different from the one we are familiar with. Plotinus' Neoplatonist successors similarly say that there are three sheaths, or, as they call them using a term of Plato's, three vehicles of the soul, the fleshly vehicle shed at death, the breath-like vehicle which houses the soul that engages in sequential reasoning and the luminous vehicle which houses the intellect.[20] Some of them believe that the breath-like vehicle can be shed, but the luminous vehicle is everlasting. I think that scholars of his Indian thought may find that Plotinus has picked up some of his ideas from India, although, in seeking to preserve some individuality, he has given them his own special deep twist.

## Bad Thoughts and Conscience

Gandhi was very conscious of the problem of bad thoughts, and he also made an idiosyncratic use of the Western idea of conscience. Both involve, though in different forms, a need for self-awareness. Bad thoughts were identified by early Christians with what the ancient Greek Stoics had earlier called

19. Jean (=Yahya) Michot, *La destinée de l'homme selon Avicenne: le retour à Dieu et l'imagination*, Leuven, 1986.

20. Richard Sorabji, *The Philosophy of the Commentators 200-600 AD*, vol. 1, *Psychology*, London and Ithaca, New York, 2005, Ch. 8, "Vehicles of soul".

"pre-passions". The Stoics meant only an initial shock which occurs when your situation appears good or bad, but which still gives you time to avoid indulging in full-scale passion. The Christians turned the Stoic theory of how to avoid passion into a theory of how to avoid sin. Bad thoughts are not yet sins, but just pre-passions, and they give you time to avoid indulging in sin. The Christian who worked this out most fully was Evagrius in the fourth century CE. He found himself as a desert hermit assailed by the eight involuntary bad thoughts of gluttony, lust, avarice, distress, anger, boredom (*akedia*), vanity (concern with others' opinions) and pride (belief in self-sufficiency).[21] The mere thoughts were not yet sins, nor even passions, only temptations. It was up to us whether they turned into sins. In attacking the bad thoughts, one must notice in what sequences they come, and at what times of the day. He worked out a science of how to nip bad thoughts in the bud. Thoughts of lust can be suppressed by thoughts of vanity, if they offend one's good opinion of oneself. Or else they will go away, if you can reduce your food intake by conquering thoughts of gluttony. But even apparently innocent thoughts may have to be conquered: for a committed hermit, for instance, thoughts of home. Evagrius had had to flee from home because he had had an illicit affair with a highly placed woman. Thoughts of home might lead one to thoughts of the woman one had left behind, or, for that matter, to angry thoughts about the brother with whom one had quarrelled. The hermit must learn to squash even the apparently innocent mental activity of thinking about home. Equally bad are thoughts of boredom. In the noonday heat of the Egyptian desert, you are meant to be studying a book, but instead you turn the pages to see how many are still left till the end. Who has not done that? But it is a bad thought.

---

21. Evagrius, *Practical Treatise, On the Eight Spirits of Wickedness, On Various Bad Thoughts* (= *On Discrimination*).

Similarly, with thoughts of avarice. Here is a desert hermit who thinks it a terrible shame how much suffering there is in the world. If only one could alleviate poverty.

> If I were to leave the desert for a few months, I could persuade some of the wealthy people in the nearest city to contribute money. I am after all admired for my holiness as a hermit, and they would surely give me a very great deal of money. I would be able to do wonderful things to alleviate poverty. And indeed there is soon going to be a vacancy for a bishop in that town, and if I had raised large sums of money, I would be the obvious candidate, and think how much more comfortable my life would be then.

Here we have moved with lightning speed from thoughts of compassion to thoughts of avarice, followed by thoughts of vanity. That is how bad thoughts develop and there is a whole science of how to counteract them.

But almost immediately after Evagrius' death in CE 399, a more famous Christian, Augustine, utterly disagreed with him. He insisted that emotions should not be got rid of either in this life or the next.[22] He denied that we can cure ourselves of bad thoughts by our own efforts without the Grace of God, though Evagrius agreed with that, or that we can be free of sin in this life.[23] And he gave as his reason an idea not discussed by Evagrius, that we have inherited sinfulness from the first human being, Adam. This is called original sin. Because Adam disobeyed God, we have all been punished with the certainty that we will sin.

In his autobiography, Gandhi agrees with Augustine. He is plagued by bad thoughts, and he says with regard to them, like Augustine, that one needs Grace,[24] and that he believes in

22. Augustine, *City of God* 14, 9-10.
23. Augustine, *Against Julian* 3.1.2, 4.3.29.
24. M.K. Gandhi, *An Autobiography*, Penguin Books, 1982, p. 291.

original sin,[25] presumably not in all its details. He further told Bajaj that one should not fret about the mere thoughts; what matters is whether they control one's actions.[26] This is very much the view not only of Evagrius, but also of Augustine.[27] He does not know of any science of combatting bad thoughts, apart from the recommendation, which is in Evagrius, of fasting and diet,[28] though Evagrius also warns against weakness derived from over-fasting. Gandhi in another writing recommends simply concentrating on one's work.[29]

Conscience originally involved another kind of self-awareness, awareness not of one's thoughts, but either of one's past faults, or of what future faults to avoid, while good conscience involved awareness of one's freedom from fault. The Greek expression in Plato meant literally to share consciousness with oneself, and in its full form is always used by Plato of a fault. But the concept grew beyond this, as it has in Gandhi, to cover awareness of what is positively right. This was encouraged when in the Christian New Testament, written in Greek 500 years later, Saint Paul, Christ's Apostle, made a loose connection between conscience and the moral law written in men's hearts.[30] In fact, Saint Paul says comparatively little about conscience. It may have been a concept introduced to him by the Greek Christians living in Corinth, who said that their conscience was clear when they ate meat that might have

25. Ibid., p. 220.

26. Rajmohan Gandhi, *Mohandas*, Delhi: Penguin Books, 2006, pp. 278-79.

27. Evagrius, *Practical Treatise* 6 and 75; Augustine, *On the Sermon on the Mount*, 1.12, 33-34; *On the Trinity* 12.12.

28. M.K. Gandhi, *An Autobiography*, pp. 198-99, 293, 300-01, 304.

29. Raghavan Iyer, ed., *The Moral and Political Writings of Mahatma Gandhi*, Oxford University Press, 1986, vol. 2, p. 116.

30. Paul, *Letter to the Romans* 2.14-15.

been sacrificed to pagan idols.[31] Conscience was much more fully mentioned by pagan philosophers, especially those writing in the Latin around Saint Paul's time such as Cicero and Seneca, and Saint Paul's comparative silence led later Christian theologians to build up the idea of conscience partly on a pagan basis.[32]

Gandhi uses the idea of conscience very frequently, and not only in the *Autobiography*. But in some ways, his concept is more reminiscent of the Greek philosopher Socrates, as presented by his pupil Plato, whose *Apology* or defence of Socrates, with its two mentions of conscience,[33] Gandhi translated out of an English version into Gujarati. Socrates also had a guardian spirit who warned him what not to do, mentioned twice in Plato's *Apology*, once as being a voice ,[34] and which he treated as infallible. Although it only told him what not to do, in the *Apology* he took the absence of a warning as a positive sign for action. Saint Paul stressed more than once that conscience may be wrong, as it was in the case of the Corinthian meat-eaters. Gandhi seems to differ from both, Socrates and Saint Paul. His conscience tells him positive things, not only, as with Socrates, what to avoid. But he treats it with a confidence closer to that of Socrates than of Saint Paul. When some orthodox priests wanted to read him texts favouring Untouchability and Child Marriage, he replied that Hinduism must be upheld not just through isolated texts, but through the inner voice of conscience.[35] He was also willing to override

31. Paul, *First Letter to the Corinthians* 8, (cf. 4.4).
32. I say more about this in *Studia Patristica*, Leuven, vol. 44, 2010, pp. 361-83, and in *Gandhi and the Stoics: Modern Experiments on Ancient Values*, Oxford and Chicago, 2012, Ch. 8, and in *Moral Conscience through the Ages*, in prepartion.
33. Plato, *Apology* 21B, 22D.
34. Plato, *Apology* 31D, 40A.
35. Bombay Chronicle, 16 September 1927, 40:105, quoted by Rajmohan Gandhi, *Mohandas, A True Story of a Man, His People and an Empire*, Penguin Books, 2006, p. 309.

virtually all his followers and expected them publicly to switch to his view, because God had spoken to him, for example when calling off rent refusal at Bardoli, and when insisting on an unexpected fast.[36] This shows a certain kind of individualism, which goes beyond the view of some Christians that one is obliged to follow one's conscience,[37] but it may be wrong, so one is obliged also to question it.[38] It is an individualism that in his case can be admirable, but in the wrong person would be very dangerous.

**No Self**

My fourth topic concerns an ancient Buddhist view that there are streams of consciousness but there is nobody who *has* the consciousness. There is no *self* who is the owner of the consciousness. And one of the best philosophers in the West, Derek Parfit in Oxford, has worked out a very similar view that there are only streams of consciousness embedded in our brains.[39] But the Buddhists went much further. They said that brain is also streams of momentary physical events. There are neither brains in the sense that we ordinarily believe nor selves. The self is a set of four streams of momentary psychological events, while bodies (brains included) are streams of momentary physical events. Some Buddhists (Nāgasena, Vasubandhu) said that momentary physical events are real enough but the rest is just a name we use for successions of these momentary events. Both Parfit and these Buddhists claim two benefits from their view. First, if we realize that

36. Rajmohan Gandhi, *Mohandas,* Delhi: Penguin Books, 2006, pp. 261, 291.

37. Thomas Aquinas, *Summa Theologiae* 1.2, q.19, a.5-6.

38. Kant, *Lectures on Metaphysics of Morals*, 1793, recorded by Vigilantius, 27, 614-20.

39. For references, see Richard Sorabji, *Self: Ancient and Modern Insights about Individuality, Life and Death*, Chicago and Oxford, 2006, Chs 15 and 16.

there is no self, we can have no occasion to be selfish. Secondly, we can have no reason to fear that death will involve a loss of self.

I find this view hard to believe, because, if there is only a stream of consciousness but nobody who *has* the consciousness, then there is suffering but nobody who *has* or *owns* the suffering. There may be beneficial acts but there is no benefactor. There is no beneficiary either, because there is nobody who is suffering and nobody who has the relief. That would surely make compassion less important. Of course, it is better if there is a universe in which suffering is relieved, so I do not say that all motivation is removed, but much of the urgency for compassion is the thought that there is *somebody* who is suffering.

I have another worry, that the whole idea of intending to do something would become an illusion, because when you intend to do something, you intend that the very same person who now *has* or *owns* the intention will later perform the action. But if the idea of the very same owner at a later date is an illusion so is the idea of intention. If all our intendings involve an illusion, so do all of our actions, and so too do all our acts of meaning; if to mean something is to intend to bring about a certain psychological states among our hearers. Also, I wonder what happens to many, I do not say all, of our ethical concepts. Rights, duties, responsibilities surely all depend on the idea that the self-same person has made the earlier promise, that is, was the owner of the promise, and is now bound by it. Will not rights, duties, and responsibilities then also become illusions?

One group of Buddhists took the subject much further again and beyond what the Western philosophers have said. This group (Nāgārjuna, Candrakīrti) produced the startling theory that even the momentary events are not fully real. There are fully real things, but not in this realm. On the contrary, the supposed momentary events are themselves empty, and there is something even more: the utterance I have just made is itself empty. What does that mean? The analogy that is given by Candrakīrti around CE 600 is that you should regard that utterance not as a statement of fact but as a medicine, a medicine to cure you of having the wrong attitudes. I believe that this explains what happened in the eighth century CE with a Buddhist in the same tradition called Śāntideva in his *Bodhicaryāvatāra*.[40] For the purposes of impartiality in compassion, he says in Book 8, one should think that there is nobody who *has* the suffering, and so no suffering is yours rather than someone else's. But then how is one to feel compassion at all, if there are no sufferers? In Book nine, he recommends that in order to feel compassion, one should think that there are sufferers after all. Has he not, then, contradicted himself on whether there are sufferers or not? No, because each of his utterances should be taken as a medicine to cure attitudes, not as a statement. That is the sense in which each of the utterances is empty, and it allows a switch of attitude without contradiction. This "medicine" theory, coupled with the deconstruction even of bodies into streams, makes the Buddhist theories more radical than any comparable Western ones.

### Being True to Your Individual Self

I shall return, finally, to individualism, but to a quite different type of individualism from that of Gandhi's conscience. This individualsim was discussed in the first centuries BCE and CE by the pagan Stoic philosophers, and again I think it has some Indian echoes. According to these later Stoics, when you make decisions in life you must ask two questions.[41] The first is very familiar in the West, because it was the question emphasized by Kant 2000 years after the Stoics introduced their two questions. But Kant treated this first question as the only

40. Śāntideva, *Bodhicaryāvatāra* 8.102-103, 9.75.

41. Cicero, *On Duties* (reporting the Stoic Panaetius) 1.107-125, Epictetus *Discourses* 1.2.

question, not one of two. The thing you need to consider is how to act as a rational being, and that involves being consistent, and accepting that what is right for one is right for all in the same circumstances. That may be true as far as it goes. It calls for impartiality as a form of consistency and hence of rationality. The Stoics and Kant would agree (rather optimistically, I believe) that that would rule out immoral conduct, which they both see as involving irrationality.

But so far, that does not give very much guidance. Kant expects you to formulate further maxims to deal with particular circumstances, but how is one to formulate them? This is where the Stoic second question is helpful. You have got to consider your own individual nature. Imagine you are choosing a career. The first requirement of making a rational choice rules out becoming a burglar, according to the Stoics. But that leaves it unanswered what positive choice to make. Some people want to please their parents when choosing their career. Their father was a famous lawyer, so they try to become a lawyer. But you have got to ask yourself, would I be any good as a lawyer. You have got to consider your own personal, individual talents, to make a good decision, even in a non-moral question like choosing a career. If you will be no good at being a lawyer, it is no good trying to please your parents. You will make a mess of it. You have got to consider your individual self in each thing you do.

Some choices are always unique. In the first century BCE, Julius Caesar won the civil war and introduced a tyranny in place of the Roman Republic. One of the great Stoics, Cato, committed suicide rather than compromise with the tyrant Julius Caesar. And what the view Stoics held was that it was right for Cato to commit suicide, but it would not be right for anybody else, even in the same circumstances. It sounds like a complete contradiction of Kant. I don't think it is logically a contradiction, but it is in the opposite spirit from Kant's. What is being said is that while considering what a rational being would do when a tyrant defeats you and ruins the Roman Republic, you must consider how to be true to your individual self, while still being rational. And Cato had stood throughout his life for a kind of uncompromising austerity. It is his peculiar, individual life history which made it right for him to commit suicide but for nobody else on the losing side to commit suicide in the same circumstances. Had Cicero been captured, for example, suicide would not have been right for him, even though he is the one who tells us this story and who had something of the same character and had done everything to oppose Caesar. So this theory gives a tremendous importance to the uniqueness of the individual.

Kant had heard of the example of Cato and made some concessions towards it. But if he had tried to say that anyone in Cato's circumstances would (as part of the circumstances) have Cato's character and so should commit suicide like Cato, he would run into the problem how to formulate this as a maxim. Anyone captured by a person who is replacing your beloved constitution with tyranny should commit suicide rather than compromise, if his character is — what? Cato's character could hardly be displayed in all its uniqueness except by telling many anecdotes about him, or reading half his biography. It cannot be described in half a dozen adjectives. That is why the Stoics rely on proper names like "Cato", which can conjure up dozens of stories through the single name, whereas trying to use descriptions to differentiate Cato from Cicero and others would never succeed. Proper names, however, are of no use to Kant, because he wants his maxims to be universal,[42] whereas with their proper names the Stoics are emphasizing that individuality must be taken into account

42. Peter Winch criticizes Kant this way, in "the universalisability of moral judgement", *Monist* 49, 1965, 196-214.

in decisions, even when it is unique. The morally interesting point about Cato is that there was nobody else like him.

One interesting point is that when the Stoics ask you to take your individual nature into account, they talk about your capabilities, e.g. in choosing a job, about the role you were born to play, e.g. as a ruler or slave, about your choices, such as becoming a philosopher. But funnily enough they do not, like modern communitarian theory, mention your ethnicity, culture or religion. Excessive stress on these issues has been criticized by Amartya Sen as being divisive in society.[43] And I would add that it can have a very conservative tendency if you identify yourself too exclusively with the existing culture. In the Stoic theory there are at least some anti-conservative elements, because you can go against the professional choice of your father, and your choices are as important as the roles you were born into, though they need to be consistent with them. Of course, culture is presupposed, but the fact that it is not mentioned in the list of things to consider when deciding how to make decisions fit with a fact about the Roman Empire. That empire seems not to have had much problem with strife concerning culture or religion. It took the view that so long as you were willing to offer a little bit of incense to worship the emperor, you could have whatever religion or culture you liked.

Is there any analogue for the Stoic theory in Indian thought? Well, I think there may be an analogue in the *Mahābhārata*. It has been pointed out that when Karṇa is offered the kingdom, he refuses it.[44] It would have been wonderful if he had accepted kingship because it would have made unnecessary that terrible war in which so many people killed

43. Amartya Sen, *Identity and Violence*, Norton, New York, 2006.

44. Aditya Adankar, "Karna's Choice: Courage and Character in the Face of an Ethical Dilemma", in T.S. Rukmani, ed., *The Mahabharata: Whatever is Not Here is Nowhere Else*, Delhi 2005, Ch. 9.

each other. Why did he not accept the kingdom? Because to accept the kingdom, he would have had to deny the two people who brought him up. What a very individual and personal reason for refusing kingship. He had thought about how to be true to his individual self. He was doing what the Stoics are recommending. Of course, some people might say that it is not really a strict analogue because had he sufficiently considered the first Stoic requirement of considering what a rational being should do? Was it rational to make a decision which would lead to such a terrible war? I do not know, I am not making a judgement on it. But at least on being true to his individual self, he is adopting the second part of what the Stoics would say. Of course, the first of the two Stoic requirements is very important, and it is important in the following way.

Charles Taylor has talked about the malaise of modernity in the West.[45] The malaise of modernity is to think that in making decisions all you do is to consult your individual self, and that that is all that matters. Of course, the Stoics utterly reject that. You have got to ask the first question, what a rational being would do, which they think will rule out being a plague to society. So the Stoics are not in favour of the malaise of modernity.

I think the Stoic version of individualism is valid; that of the malaise of modernity is not. And individualism of conscience is good in a case like Gandhi's, but carries dangers in the wrong hands, so needs scrutiny.

That is my last topic. I hope that each of my Western analogues has resonance for readers who know much more than I do about Indian literature and Indian thought.

---

45. Charles Taylor, *The Malaise of Modernity*, Concord, Ontario, 1991, pp. 15, 24-28, 74. I thank Vasanthi Srinivasam for the reference.

# 12

# Self and Morality

## Some Indian Perspectives on Sorabji

*Jonardon Ganeri**

THE Indians have indeed, I think, many interesting things to say about the five topics Richard Sorabji has selected. My comments are in no way comprehensive, but I hope that they give a flavour of the sorts of discussions that have taken place.

### Reincarnation

In Martin Amis's novel *Money*, the lead protagonist, John Self, leads a debauched life but promises himself that one day he'll take himself off to a clinic in California and get himself a new body, to replace the one he has abused and ruined. In the *Bhagavad-Gītā*, Kṛṣṇa tells Arjuna not to worry about the people whose bodies he is about to pierce with arrows, because, after all, "As a man casts off his worn-out clothes and takes on new ones, so does the embodied [self] cast off its worn-out bodies and enter other new ones".[1] There is something obviously wrong about thinking of either of these examples as a case of reincarnation. Reincarnation isn't simply a matter of getting a new body, as one might get a new suit from the shop. The problem is that bodies are not just hanging around, waiting to be inhabited by a friendly soul; the body into which one is

---

* I am very grateful to Richard Sorabji for his comments on an earlier draft of this paper.

1. *Bhagavad-Gītā*, 2.22.

reincarnated is itself a person. The Emperor Julian believed that he was the reincarnation of Alexander the Great,[2] but he was not like the deranged persons who believe that they really are Napoleon, nor was his case like the case of the woman who really believed that she was her father, even when she was shown her reflection in a mirror.[3] So, as Plotinus said, it looks more as if reincarnation implies that two *different* persons, for instance Pythagoras and Socrates, share a common soul.[4]

Sorabji points out, however, that this cannot be very satisfactory either, because it would imply that one person's soul could be taken off in a different moral direction by someone else. But if sharing a soul does after all imply preservation of personal identity, then we need at least to have an account of the psychological linkages between Pythagoras and Socrates that would make them be the same person, at different times in different bodies. Sorabji observes that the Indians provide a richer description of such person-shaped psychological linkages, including dispositional traces, habits, talents, and, most interestingly, the category of linkage that includes one's memory of past future-directed aspirations. It is one thing for Julian to claim to remember some of Alexander's experiences and exploits as his own, but something else and deeper for him to remember Alexander's plans and projects and to feel them as past aspirations which are his to fulfil.

2. See Alexander Alexakis, *Was There Life Beyond the Life Beyond? Byzantine Ideas about Reincarnation and Final Restoration*, "Dumbarton Oaks Papers", 55 (2002), p. 164; reporting the Church History of Socrates.

3. See N. Breen, D. Caine, M. Coltheart, J. Hendy and C. Roberts, "Towards an Understanding of Delusions of Misidentification: Four Case Studies", in M. Coltheart and M. Davies (eds), *Pathologies of Belief*, Oxford: Blackwell, 2000, 4 Plotinus, *Ennead* 5.7.1 (1-6).

4. Plotinus, Enneads 5.7.1, trans. A.H. Armstrong, Loeb Classical Library edition (Cambridge, MA: Harvard University Press, 1966), pp. 1-6.

I think that Sorabji is right that the memory of a past anticipation is a particularly important vehicle in weaving a psychology into a person. Vaiśeṣika philosophers distinguish between various sorts of pleasures, and identify the anticipation of a future pleasure as itself pleasurable in a certain way.[5] One might, for example, anticipate the pleasure of victory while still in the midst of the battle. And when one is enjoying that pleasure later, one might think back to the time when one anticipated it, and look upon one's present happiness as realizing or fulfilling that earlier anticipation. I think one can certainly say that being in such a mental state is quite different from simply enjoying the pleasure of victory as such. A distinctive phenomenology of satisfaction (and frustration; cf. the Indian terms *sukha* and *duḥkha*) is characteristic of the psychological life of a single person.

Psychological linkages across incarnations are discussed by the commentators on *Nyāya-Sūtra* 3.1.18. This *sūtra* argues that a neonate experiences the emotions of fear (*bhaya*), sorrow (*śoka*) and delight (*harṣa*), emotions which it says follow on the heels of a memory of some repeated experience in the past. A later philosopher analyses these emotions as follows. Delight is the experience of pleasure one has on fulfilling a longing for something desired. Fear is an inability to rid oneself of the wish to flee in the presence of what will lead to something undesired. Sorrow is the unfulfillable longing for something

5. Praśastapāda, *Padārthadharmasaṁgraha* 2.13, and the commentaries of Śrīdhara and Udayana on the sentences *atīteṣu viṣayeṣu smṛti-jam | anāgateṣu saṁkalpa-jam | Praśastapādabhāṣya*, text and index in Johannes Bronkhorst and Yves Ramseier, *Word Index to the Praśastapādabhāṣya*, Delhi: Motilal Banarsidass, 1994, p. 58; see also *Praśastapādabhāṣyam of Praśastapāda with the Commentary Nyāyakandalī by Śrīdhara Bhaṭṭa*, ed. Durgadhara Jha, Varanasi: Sampurnanand Sanskrit University, 1997.

desired from which one is separated.[6] Elsewhere, desire is defined as an unfulfilled longing for something one wants but does not have, a category that includes the anticipation (*saṁkalpa*) of a future pleasure.[7] So, for example, one feels delight when one obtains something which one remembers longing for. Experiences like these are complex psychological events, and only occur as part of a richly woven psychological life. The argument of *Nyāya-Sūtra* 3.1.18-26 is that they do occur in newly born infants, and this proves that the newborn has a soul from a past life. We know that they are felt by newly born infants because such infants smile, cry and flinch. It is only with this last inference, it seems to me, that the argument runs into trouble.

If one feels, as I think many of the Indians do, that it would still be good to be able to distinguish between a person who is the reincarnation of someone else, and a person who is that very person but just in another body (the difference between Julian as the reincarnation of Alexander, and Alexander himself, alive and well, but in the body of Julian), one might retain the distinction by thinking of a person as a continuous body within which these kinds of person-shaped psychological linkages occur. In cases of reincarnation, when the person-shaped psychological linkages span discrete bodies, the distinction between being-that-person and being-a-reincarnation-of-that-person would be preserved, but it would

6. These definitions are provided by Uddyotakara in his *Vārttika* on *Nyāya-sūtra* 3.1.18. The text reads: *abhipretaviṣaya-prārthanāprāptau sukhānubhavo harṣaḥ* | *aniṣṭa-viṣaya-sādhana-sannipāte tajjihāsorhānāśakyatā bhayam* | *iṣṭaviṣaya-viyoge sati tatprāptyaśakya-prārthanā śokaḥ* | Anantalal Thakur, ed., *Nyāyabhaṣyavārttika of Uddyotakara*, Delhi: Indian Council of Philosophical Research, 1997, pp. 344, 9-11.

7. Praśastapāda, *Padārthadharmasaṁgraha* 2.15: *svārtham. parārtham. vā 'prāpta-prārthanecchā* | ... | *kāmo 'bhilāso ... rāgahsaṁkalpahkārunya-mvairāgyam upadhā bhāva ity evamādaya icchā-bhedāh* |

also be intelligible why reincarnation presents itself as like a case of "same person, different body". I think that such an account would be consistent with the Buddhist view that a person is an aggregate of the physical *and* psychological streams, and that it would also explain why belief in reincarnation seems to be independent of belief in substantial souls; for, as both Kant and Locke pointed out, the presence of a substantial soul does not help with the problem of the identity of the person. One might also argue that the psychological linkages that must exist for a person to be the reincarnation of an earlier individual are similar in kind, but not as strong as, the ones that hold within a single person.

**Higher and Lower Selves**

There are certainly close similarities between Plotinus' quest to identify himself with the divine intellect within him, and the Upaniṣadic ambition of asserting the identity of *ātman* with *Brahman*. But what about the more specific and fascinating question which Sorabji raises, whether in any sense one's individuality would survive such an identification? Plotinus says, metaphorically, that one would be like a theorem in a mathematical system,[8] and Sorabji has a very illuminating explanation of the way the metaphor works: although all the disembodied minds will think the same thoughts about the Platonic system of universals, each will have a distinctive focus of attention with respect to the system. In this way they will be discriminable from one another.

In the Indian situation, it is not so much that one manages to identify oneself with *Brahman* as that one successfully frees oneself of the illusion that one is different (the injunction "Know thyself" would have, on this view, a clear epistemology). This implies, first of all, that one was identical with *Brahman* all along, and second that the individuality which one possesses

8. Plotinus, *Ennead* 4.3.2 (49-58).

is the result of a mistake. That would suggest that it is a mistake that each individual can make in one's own distinctive way, and there is also the possibility that some residue of this mistake, or rather the distinctive way it was made, might remain even when the mistake has been seen through, just as coming to know that something is simply a *trompe l'oeuil* does not completely dispel the appearance. Philosophers in the tradition of Advaita Vedānta have tried to make sense of this complex situation by appealing, as did Plotinus, to metaphors. For some of them, the right metaphor to choose is as follows.[9] We say that within a house there are many different spaces, because there are many rooms separated off by walls. In reality, however, there is just one space, and the walls are merely imposed delimitations upon it (just as one divides up time into days and years).[10] The relation between individuals and *Brahman* is just the same. Perhaps it is possible to see how, even after one has come to understand that one is just a delimited "region" of *Brahman*, the seen-through illusion can persist enough for some sense of individuality to remain.

Other philosophers experimented with another metaphor, saying that the relationship between *Brahman* and individual selves is akin to the situation in which the moon is reflected in a pond. Different people see different reflections, even though there is just one moon. So individuality is an illusion of perspective.[11] I think that this metaphor is in some ways closer to the one used by Plotinus, especially if, as Sorabji says, that

9. For details see Srinivasa Chari, *Advaita and Viśiṣṭādvaita*, Delhi: Motilal Banarsidass, 1999, rev. 2nd edn., pp. 69-74; K. Narain, *The Fundamentals of Advaita Vedānta*, Varanasi: Indological Research Centre, 2003, pp. 223-32.

10. Śaṅkara, *Brahmasūtra-bhāṣya* 1.1.31, 1.4.22. *Brahmasūtra-bhāṣya* of Śaṅkara. ed. with commentaries N.A.K. Shastri and V.L. Shastri Pansikar, Bombay: Nirnaya Sagar Press, 1917.

11. Śaṅkara, *Brahmasūtra-bhāṣya* 2.3.50.

one works by appealing to the idea of a distinctive focus of attention. One difference is that here, again, the element of illusion plays an important part, as is indicated by the reference to reflections which are, in some sense, not really there (or at least, not where they appear to be). This metaphor is especially amenable to the suggestion I am making, that some residue of the illusion persists even when it has been consciously recognized as just an illusion, because of the well-known fact that visual illusions continue to trick the eye even when the perceiver knows of their illusory nature, like the submerged stick continuing to look bent.

Philosophers in the Vaiśeṣika tradition do not agree that there is an identity between individual and divine self, either actual or strived for, and they explain those Vedic passages which seem to countenance such an identity as having the therapeutic function of encouraging us to engage in an imaginative exercise.[12] These philosophers argue that what such exercises help us towards is not identification with *Brahman*, but rather a state of disembodied existence (actual or imagined), such a state being the one in which one is free from all the emotional and cognitive turmoils associated with embodiment. This leads them to address the problem of individuality in a different guise, however, because the disembodied selves retain their individuality but can no longer be told apart by way of their by now rather minimal psychological properties (it isn't wholly clear to me whether the Vaiśeṣika can permit their disembodied individual selves anything analogous to thinking about universal Platonic forms, but the consensus of opinion seems to be that they do not).[13] For the Vaiśeṣika philosopher, the problem is similar to that

12. Viśvanātha, *Kārikāvalī*, ed. with five commentaries by C.S.R. Shastri, Delhi: Chaukhamba Sanskrit Pratishthan, 1988, p. 399.

13. Vyomaśiva, *Vyomavatī*, ed. by Gaurinath Sastri, Varanasi: Sampurnanand Sanskrit University, 1983, p. 285.

of distinguishing between different individual atoms of a single substance. The fact that each atom moves along its own individual spatio-temporal path is not enough to individuate it, because — they claim — an atom can be reidentified without having been tracked, and they therefore conclude that each atom, and likewise each self, has its own special uniquely individuating feature, a *viśeṣa*, something possibly akin to the mediaeval haecceities proposed by Duns Scotus in the thirteenth century.

### Bad Thoughts and Conscience

If conscience means an acquaintance with the moral value of one's own thoughts, traits, and deeds, then it might fairly be said that much of Indian philosophy consists in the science of its cultivation. In Buddhism, the term *tṛṣṇā* (Pāli: *taṇhā*) denotes all those "cravings" which lead us into distress, and the fourth noble truth describes the various forms of self-knowledge which eradicate them. The Indian discussion bears greater resemblance, I feel, to the pagan Greek theory of the concept than to the subsequent Christian reworking, especially because notions of sin, temptation, and evil are not as central in the Indian framework. In Nyāya, for example, God's function is to fashion the cosmos out of its atoms, as a potter fashions a piece of clay into a pot; his role is not to relieve us of our bad thoughts through his good Grace. Our bad thoughts are a product of our culpable ignorance, and the way to eradicate them is to become better informed.

The understanding of conscience as an inner voice speaking to me, or a guardian spirit telling me what not to do, is not one I have so far found much evidence of in the Indian thought, except possibly in the epic references to a state of mental anguish (*mānas-tāpaḥ*), which might be regarded as being indicative of an inner moral discomfort. I think that Sorabji is exactly right when he traces Gandhi's own use of this idea of conscience back to his eclectic awareness of the Western literature. In two places, however, Manu states that the moral law has four foundations, and includes as the last of them "that which is pleasing to oneself".[14] The thought appears to be that when confronted with an otherwise insuperable moral conflict, when the declarations of the law books contradict one another, or else are completely silent, and when no guidance is to be had either from the way good people conduct themselves or from the use of reason, then consulting one's own inner moral feeling is permissible. Yājñavalkya even adds that it is sometimes morally permissible to consult one's "appropriate" desires.[15] As far as I am aware, little use seems to have been made by later Indian thinkers of the possibilities these texts open up. Only Vīramitrodaya (commenting on Yājñavalkya) develops the idea, saying that the consultation of one's inner feeling is decisive in scenarios such as deciding when one has done enough penance for some past misdemeanour, and he notes that this is an entirely individual matter and that what one decides applies only to oneself and to nobody else.[16]

There are echoes of Stoic theory and also of Evagrius in a chapter of the *Mahābhārata* near the end of that great epic, the

---

14. *Manu-smr̥ti* 2.6 uses the expression *ātmanas tustir*, while at *Manu-smr̥ti* 2.12 the phrase is *svasya priyam ātmanah* . . . (this is also the phrase used by *Yājñavalkya* 1.7) see Patrick Olivelle, *Manu's Code of Law: A Critical Edition and Translation of the Mānava-Dharmaśāstra*, New York: Oxford University Press, 2005, pp. 404, 405. Robert Lingat is willing to paraphrase these expressions as "approval of one's conscience", in his *The Classical Law of India*, California: University of California Press, 1973, p. 6.

15. *Yājñavalkya* 1.7, *samyak-saṁkalpahkāmaḥ*. *Yājñavalkya's Smr̥ti with the Mitākṣarā*, ed. by S.C. Vasu, Allahabad: The Panini Office, 1909, p. 16.

16. The commentaries on *Manu* 2.6 and *Yājñavalkya* 1.7 are helpfully surveyed by Ganganatha Jha in his *Studies in Hindu Law*, Varanasi: Sampurnanand Sanskrit University Press, 1992, pp. 53-55.

part of the text that deals with philosophical ideas.[17] The fundamental source of all bad thoughts here is declared to be greed (*lobha*): greed produces lust (*kāma*) and anger (*krodha*) in the first instance; anger at who or what prevents one from getting the things one lusts after. From these follow envy (*akṣamā*), shamelessness (*hrī-parityāga*), loss of dignity (*śrī-nāśa*), loss of morals (*dharmasaṁkṣaya*), covetousness (*abhidhyā*) and so on. The text now states that greed is on the same footing as (culpable) ignorance (*ajñāna*). Ignorance produces, in the first instance, distress (*duḥkha*), and a host of emotions, including passion (*rāga*), dread or aversion (*dveṣa*), delight (*harṣa*), sorrow (*śoka*), pride (*abhimānitā*; thinking well of oneself); and thereafter lust (*kāma*), anger (*krodha*), haughtiness (*darpa*) also follow on. Ignorance and greed, going hand in hand, are the root causes of all bad thoughts and emotions. These must be counteracted, and what counteracts them are self-control (*dama*) and self-restraint (*tapas*). Self-control consists in having a tranquil, calm, state of mind. Self-restraint includes a variety of things, but the best and highest form of self-restraint is said to be abstinence from food. The discussion is wound up by reiterating that anger and lust give rise to thirteen sorts of badness, including the ones already listed above, and that tranquillity of soul (*praśama*) is what, ultimately, destroys them.

All this certainly has intriguing similarities with the Stoic theory as adapted by Evagrius. Anger and lust are two of the eight sorts of involuntary bad thoughts he has identified, avarice and gluttony (forms of greed) being the others two. He also mentions distress, pride and vanity, which find a place in the above system. But he does not mention ignorance; and of his eighth kind of bad thought, boredom, there does not seem to be an analogue in the *Mahābhārata* scheme. Boredom

17. *Mahābhārata*, book 12 (Śānti-parvan), chapters 152-57; critically ed. by S.K. Belvalkar, Poona: Bhandarkar Oriental Research Institute, 1954, vol. 14, pp. 841-62.

and ignorance are perhaps related, in that both imply a certain mental idleness. Or perhaps, it is just that boredom was an exceptionally serious issue for the desert hermit.

**No Self**

The Buddhists say that there are no selves, and, since wrong beliefs lead to "craving" (*tṛṣṇā*), and craving leads to distress, it is ethically incumbent on us to identify and address the false idea of self. Other philosophers in India were not slow to point out that without persisting selves, the idea that we can be held morally responsible to account for what we have done or will do, is deprived of a solid foundation; the idea of individual moral responsibility seems to have been undermined.[18] Sorabji raises the stakes still further. He argues that a no-self theory also loses purchase on (i) the idea that there can be compassion for the suffering of *others*, (ii) the idea that one can intend now *oneself* to perform an action later, (iii) the idea that one can be bound by a promise *one* has made in the past. Without compassion, the altruistic ethics to which Buddhism aspires is compromised; without intentions, actions and language do not have meaning; and without promises, there are no rights, duties and responsibilities. Sorabji is surely right that much of our ordinary moral vocabulary presupposes that there are moral agents who are the enduring owners of their acts and intentions.

I think the Buddhists will have to agree that the whole conceptual scheme of what we might call "folk ethics" is interrelated with and dependent on the notion of persisting selves. That leaves three possible strategies for the Buddhists, and I think they take advantage of all of them. If any one of these moves is successful, it will diffuse the line of objection to the Buddhist view without itself constituting a positive reason in

18. For example, Kumārila's *Ślokavārttika, Ātmavāda* 32-33. K. Sāmbaśiva Śāstrī, ed., *The Mīmāṁsā Ślokavārttika, with the commentary Kāśikā of Sucaritamiśra*, Trivandrum, 1926, Trivandrum Sanskrit Series, no. 90.

favour of that view. One move is to say that the resources of folk ethics, embedded as it is in most people's thinking, should be exploited in order to help improve their lives. In the *Lotus Sūtra*, the Buddha is reported to have illustrated the idea with the story of a father whose children are playing inside a house that has caught fire. In order to entice them to come out, he tells them that there are toys and sweets waiting for them if they do so, even though in reality there are none. Thus even false ideas can lead one to do what is right.

Another strategy is to seize the dilemma by its horn, and agree that the whole system of everyday ethical concepts is, ultimately, in need of repair. This is an idea that the Buddhist texts say is hard to grasp and easy to misinterpret, and that it requires a lot of preparatory work before one can understand it properly. One way to approach it, perhaps, is in comparison with the advice of the Stoics that one should aim to cultivate a "view from above", or perhaps a "view from nowhere", and to think about the whole world and all that goes on in it, dispassionately and impartially. It is true that someone who manages to do that will not feel the force of individual moral responsibility to the same degree as before, but this does not mean that one will cease to be ethical. It is rather that their ethical concern will be for the whole, rather than for anyone part, even the part that is themselves. And perhaps that is what the Buddhists have in mind when they speak about *karuṇā*, which would then not altogether happily be rendered by the English word "compassion", though this is how it is invariably translated. Someone who manages to free his thinking entirely of the notion of self and what depends on it, will see the suffering in the world, and will judge that it would be better if there were less, without apportioning blame.[19]

19. On the possibility of an entirely self-free consciousness, see Thomas Metzinger, *Being No One: The Self-Model Theory of Subjectivity*, Cambridge, Mass.: Bradford Books, 2003, pp. 565-66. Metzinger's →

A final possibility is that the illusion that there are selves should be regarded as having the same status as Kant's transcendental illusions of pure reason. Kant said that there are certain illusions which are inseparable from the use of reason, even after their deceptiveness has been exposed.[20] If the conviction that there are enduring selves is an illusion of that sort, then we can never fully escape from it, but we can become self-aware about the way it entraps our thinking, and we can adapt accordingly. In other words, it is a disease for which there is no cure, but only an accommodation, and knowing it for what it is, the first step is learning how to live with it as best one can.

**Being True to Your Individual Self**

I have spoken about the pandemic illusions that the Indians tell us we are suffering from, and about the benefits that accrue to those who achieve self-consciousness. Individuality has had a role to play in the story, but not a very prominent one. Where does that leave what Sorabji has called "individual reasons", an individual reason being, roughly, a reason that bears on *that very* individual and on nobody else? Sorabji argues very convincingly that we should not treat individual reasons

---

→ book is a defence of the thesis that "there are no such things as selves"; there are only "self-models" in the representational systems of organisms. Ownership, "mineness" and subjectivity are likewise properties modelled by the system, phenomenal properties of a merely phenomenal self. He speaks to the argument from ethics only very briefly, stating that the representational systems are capable of conscious suffering, and affirming a negative utilitarian principle, that "the *overall amount of conscious suffering* in all beings capable of conscious suffering should be minimized" (p. 570; his italics). It is not clear to me how he would answer Sorabji's criticism of that position.

20. Immanuel Kant, *Critique* A298/b355.

as special cases of general ones, even were it formally possible to do so. Even if anyone else like Cato should have done what he did, "the morally interesting point about Cato is that there was nobody else like him". And where does it leave the point Amartya Sen makes, that everyone is presented with a range of "identities", and to be an individual is to exercise one's right to choose which parts of one's overall identity to make one's own. Sen sums this up by saying that "reason is before identity" — it is for me to choose what relative prominence to give to my class, gender, vocation, hobbies, religion, family, ethnicity, and so on.[21] We might say that the point is that there are more individual reasons than there are individuals, and so individual choices are still there to be made (as Arjuna discovered in the *Bhagavad-Gītā,* one's *svadharma,* one's individual duties and responsibilities, do not deprive one of the freedom to make choices). Sorabji mentions Karṇa, a character in the *Mahābhārata* who chose to remain true to his exceptionally unusual ancestry and upbringing rather than to accept the kingdom and forestall the calamitous war. Now the important point about Sorabji's "individual reasons" is that they do not merely explain why the individuals acted in the way that they did, but rather that they provide the action with moral justification (they are *normative* reasons and not merely *explanatory* reasons). The claim is that Cato was *right* to commit suicide, even if nobody else was; that Karṇa was *right* to forego the kingdom, even though the consequences were disastrous. The point is not simply that there is such a thing as being true to one's individual self. Rather, the argument must be that being true to one's individual self is a way to provide one's own acts with moral sanction.

One of the stories about Karṇa does, I think, confirm that this idea is present in the *Mahābhārata*. Karṇa wanted to learn

21. Amartya Sen, *Reason Before Identity: The Romanes Lecture of 1998*, Oxford: Oxford University Press, 1999.

military skills, and in order to do so pretended to be a brāhmaṇa. When the deception was uncovered, his teacher wished him that whatever skills he had learned would let him down when he most needed them; and that is indeed what happened, resulting in Karṇa's death in the battle. This episode seems designed to inform us that in failing to be true to his individual self (in this case, deriving from his caste), Karṇa did something wrong for which he would later pay the price. An interesting point is that Karṇa was also renowned for his exceptional generosity, i.e. for his commitment to a recognized moral universal. Indeed, his generosity was often taken advantage of, and caused him much suffering. So it seems to me that the story of Kaṛṇa nicely demonstrates the existence of both, the two questions Sorabji talks about, namely how to behave from an impartially rational perspective, and how to behave in a way that is true to oneself. If the *Mahābhārata* is illustrative of anything, it is that circumstances rarely permit these two questions to receive a univocal answer. Perhaps one's individuality emerges in the way one balances his or her conflicting calls.

It does seem that the moral framework of the *Mahābhārata* allows for individual reasons, I will conclude by mentioning that the Indian logicians discuss the general principles underlying the topic in great detail. Diṅnāga, the famous Buddhist logician, considers the possibility that one might draw inferences about the properties of a thing based on its unique characteristics. His example is: Sound is eternal because it is audible. He describes this a logical fallacy, the fallacy of the "specific indeterminate" (*asādhāraṇa anaikāntika*).[22] His point is that we have no way of knowing whether audibility is a good sign of eternality or anything else, since we cannot observe it anywhere else or make inductions based on observable

22. Diṅnāga, *Pramāṇasamuccayavr̥tti*, chapter 2.

correlations. Likewise, Diṅnāga would ask: how do we know that Cato's unique individuality made it right, rather than wrong, for him to commit suicide? Precisely because his individual features are unique to him, there seems to be no way to answer the question. Other Indian logicians, however, were not quite convinced by Diṅnāga's argument. The Nyāya philosopher Uddyotakara thought that we could get a valid inference if we just turn things around. He used the idea to try to demonstrate the existence of the enduring self, as follows: A living body is not without a self, because if it were it would be without life-breath. The point is that we can confirm empirically that things like stones, which do not have a self, also do not have life-breath, and Uddyotakara's claim is that such negative correlations are sufficient.[23] The logical dispute about the status of the so-called "specific indeterminate" reason rumbled on and became very intricate in the work of later Buddhist and Nyāya philosophers, and attention shifted to the question of whether there can be "inner" correlations (*antarvyāpti*) between the unique characteristics of something and its other properties. But perhaps one can derive some sense from the application to Cato and Karṇa that there were real practical motivations behind all the abstruse theorizing.

23. Uddyotakara, *Nyāyavārttika* on *Nyāyasūtra* 1.1.35.

# Contributors

**Prasenjit Biswas** is currently Associate Professor of Philosophy at North Eastern Hill University, Shillong. Has published books entitled, *Ethnic Life-worlds in Northeast India* (2008), *The Post-modern Controversy* (2005) and many papers in edited books and journals. His areas of interest are Ethnophilosophy, Human Rights, Philosophy of Anthropology and Post-modern Philosophy. [*address*: Department of Philosophy, North Eastern Hill University, SHILLONG, *e-mail*:<prasenjitbis@hotmail.com>].

**Bijoy Boruah** teaches Philosophy in Indian Institute of Technology, Delhi. Until 2010 he was teaching in Indian Institute of Technology Kanpur. He has authored one book in the area of philosophical aesthetics and co-edited two books on ethics. His current area of research is the nature of self-awareness and the metaphysical foundations of virtue ethics. He was a Senior Fulbright Fellow in the University of Texas, Austin during 2000-2001 [*address*: Professor of Philosophy, Department of Humanities and Social Sciences, Indian Institute of Technology, Hauz Khas, NEW DELHI - 110 016, *e-mail*: <boruah@iitk.ac.in>].

**Monima Chadha** is a Senior Lecturer, at Monash University, Australia. She works in Philosophy of Mind and Language and Classical Indian Philosophy and has published in journals including *Philosophy East and West*, *Consciousness and Cognition*, *Philosophical Psychology*, etc. [*address*: Philosophy Section, School of Philosophical, Historical and International Studies, Monash University, CLAYTON, Victoria 3800 (Australia); *e-mail*: <monima.chadha@arts.monash.edu.au>].

**Amita Chatterjee**, Emeritus Professor in the School of Cognitive Science in Jadavpur University, was formerly Professor of Philosophy and co-ordinator of the Centre for Cognitive Science in Jadavpur University, as well as the First Vice-Chancellor of Presidency University, Kolkata. She has written scholarly articles in the areas of Philosophy of Logic, Indian Logic, Philosophy of Language, Fusion Philosophy, Philosophy of Mind, and Philosophy of Cognitive Science both in International and National journals and anthologies. Her books include *Understanding Vagueness* (1994), *Mental Reasoning: Experiments and Theories*, co-authored with Smita Sirker (2009), *Bharatiya Dharmaniti* (ed.) (1998), *Perspectives on Consciousness* (ed.) (2003), *Physicalism and its Alternatives* (Bengali), co-edited (2003), *Some Philosophical Issues in Indian Logic*, co-edited (2003), and co-edited two volumes on *Philosophical Concepts Relevant to Sciences in Indian Traditions*, PHISPC Project of Centre for Studies in Civilizations, New Delhi, 2006 and 2008. [*address:* Department of Philosophy and Centre for Cognitive Science, Jadavpur University, KOLKATA - 700 032, *e-mail:* <amita_ju@yahoo.com>].

**MEENA DHANDA** migrated to the U.K. as a Commonwealth Scholar at Oxford University in 1987 and is currently a Reader in Philosophy and Cultural Politics at the University of Wolverhampton. Her publications include *The Negotiation of Personal Identity* (2008), an edited book *Reservations for Women* (2008) and several papers. She was awarded a Leverhulme Research Fellowship (2010-12) for primary research on her project: 'Caste Aside: Dalit Punjabi Identity and Experience' [*address:* School of Law, Social Sciences and Communication, Millennium City Building, University of Wolverhampton, Wulfruna Street, WOLVERHAMPTON, WV1 1LY (UK) *e-mail:* <m.dhanda@wlv.ac.uk>].

**PAUL FLETCHER** taught Philosophy and Religion in the Department of Religious Studies at Lancaster University. As well as writing within the context of philosophical theology, he has also published extensively in political theory and cultural theory. His main publications include, *Disciplining the Divine: Towards an (Im)political Theology* (2009), and works edited with Arthur Bradley, *Politics to Come: Power Modernity and the Messianic* (2010), *The Messianic Now:Philosophy, Religion, Culture* (2010).

**JONARDON GANERI**'s work has focussed primarily on a retrieval of the Sanskrit philosophical tradition in relationship to contemporary Anglo-American analytical philosophy, and he has done work in this vein on theories of self, concepts of rationality, and the philosophy of language, as well as on the idea of philosophy as a practice and its relationship with literature. He has also worked extensively on the social and intellectual history of early modern

South Asia and the political conception of identity. He is the author of *The Self: Naturalism, Consciousness, and the First-Person Stance* (2012) [*address*: Professor of Philosophy, Department of Philosophy, University of Sussex, Arts Road, BRIGHTON, BN1 9QN (UK), *e-mail*: <jonardon@gmail.com>].

**Rachana Kamtekar** is Associate Professor of Philosophy at the University of Arizona, where she mainly teaches ancient Greek and Roman Philosophy. She has written extensively on ancient political Philosophy, ethics, and moral psychology, and is currently working on a book entitled *The Powers of Plato's Psychology* [*address*: Department of Philosophy, University of Arizona, Social Sciences 213, TUCSON, AZ 85721 (USA), *e-mail*: <kamtekar@email.arizona.edu>].

**Fiona Macpherson** is Professor of Philosophy at the University of Glasgow, where she is director of the Centre for the Study of Perceptual Experience. She is also co-director of CenSes: Centre for the Study of the Senses, Institute of Philosophy, University of London. She has written many papers and published many edited volumes on philosophy of mind, perception and consciousness. [*address*: Department of Philosophy, University of Glasgow, GLASGOW, G12 8QQ, (UK), *e-mail*: <fiona.macpherson@glasgow.ac.uk>].

**Bhaskarjit Neog** had his doctoral degree in Philosophy from IIT Kanpur. His area of specialization is Ethics. Prior to the completion of his PhD, he was also a recipient of the Erasmus Mundus Fellowship of the European Union and had obtained the degree of Master of Applied Ethics from the University of Utrecht. He has published in both national and international journals in different areas of ethics. He is currently Assistant Professor of Philosophy, Assam University, Silchar. [*address:* Assistant Philosopher, Department of Philosophy, Assam University, SILCHAR 788 011 (Assam), *e-mail:* <bhaskarjit@gmail.com>].

**Madhucchanda Sen** teaches Philosophy at Jadavpur University, Kolkata. She has been educated in Jadavpur University, Kolkata and University College, London. She works in the area of Philosophy of Mind, Philosophy of Language and Epistemology. She is the author of *Introduction to Critical Thinking*, and has co-authored with Stan Baronett *Logic* (2009), and with Marilyn Anderson and Pramod Nayar *Critical Thinking, Academic Writing and Presentation Skill*. She has co-edited E*mpiricism and the Two*

*Dogmas* (2006), *Language and Communication — A Philosophical Study* (2005), *Truth and Realism — Essays in Philosophical Analysis* by Pranab Kumar Sen (2007). She is a Trustee of Anando — an NGO working for underprivileged children in Kolkata [*address*: Department of Philosophy, Jadavpur University, KOLKATA, 700 032 *e-mail*: <madhucchandasen@gmail.com>]

**MANIDIPA SEN** is an Associate Professor in the Centre for Philosophy, School of Social Sciences, Jawaharlal Nehru University, New Delhi. Her research interests are in the areas of Philosophy of Mind, Philosophy of Language and Epistemology. Her publications include *Knowledge, Truth and Realism: Essays in Philosophical Analysis* by Pranab Kumar Sen (2007), which she co-edited with Nirmalya Narayan Chakraborty and Madhucchanda Sen, and *Thinking about the World: An Essay in De Re Thought and the Externalist-Internalist Debate* (2008) [*address*: Centre for Philosophy, School of Social Sciences, Jawaharlal Nehru University, NEW DELHI - 110 067, *e-mail*: <manidipasen@gmail. com >].

**RICHARD SORABJI** is Honorary Fellow of Wolfson College, Oxford. He has edited well over 100 books and written 12, including *Aristotle on Memory, Necessity, Cause and Blame; Time, Creation and the Continuum; Matter, Space and Motion; Animal Minds and Human Morals; Emotion and Peace of Mind; Self; Gandhi and the Stoics; The Ancient Commentators on Aristotle* (3 vols.), and (ed.) *Ethics of War: Shared Problems in Different Traditions*. His next book is *Moral Conscience through the Ages* [*address*: Wolfson College, OXFORD, OX2 6UD, UK].

# Index